Artificial Intelligence in Mental Healthcare

As the healthcare industry begins to digest recent advances in artificial intelligence (AI), this book unveils the potential impact of AI on mental and behavioral healthcare. It covers existing and potential applications of AI in addition to its main subfields of machine learning (generative AI included), natural language processing (NLP), and predictive analytics.

This book navigates the intricacies of AI in all stages of the patient journey from diagnosis, treatment, and prevention, offering a holistic view of the future of mental and behavioral healthcare. It explores how AI is revolutionizing key therapeutic areas within mental health, like substance misuse, anxiety disorders, and mood disorders. It also assesses use cases in back office and non-patient-facing areas including reimbursement processes, data collection and management, and revenue cycle management. Chapters are supplemented with a variety of real-world case studies that highlight the practical implications of AI in clinical and non-clinical settings.

This work is relevant for healthcare clinicians, innovators, researchers, healthcare executives, and students navigating the intersection of AI and mental and behavioral healthcare.

Artificial Intelligence in Mental Healthcare

Potential Applications and New Frontiers

Shivan Bhavnani and Ryan McKim

CRC Press
Taylor & Francis Group
Boca Raton London New York

CRC Press is an imprint of the
Taylor & Francis Group, an **informa** business
A CHAPMAN & HALL BOOK

First edition published 2026
by CRC Press
2385 NW Executive Center Drive, Suite 320, Boca Raton, FL 33431

and by CRC Press
4 Park Square, Milton Park, Abingdon, Oxon, OX14 4RN

CRC Press is an imprint of Taylor & Francis Group, LLC

ISBN: 9781032932880 (hbk)
ISBN: 9781032932859 (pbk)
ISBN: 9781003565215 (ebk)

DOI: 10.1201/9781003565215

Typeset in Sabon
by KnowledgeWorks Global Ltd.

For my wife, Brittany, for her endless patience and support,
and to my parents, for everything.

Shivan Bhavnani

Contents

Authors

Shivan Bhavnani is a healthcare investor focused on reshaping mental healthcare. As a Partner at Evio VC, he backs early-stage companies innovating in mental healthcare. He also founded GIMBHI, an independent research institute whose insights have appeared in *Nature*, *Axios*, *Business Insider*, *Entrepreneur*, and Bessemer Venture Partners.

A regular speaker at global health-tech conferences, Shivan has served as a strategic advisor at various startups and organizations including One Mind Accelerator, ReKlame Health, and others. Over the past decade, Shivan has worked across venture capital, biotech, and credit.

Shivan earned an MBA from Duke University and a BA from Wesleyan University. Additionally, he completed an innovation fellowship at Columbia Psychiatry. He is also a Chartered Alternative Investment Analyst (CAIA).

Ryan McKim, Psy.D., is a Venture Advisor to Innovative Growth Capital within GIMBHI's advisor network, where he guides founders on capital strategy and market access for breakthrough mentalhealth technologies. A seasoned health-tech operator and investor with more than two decades in the sector, he has helped scale digital-therapeutic, neurotechnology, and psychedelic-medicine startups from seed through commercialization.

Alongside his investment work, Ryan remains an active clinician. Currently serving as supervisor for Marin County's substance use treatment program for adults with complex co-occurring substance use disorders and serious mental illness, as well as a private integrative psychiatry clinic, and formerly the Department of Psychiatry at California Pacific Medical Center, where he delivered comprehensive neuropsychological evaluations and evidence-based interventions for adults with neurodegenerative and CNS disorders, TBI, and mood disorders. His dual perspective – clinician and venture capitalist – allows him to translate rigorous neuroscience into scalable products that improve patient outcomes. He has contributed to the development of early digital therapeutics for executive dysfunction as part of clinical research into neuroplasticity for veterans with TBI while at the San Francisco VA in addition to providing court-ordered forensic evaluations for youth in the juvenile justice system.

Ryan earned his Psy.D. in Clinical Psychology with an emphasis in Neuropsychology from the California Institute of Integral Studies. He completed residency training at California Pacific Medical Center including postdoctoral specializations in Neuropsychology, Cognitive Rehabilitation and Health Psychology, and holds a bachelor's degree from Duke University.

Contributors

Elena Gray is pursuing her clinical psychology doctorate at PAU-Stanford, holds a master's degree in cognitive neuroscience from University College London, and holds an undergraduate degree in computer science and psychology from Duke University. With previous experience as a healthcare consultant, she is aptly positioned to capture how technology and AI can be harnessed to improve mental healthcare. Through her career, she seeks to bridge the domains of business, technology, and psychology to meet the urgent demands of the mental healthcare epidemic.

Salina Pirzada is a clinical researcher examining the intersection of public health policy, psychiatry, and end-of-life care. Her patient-oriented work focuses on vulnerable populations and the ethical dimensions of health systems and legislation, drawing on a background in global health, community-based research, and diagnostic neuroimaging. Salina's research has been widely published, and her interdisciplinary expertise has contributed to her research on AI-driven mental health systems. She is currently completing her Doctorate at the University of Manitoba, where she also serves as a University Lecturer.

Margot Wagner is a postdoctoral researcher and machine learning scientist working on neuropsychiatric applications of multimodal AI. Her research integrates neuroimaging, language, and deep learning to identify biomarkers for mental health conditions. She is passionate about scalable, interpretable, and clinically useful technologies for psychiatric care and digital mental health.

Zoë Shapiro is a psychology student whose research interests include digital media, adolescent mental health, and public engagement. She has contributed to research and presentations on technology's impact on youth behavior and serves on academic committees focused on student wellbeing, education policy, and the role of media in mental health.

Acknowledgments

Writing a book on the future of AI in mental healthcare is a collaborative act. We owe our deepest gratitude to the people who helped us throughout the process.

Our thanks go to Elena Gray, whose rare mix of clinical-psychology training and technical fluency ensured every discussion of AI remained both scientifically rigorous and deeply humane. Salina Pirzada pressed us to investigate the angle of prevention and explore policy blind spots and equity implications. Dr. Margot Wagner contributed incredible insights, perspective, and the entire analytic backbone for everything related to neuroimaging.

Lucy McClune, our commissioning editor at Taylor & Francis, championed the manuscript from pitch through proofs – thank you.

Beyond these core contributors, we are indebted to the broader community of researchers, founders, and advocates. Your late-night brainstorms and thoughtful introductions helped us immensely. And to our families, friends, and mentors: your support carried us through every rewrite.

Chapter 1

Artificial intelligence in healthcare

The intersection of artificial intelligence (AI) and mental healthcare represents one of the most promising frontiers in modern medicine. As this field rapidly evolves, with new research emerging weekly and novel applications constantly being developed, any comprehensive examination must necessarily establish clear boundaries. This book focuses on specific aspects of AI in mental healthcare while acknowledging important areas that lie beyond its scope.

This volume examines how AI is transforming mental healthcare across the continuum of prevention, diagnosis, and treatment. We explore established and emerging applications including neuroimaging-based diagnostics, behavioral and language analysis for mental health assessment, voice biomarkers, digital phenotyping, and AI-enhanced treatment prediction. The book emphasizes the clinical and research applications that are currently showing promise or have demonstrated efficacy in controlled studies.

Our approach is deliberately broad rather than deep in any single technical domain. We aim to provide readers – whether clinicians, researchers, policymakers, or informed observers – with a comprehensive understanding of how AI is reshaping mental healthcare across multiple modalities and applications. Each chapter examines current capabilities, limitations, and future potential while maintaining focus on clinical relevance and real-world applicability.

While comprehensive in its survey of AI applications in mental healthcare, this book does not attempt to cover every aspect of this vast and rapidly evolving field. Several important areas are either excluded or receive limited attention: Biotech & drug development, electroencephalogram (EEG), large language model (LLM) implementation, commercial application analysis, healthcare system integration, operational and administrative issues, and limited ethical review. These scope limitations reflect both practical constraints and deliberate choices. The excluded areas each represent substantial fields that would require dedicated volumes to address adequately. Our goal is to provide a coherent survey of AI's impact on core mental healthcare practices rather than an exhaustive technical manual or commercial guide. Furthermore, the rapid pace of development in AI technology means that highly detailed technical discussions risk becoming outdated quickly, while the fundamental

DOI: 10.1201/9781003565215-1

concepts and applications we focus on provide a more stable foundation for understanding this evolving field.

RECENT BREAKTHROUGHS

Artificial intelligence is a term that refers to the simulation of human intelligence using machines. In 1950, Alan Turing explored the question of whether machines could think, and he devised a test. A few years later in 1956, John McCarthy, a professor at Dartmouth, introduced the term "artificial intelligence" for the first time.

By the 1960s and 1970s, researchers developed systems which duplicated the choice procedures of medical experts through programs like the MYCIN system, which diagnosed infectious diseases. The rule-based system design had shortcomings. It was difficult to maintain and also remaining unstable under certain conditions. It was impractical because extensive medical knowledge could not be transformed into explicit rules. During the 1980s, the Cyc project engaged in massive data entry of commonsense facts into knowledge bases

Other notable developments include Frank Rosenblatt's Perceptron during the late 1950s, while Geoffrey Hinton conducted work on backpropagation during the 1980s. In 1988, Yann LeCun joined AT&T in New Jersey. Yann LeCun was a researcher who joined a research department at AT&T in 1988 in New Jersey. His research showed that neural networks could recognize patterns. More specifically, he developed a convolutional neural network that could read handwritten digits (LeNet-5). However, in general, neural networks did not outperform less advanced methods on real-world tasks. This was mainly due to limited computing power at the time.

It wasn't until the 2010s that neural networks (now with many layers) started to decisively beat prior approaches on complex tasks. The contributions of Geoffrey Hinton, Yann LeCun, and Yoshua Bengiowe were so foundational that they were collectively awarded the 2018 ACM Turing Award (often called the "Nobel Prize of Computing") for "conceptual and engineering breakthroughs that have made deep neural networks a critical component of computing."[1] They demonstrated that layered neural networks trained on large data could finally realize some of AI's early promises.

Why has AI exploded in the last decade?

Several factors are responsible:

Data: The world is generating digital data at an unprecedented scale (clinical records, medical images, lab results, genomic sequences, etc.). Large datasets are the fuel for AI models.

In healthcare, for example, electronic health records (EHRs) and medical imaging datasets have grown exponentially. In 2009, ImageNet was created which was a public dataset of 15 million labeled images. Hinton's team trained a deep CNN called *AlexNet* on ImageNet, and AlexNet began to successfully recognize images in 2012, surpassing previous benchmarks.[2] In medicine, datasets including collections of retinal images for diabetic retinopathy or millions of histopathology slides became available, which made it possible to train AI for specific clinical tasks.

Compute: Around 2010, computing power exploded. Strangely enough this was due to advances in graphics processing units (GPUs). GPUs were originally designed for video games, but coincidentally, they were effective for the parallel mathematical operations needed for neural network training. Researchers like Andrew Ng showed that GPUs could accelerate deep learning by orders of magnitude.[3] By 2015, companies were designing custom AI chips like Google's Tensor Processing Units.

Algorithms/Architectures: In addition to data and hardware, there were important breakthroughs involving algorithms.

Deep learning uses layers of neural networks with non-linear activation functions. In addition, deep learning utilizes efficient algorithms like backpropagation to train models. In deep learning, the models learn features directly from data instead of relying on human input. Different architectures began to be used for different data types. For example, Convolutional Neural Networks (CNNs) for image data. Recurrent Neural Networks (RNNs) were helpful with sequential data like time series or language. Beyond this, the introduction of the Transformer architecture in 2017 was groundbreaking. Unlike RNNs, transformers employ an attention mechanism to handle long sequences. This enables much larger models to be trained in parallel. The seminal paper "*Attention Is All You Need*" (2017) showed the power of transformers for language-based tasks. Soon transformers became the basis for many language models[4] like BERT (Google) and GPT (OpenAI). Beyond text, transformers were adapted for image analysis, protein folding (AlphaFold), and more.[5]

Open-Source Ecosystem: The AI boom definitely benefited from open-source tools. Frameworks like TensorFlow and PyTorch (open-sourced by Google and Facebook) made it easier for students, researchers, and industry practitioners to build neural networks.[6] This democratization of tools versus siloed efforts created rapid progress. Combining these factors, the past decade (2010–2020s) has indeed been described as a "golden decade" of AI[7] – milestones included IBM's Watson winning the quiz show *Jeopardy!* in 2011 (showcasing natural language question-answering), DeepMind's AlphaGo defeating the world champion at Go in 2016 (demonstrating reinforcement learning in a complex game), and more recently the emergence of generative AI systems like GPT-3/4 and DALL·E that can produce human-like text and images. The convergence of big data, big models, and big compute has created a cycle. AI systems get better as they get more usage and data, which attracts more usage.

THE CASE FOR AI IN HEALTHCARE

Healthcare has always been an exceptionally challenging industry.

These challenges typically could be characterized as a problem of **scale, complexity, and efficiency.** Coincidentally, AI is uniquely positioned to help address these issues.

We will outline some of the major problems in the U.S. healthcare system and discuss why traditional approaches have fallen short, making a compelling case for why AI offers new hope.

Major challenges in U.S. healthcare

- **Diagnosis:** Despite medical advances, diagnosing illnesses correctly and in a timely manner remains a widespread problem. It is estimated that about *5% of U.S. adults experience a diagnostic error each year in outpatient settings.*[8] Diagnostic mistakes can lead to serious harm. A National Academy of Medicine Committee in 2015 concluded that approximately 64,000 deaths per year in the United States may be attributable to diagnostic errors in hospitals and clinics.[9] Roughly one in four medical error-related deaths stem from diagnostic failures.[10] Traditional safeguards like manual double-checks, follow-up protocols, and clinician education help of course, but these are not enough.
- **Administrative Burden:** The United States spends more on healthcare than any other country per capita. One of the major reasons for the high expenditures is administrative expenses. Studies have found that administrative expenses account for roughly 15–25% of total healthcare spending[11] – hundreds of billions of dollars that do not directly contribute to patient care. An observational study in ambulatory care famously found that physicians spend nearly half their work time (49%) on EHRs and desk work, compared to only ~27% on direct clinical face time with patients.[12] This imbalance reduces efficiency in addition to contributing to burnout among healthcare workers. Traditional health IT systems often add to the burden as well.
- **Workforce Shortages:** Even if we eliminated waste, we need *more* healthcare professionals to meet patient needs. The United States faces a **physician shortage**; projections by the Association of American Medical Colleges indicate a shortfall of up to 124,000 physicians by 2034, spanning primary care and specialties.[13] Among these, the shortage of certain specialists (e.g., radiologists, pathologists, psychiatrists) is acute. For instance, more than half of U.S. counties do not have a single psychiatrist practicing[14] – a dire gap as mental health needs rise. Nursing shortages and clinician burnout further strain the system. The COVID-19 pandemic exacerbated these issues by increasing demand (more patients, including those with long-term complications) while many providers retired early or reduced hours.

Training new clinicians is slow and expensive, and the United States is not projected to fill the gap quickly enough.[15] This shortage leads to long wait times, reduced time per visit, or even the inability to access specialists for patients

- **Complexity of Data:** Modern medicine generates an enormous amount of data per patient. Let's take the example of a hospitalized patient. This patient might have continuous vital sign streams, dozens of lab results, imaging studies, genetic tests, and a long medical history. No human can synthesize all these data points in real-time without overlooking something. Traditional clinical decision support systems are rigid and prone to alarm fatigue. The complexity often manifests in information overload for clinicians, who may miss a critical pattern (say, subtle lab trends indicating sepsis) among the noise. Moreover, treatments themselves are growing more complex. This requires risk-benefit calculations personalized to each patient.

Inadequacy of traditional technology

Conventional health technology and analytical methods have struggled with these challenges we outlined for several reasons.

First, much of medicine does not lend itself to simple rules. There are countless exceptions and interacting factors. Rule-based expert systems built in the 1980s and 1990s (e.g., early diagnostic decision aids) could handle narrow, well-defined problems but failed in real-world complexity.

Developers found that enumerating every if-then rule for something as nuanced as diagnosing abdominal pain was impossible. Approaches reliant on "hand-curation of millions of pieces of human knowledge" proved "very labor-intensive" and couldn't scale or adapt.[16]

Second, older statistical methods (like regression models or simple scoring systems) were limited in the number of variables they could reasonably include and often assumed linear relationships. They might flag one or two risk factors (e.g., an early warning score for sepsis might add points for high heart rate and fever), but they couldn't capture complex non-linear interactions in data.

Third, legacy software in healthcare has often been siloed and unintuitive. EHR systems primarily serve billing and record-keeping; they were not designed with advanced real-time analytics in mind. Integration between systems (e.g., a radiology Picture Archiving and Communication System communicating with an EHR) has been clunky, hindering a comprehensive view of patient data.

OPPORTUNITIES FOR AI

Modern AI (new machine learning and deep learning techniques) brings several capabilities to the challenges we referenced above:

- **Pattern Recognition:** Deep neural networks are excellent at finding patterns in large datasets that humans might miss. For example, CNNs can detect subtle features indicative of disease in medical images. In radiology and pathology, AI can act as a second pair of eyes, reducing diagnostic errors. Studies have shown that for certain tasks like identifying melanoma in images of skin lesions, a CNN can match the performance of board-certified dermatologists.[17] Similarly, AI algorithms have been developed that detect diabetic retinopathy from retinal photographs; one such system achieved sensitivity and specificity on par with ophthalmologists and was approved for autonomous use (without a physician).[18] These achievements suggest that AI can help catch diagnoses that clinicians might overlook, especially in image-heavy fields. Beyond images, pattern recognition extends to temporal data: RNNs and transformer models can analyze multi-year histories in EHR data to flag risk patterns (like a combination of lab value changes, vital sign trends, and symptoms that collectively indicate a patient is decompensating). AI's ability to handle dozens or hundreds of variables simultaneously means it can weigh complex combinations of risk factors more effectively than a human using a mental shortcut or a simple scoring checklist.
- **Automation:** AI can shoulder some of the rote tasks that consume clinician time. For instance, speech recognition combined with natural language processing can transcribe and even summarize doctor-patient conversations into structured notes. LLMs like GPT-4 are now being piloted to draft clinical documentation and letters. Major electronic record vendors have begun integrating these capabilities – *Epic Systems* announced integration of GPT-4 for drafting responses to patient messages and assisting in note-writing.[19] Likewise, AI-powered voice assistants can listen during patient visits and automatically fill in required fields in the EHR (a task that otherwise takes physicians hours). By offloading administrative burden, AI allows clinicians to focus more on direct patient care. Early implementations (like Nuance's DAX ambient documentation system) report significant time saved on paperwork. Another area is scheduling and triage: AI algorithms can handle appointment scheduling optimally, or triage digital patient queries (deciding which need urgent physician attention versus which can be answered with automated advice). These use cases attack inefficiency directly, potentially reducing overhead costs and burnout. A Harvard Business Review piece noted that companies are embedding "AI assistants" in office tools to automate tedious tasks like scheduling meetings or parsing emails[20] – healthcare is doing the same for scheduling surgeries or following up normal test results.
- **Clinical Decisions:** AI, especially LLMs and knowledge graph-based systems, can serve as an instantaneous reference and recommendation engine at the point of care. Consider diagnostic decision support: An AI

system can instantly cross-reference a patient's unusual combination of symptoms and findings against millions of cases or medical literature to suggest possible diagnoses, including rare diseases a busy clinician might not consider. Unlike static clinical guidelines, an AI can personalize recommendations to the patient by taking into account a broader context. Transformer-based models can summarize or extract relevant information from unstructured text. This could be used for patient histories or understanding the latest research. For example, an oncologist asks about off-label therapies for a patient's tumor genetic profile, and the AI could return summarized evidence from trials and databases. This would have taken hours without AI. Traditional search or decision support systems weren't sophisticated enough to do this context-specific synthesis. LLMs trained on medical text (like *Med-PaLM* from Google or others) are reaching the point where they can score at a clinician-level on medical exam questions,[21] indicating they have absorbed a significant amount of medical knowledge. In fact, when tested on the U.S. Medical Licensing Exam (USMLE), Pathway's Deep AI model achieved 96% accuracy, significantly outperforming other medical AI systems including GPT-4, Med-Gemini, OpenEvidence, and Hippocratic AI, setting a new benchmark for specialty medical AI.[22]

- **Predictive Analytics:** AI enjoys predicting future events based on past data. You could, say, use predictive analytics to pinpoint patients most likely to experience an event like a hospital readmission, sepsis, or complications before those events occur. In traditional risk scoring, a handful of criteria were included, but AI-driven analytics are capable of including hundreds of data points. Take, for instance, researchers at Duke University have come up with a deep learning system called Sepsis Watch that is always looking out for danger signs like the symptoms of sepsis in hospitalized patients and sends an alert to the clinician hours before the issue manifests. This model was developed from 32 million data points from 42,000 patient cases and monitors 86 variables per patient in real-time. This enabled Duke clinicians to spot sepsis early, resulting in a large 27% decline in sepsis.[23] Similarly, AI can perform functions like forecasting patient volumes in emergency rooms, staffing needs, or supply shortages. Traditional analytics could not handle the complexity or provide the real-time adaptability like this.

Traditional technologies have reached their limits in solving the above challenges, but AI offers a fundamentally different approach that can learn/adapt, handle high-dimensional data, and one that is capable of personalization.

Within the field of healthcare, AI has potential in a few specific therapeutic areas. One of those areas is mental healthcare. Fundamentally, there is a shortage of mental health professionals, creating a clear need for technological solutions. From a therapeutic perspective, the language capabilities of modern AI systems create natural synergies with therapeutic approaches used in mental healthcare. We will explore the challenges of mental healthcare and how AI can be leveraged to drive efficiencies and better outcomes.

NOTES

1 "2018 ACM A.M. Turing Award." *Association for Computing Machinery*, ACM, https://awards.acm.org/about/2018-turing.
2 Hennessy, John L., and David A. Patterson. "The Golden Decade of Deep Learning: Computing Systems and Applications." *Dædalus*, vol. 152, no. 2, 2023, pp. 12–28. American Academy of Arts & Sciences, https://www.amacad.org/publication/daedalus/golden-decade-deep-learning-computing-systems-applications.
3 Hennessy, John L., and David A. Patterson. "The Golden Decade of Deep Learning: Computing Systems and Applications." *Dædalus*, vol. 152, no. 2, 2023, pp. 12–28. American Academy of Arts & Sciences, https://www.amacad.org/publication/daedalus/golden-decade-deep-learning-computing-systems-applications.
4 Hennessy, John L., and David A. Patterson. "The Golden Decade of Deep Learning: Computing Systems and Applications." *Dædalus*, vol. 152, no. 2, 2023, pp. 12–28. American Academy of Arts & Sciences, https://www.amacad.org/publication/daedalus/golden-decade-deep-learning-computing-systems-applications.
5 Hennessy, John L., and David A. Patterson. "The Golden Decade of Deep Learning: Computing Systems and Applications." *Dædalus*, vol. 152, no. 2, 2023, pp. 12–28. American Academy of Arts & Sciences, https://www.amacad.org/publication/daedalus/golden-decade-deep-learning-computing-systems-applications.
6 Hennessy, John L., and David A. Patterson. "The Golden Decade of Deep Learning: Computing Systems and Applications." *Dædalus*, vol. 152, no. 2, 2023, pp. 12–28. American Academy of Arts & Sciences, https://www.amacad.org/publication/daedalus/golden-decade-deep-learning-computing-systems-applications.
7 Hennessy, John L., and David A. Patterson. "The Golden Decade of Deep Learning: Computing Systems and Applications." *Dædalus*, vol. 152, no. 2, 2023, pp. 12–28. American Academy of Arts & Sciences, https://www.amacad.org/publication/daedalus/golden-decade-deep-learning-computing-systems-applications.
8 "The Current State of Diagnostic Safety in the U.S." *Agency for Healthcare Research and Quality*, U.S. Department of Health and Human Services, Feb. 2022, https://www.ahrq.gov/diagnostic-safety/resources/issue-briefs/dxsafety-current-state1.html.
9 Dzau, Victor J., and Cato T. Laurencin. "Advancing Antiracism, Diversity, Equity, and Inclusion in STEMM Organizations: Beyond Broadening Participation." *Health Equity*, vol. 6, no. 1, 2022, pp. 798–802. *PubMed Central*, https://www.ncbi.nlm.nih.gov/pmc/articles/PMC9480522/.
10 Dzau, Victor J., and Cato T. Laurencin. "Advancing Antiracism, Diversity, Equity, and Inclusion in STEMM Organizations: Beyond Broadening Participation." *Health Equity*, vol. 6, no. 1, 2022, pp. 798–802. *PubMed Central*, https://www.ncbi.nlm.nih.gov/pmc/articles/PMC9480522/.
11 Shrank, William H., Teresa L. Rogstad, and Natasha Parekh. "Waste in the US Health Care System: Estimated Costs and Potential for Savings." *JAMA*, vol. 322, no. 15, 7 Oct. 2019, pp. 1501–1509. *JAMA Network*, https://jamanetwork.com/journals/jama/fullarticle/2785479.

12 Sinsky, Christine, et al. "Allocation of Physician Time in Ambulatory Practice: A Time and Motion Study in 4 Specialties." *Annals of Internal Medicine*, vol. 165, no. 11, 6 Dec. 2016, pp. 753–760. *American College of Physicians*, https://www.acpjournals.org/doi/10.7326/M16-0961.

13 "AAMC Report Reinforces Mounting Physician Shortage." *Association of American Medical Colleges*, 11 Apr. 2023, https://www.aamc.org/news/press-releases/aamc-report-reinforces-mounting-physician-shortage.

14 "A Growing Psychiatrist Shortage and an Enormous Demand for Mental Health Services." *Association of American Medical Colleges*, 3 Mar. 2020, https://www.aamc.org/news/growing-psychiatrist-shortage-enormous-demand-mental-health-services.

15 "A Growing Psychiatrist Shortage and an Enormous Demand for Mental Health Services." *Association of American Medical Colleges*, 3 Mar. 2020, https://www.aamc.org/news/growing-psychiatrist-shortage-enormous-demand-mental-health-services.

16 Hennessy, John L., and David A. Patterson. "The Golden Decade of Deep Learning: Computing Systems and Applications." *Dædalus*, vol. 152, no. 2, 2023, pp. 12–28. American Academy of Arts & Sciences, https://www.amacad.org/publication/daedalus/golden-decade-deep-learning-computing-systems-applications.

17 Shashank, Rajesh. "Algorithm Matches Dermatologists' Ability to Identify Skin Cancer." *Stanford Medicine News Center*, 1 Feb. 2017, https://med.stanford.edu/news/all-news/2017/02/algorithm-matches-dermatologists-ability-to-identify-skin-cancer.html.

18 Basen, Matt. "FDA Clears 692 AI-Enabled Medical Devices, Reflecting Explosive Growth." *MedTech Dive*, 20 Mar. 2024, https://www.medtechdive.com/news/fda-ai-medical-devices-growth/728975/.

19 Lash, Alex. "Epic Expands AI Partnership with Microsoft, Rolls Out Copilot Tools to Help Clinicians." *Fierce Healthcare*, 27 Mar. 2024, https://www.fiercehealthcare.com/ai-and-machine-learning/epic-expands-ai-partnership-microsoft-rolls-out-copilot-tools-help.

20 "The AI Explosion, Explained." *Duke Today*, 26 Feb. 2024, https://today.duke.edu/2024/02/ai-explosion-explained.

21 Patel, Bhavik N., et al. "Human–Machine Partnership with Artificial Intelligence for Chest Radiograph Diagnosis." *NPJ Digital Medicine*, vol. 6, 2023, article no. 28, https://www.ncbi.nlm.nih.gov/pmc/articles/PMC9931230/.

22 "Pathway Sets a New Benchmark for Specialty Medical AI with Transparent Just-in-Time Reasoning." *Business Wire*, 2 May 2025, https://www.businesswire.com/news/home/20250502879071/en/Pathway-Sets-a-New-Benchmark-for-Specialty-Medical-AI-with-Transparent-Just-in-Time-Reasoning.

23 "Duke's Quantum Leap in AI." *Duke Today*, 2 Aug. 2024, https://today.duke.edu/2024/08/dukes-quantum-leap-ai.

Chapter 2

Mental healthcare patient journey and AI use cases

When attempting to define mental healthcare, the concept of the continuum of care is relevant. This ranges from a patient's efforts to maintain their well-being and prevent illness, then through the process of identifying and diagnosing mental health conditions, and finally to treating and managing those conditions over time.

In this book, we separate the key phases of this mental healthcare patient journey into prevention, diagnosis, and treatment.

We will explore the role of technology in each phase, identify several conceptual Technology Application Areas (TAA) relevant to each phase. And finally, we explore the specific AI use cases in each TAA.

- Prevention Phase: Involves all efforts to *promote mental well-being* and *prevent the onset/development* of mental health issues. We are defining prevention as a phase that happens before a clinical disorder or diagnosis fully manifests. This includes mental health promotion in the general population, early identification of those at risk, and early interventions to mitigate emerging problems.
- Diagnosis Phase: Encompasses the *recognition, assessment, and formal identification* of a mental health condition. In this phase, a person (often with the aid of health professionals) moves from experiencing symptoms to receiving an official diagnosis or clinical understanding of their condition.
- Treatment Phase: Treatment will refer to any intervention or management after a diagnosis is made. In this context, the treatment phase can include acute treatment, long-term maintenance, and relapse prevention.

Given these are artificial delineations in the patient journey, these phases are not always mutually exclusive. For example, prevention activities can continue during treatment to avoid relapse (a form of tertiary prevention), and assessment is an ongoing process throughout treatment to monitor progress. Nonetheless, distinguishing these phases is useful for conceptual clarity and for pinpointing where different technologies and AI applications fit into the care continuum.

DOI: 10.1201/9781003565215-2

WHY TODAY'S PATIENT JOURNEY MATTERS

Until the mid-1950s, public psychiatric hospitals warehoused more than 558,000 people; overcrowding and abuse were endemic. The arrival of chlorpromazine and the Community Mental Health Centers Act of 1963 triggered mass deinstitutionalization, shrinking the inpatient census to roughly 72,000 by 1994 – a 486k decline that scattered care across community clinics, nursing homes, shelters, and jails. That dispersal explains why today's "single" patient journey often goes through emergency rooms, primary-care offices, teletherapy apps, and criminal-justice settings instead of one coherent system.

Policy

Policy is not background noise; it sets the guardrails for insurance coverage, network adequacy, and reimbursement:

- Mental Health Parity Act (1996) and Parity & Addiction Equity Act (2008) bar dollar or visit limits stricter than those for medical–surgical care.
- Affordable Care Act (2010) makes mental-health and substance-use treatment "essential benefits," bans pre-existing-condition exclusions, and expands Medicaid for most states.
- 21st-Century Cures Act (2016) injects new federal grants and leadership.

Whether a patient is billed a $15 co-pay or a $150 out-of-network fee – and whether a telepsychiatry visit is reimbursed at all – still turns on those statutes.

Epidemiology

Prevalence. In 2022 about 59.3 million U.S. adults (23.1%) experienced any mental illness, and 15.4 million (6%) lived with a serious mental illness. Roughly half of all lifetime mental disorders emerge by the mid-teens and 75% by the mid-20s. Yet treatment is delayed a median 6–8 years for mood disorders and 9–23 years for anxiety disorders – an invisible "pre-clinical" leg of the journey that technology now tries to shorten.

Youth surge. Among U.S. high-school girls, 57% reported persistent sadness in 2021 and 30% seriously considered suicide. Any map of the journey that ignores adolescents is obsolete.

Disparities

Only 38% of Black adults and 36% of Asian adults with mental illness receive care versus 56% of White adults. Language barriers, provider mistrust, and insurance churn widen those gaps. Poverty compounds them: adults below the federal poverty line face far higher psychological distress yet remain least likely to find treatment. LGBTQ+ youth shoulder disproportionate risk, while rural residents often commute hours for a single appointment. These inequities ensure that two patients with identical symptoms can face wildly different itineraries.

Workforce

The United States has only ~50,000 psychiatrists (≈15 per 100 k residents); more than half of counties have none at all, and over 169 million Americans live in formally designated mental-health professional shortage areas. Child-adolescent psychiatrists are scarcer still, leaving pediatricians and school counselors to shoulder specialty care. Federal projections warn of a 14k-plus psychiatrist deficit by 2035. No digital triage tool or AI chatbot described later is a luxury; each is a workaround for this structural shortfall.

Insurance

Parity exists on paper, but the checkout counter tells another story: only 36% of psychiatrists accept new Medicaid patients, fewer than half take Medicare or major commercial plans, and cash-pay therapy regularly tops $150–250 per session. Narrow insurance networks and prior-authorization hurdles push many toward out-of-network bills or emergency departments. Financial detours are therefore baked into the journey, not anomalies.

Stigma

Ninety percent of Americans now say the nation faces a mental-health crisis, yet stigma still slows help-seeking – especially in certain racial-ethnic communities, military culture, and older cohorts. Shortfalls of culturally concordant or multilingual providers translate that stigma into real dropout rates and missed diagnoses. Anonymous chat therapy, peer-support apps, and school-based screening thus become early on-ramps for groups wary of traditional clinics.

Death

Nearly 46.3 million Americans met criteria for a substance-use disorder in 2022, and drug-overdose deaths topped 107k. The same year recorded almost 50,000 deaths by suicide – the highest on record. Because roughly half of those with Serious Mental Illness also have a substance-use disorder, single-lane care models fail; integrated mental-health and addiction pathways are mandatory for true continuity.

Each pain-point you will read in the forthcoming journey chapter – mis-triage, non-adherence, inequitable access – echoes one of the systemic patterns above. Conversely, every promising AI-driven or digitally enabled fix should be judged by its power to bend those trends toward earlier help, better outcomes, and true equity.

By keeping the historical shifts, prevalence curves, disparity fault lines, workforce math, cost hurdles, cultural headwinds, and comorbidity shadows in mind, readers can follow an individual's journey.

PREVENTION PHASE

In the patient journey, this phase is involved with *preventing clinical mental health issues from arising or escalating.*

Primary prevention is aimed at the general public or high-risk groups to avert the initial onset of a disorder, secondary prevention involves early detection and intervention to address emerging problems at the earliest stage, and tertiary prevention could be categorized as intervening to prevent relapse or complications in those who have already experienced a mental illness.

During this phase, mental health promotion and awareness-building are key objectives.

This includes education about mental health, stigma reduction, and activities that involve emotional resilience like regular exercise, sufficient sleep, social connection, and stress reduction techniques. Public health campaigns and school-based programs attempt to improve mental health literacy and teach coping skills, so that individuals are better equipped to handle stressors and seek help when needed.[1] Effective promotion and preventive strategies can have a broad impact: *evidence suggests that focusing on promotion, prevention, and early intervention may yield the greatest improvements in population mental health outcomes*, by addressing issues long before they become severe.[2] *About half of all mental disorders first emerge by the mid-teens*,[3] often preceded by milder symptoms or psychosocial difficulties. Catching and managing these early signs in youth through preventative programs could significantly alter illness trajectories and reduce the lifetime burden of disease.[4]

Another crucial aspect of prevention is identifying at-risk individuals or early symptoms. This involves *screening* in schools, primary care clinics, and workplaces. For example, a primary care practice might use a short questionnaire (such as the PHQ-9 for depression) for all adult patients to spot those with elevated symptoms and intervene early. The aim of such secondary prevention efforts is to enable quicker intervention – ideally offering support or referral to those in need *months or years earlier* than they would otherwise receive help.[5] Early action is critical because it can prevent a mild condition from becoming moderate or severe; it may even avert some crises like suicide attempts by addressing problems upstream.

Despite the clear benefits of prevention, engagement involves convincing people who are not yet ill (or do not realize they are) to participate in preventive programs or use tools designed to monitor their mental well-being, and this is difficult. Stigma and lack of awareness typically stop individuals from taking preventive steps, and many people do not seek any help until a condition has significantly impacted their lives.

Studies have found that even in developed countries, a majority of individuals with emerging mental health problems delay seeking care – contributing to the average decade-long gap between onset and first treatment for disorders like anxiety or depression.[6] Additionally, healthcare systems traditionally invest far less in prevention than in treatment, leading to an underdeveloped infrastructure for preventive mental health care. The result is that opportunities for early intervention are frequently missed: for example, one review highlighted that only about 37.5% of people undergo any screening for depression in certain populations, and fewer than one-fifth ultimately receive a diagnosis and treatment, even when the prevalence of depression is high.[7] This demonstrates a large drop-off between the prevention/intake stage and clinical care.

DIAGNOSIS PHASE

The Diagnosis Phase is when an individual's mental health problem is formally identified and labeled by healthcare professionals (or by the individual themselves through self-assessment). This phase is pivotal, as it transforms a person's experience of distressing thoughts, feelings, or behaviors into a recognized clinical condition for which appropriate treatments can be planned. In traditional mental healthcare practice, diagnosis typically involves several components:

- Recognition of a Problem: The person (or people around them) realizes that something is wrong like moods are persistently depressed, anxiety is overwhelming daily life, or odd perceptions/thoughts occur. Often this recognition triggers an initial help-seeking step.
- Clinical Assessment: A healthcare provider conducts an evaluation, which may include an in-depth clinical interview, functional impairment, personal/family history, medical history, and psychosocial context. Scales or questionnaires are employed to quantify symptom severity.
- Application of Diagnostic Criteria: Using classification systems such as the DSM-5 (Diagnostic and Statistical Manual of Mental Disorders, 5th ed.) or ICD-11, the clinician determines which diagnosis (if any) best fits the person's symptoms and history. For example, criteria for major depressive disorder include a certain number of depressive symptoms persisting for at least two weeks causing clinically significant distress or impairment. The clinician must use judgment to ensure symptoms are not better explained by other conditions or substance effects, etc.

Diagnosis typically includes some type of subjective reports/clinical judgment unlike many areas of medicine. Mental disorders are diagnosed based on symptomatology and observed behavior, which introduces a degree of uncertainty. As a result, misdiagnosis or delayed diagnosis is common. For example, an initial diagnosis of unipolar depression might later be revised to bipolar disorder after a manic episode occurs, or anxiety symptoms might be missed in a patient primarily reporting insomnia and fatigue. Furthermore, conditions such as Post-Traumatic Stress Disorder (PTSD) or substance use disorders may go unrecognized if the clinician does not probe those areas. The lack of objective biomarkers for most psychiatric disorders has long been cited as an impediment to diagnostic accuracy.[8] As one recent review noted, *psychiatry is hampered by a paucity of reliable biological markers that could help objectively diagnose patients*.[9] Traditionally, diagnoses are made based on clinical interviews and symptom checklists, which can be subject to biases and variability between clinicians.[10]

Another major challenge during the Diagnosis Phase is that many individuals never receive any formal diagnosis despite meeting criteria for a mental disorder. Epidemiological studies have revealed large treatment gaps stemming from underdiagnosis. For example, one analysis showed that *fewer than half of people with depression in a given year receive a diagnosis or treatment*.[11] For anxiety disorders, the treatment gap can be even larger, and for disorders like alcohol use disorder, it often exceeds 80%. In global terms, as mentioned earlier, over 50% of those with any mental disorder get no treatment – implicitly meaning no diagnosis is made or disclosed – and in some regions this figure is far higher.[12] These gaps reflect both health system limitations (shortage of specialists, brief primary care visits that miss mental health issues) and individual barriers (stigma, denial, lack of mental health literacy).

Even when a patient is in care, the diagnostic process can be long and complex. Given the fickle nature of many mental health symptoms, it is common for patients to see multiple providers before a clear diagnosis. For example, a patient may report headaches and poor sleep to their primary care provider. But mood and anxiety symptoms can wax and wane, evading detection from the provider. One study reported that among those who eventually receive mental health treatment, the median delay was 6–8 years for mood disorders and 9–23 years for anxiety disorders.[13] Such delays underscore the difficulty in promptly identifying the condition.

TREATMENT PHASE

The Treatment Phase encompasses the wide array of interventions and ongoing support provided to an individual following a mental health diagnosis. Of course, the overarching goals of treatment are to reduce or eliminate symptoms, improve the individual's ability and quality of life, and/or achieve sustained recovery of the condition. Treatment can include some of the categories of intervention below:

- Psychotherapy: This is mainly therapeutic modalities delivered by mental health professionals such as cognitive behavioral therapy, psychodynamic therapy, interpersonal therapy, dialectical behavior therapy, and others. Psychotherapy can be delivered 1-on-1 or group-based. Typically, this involves regular sessions with a practitioner over a period of months or longer.
- Pharmacotherapy: Psychiatric medication is a core part of treatment for disorders including depression, anxiety, bipolar disorder, schizophrenia, ADHD, and others. Medications include antidepressants (SSRIs, SNRIs), mood stabilizers, antipsychotics, anxiolytics, and stimulants. A psychiatrist or other licensed prescriber selects the medication, determines dosing, and monitors for side effects. Finding the right medication is usually some form of a trial-and-error process. Beyond finding the correct medication, patients may need to adjust or switch. In depression, for instance, about 40–60% of patients do not respond to the first prescribed antidepressant, necessitating alternative treatments.[14] Indeed, up to *30% of patients with major depression exhibit treatment-resistant depression (failure to respond to at least two different antidepressant trials)*,[15] highlighting the challenges in pharmacological management.
- Rehabilitation and Long-term Follow-up: After initial treatment of an acute episode, many patients need ongoing follow-up to prevent relapse. This may involve maintenance medication, periodic therapy "booster" sessions, regular monitoring of symptoms, and quickly addressing any early signs of recurrence. For some chronic conditions, rehabilitation services (such as cognitive remediation for cognitive deficits, or social skills training for schizophrenia) are part of treatment. The focus is on helping individuals regain or maintain social and occupational functioning and independence.

The Treatment Phase is unique because it needs continuous engagement and adherence from the patient over an extended period. Unlike a time-limited diagnostic evaluation, treatment for mental health can be ongoing or recurrent throughout a person's life which presents challenges:

- **Adherence:** Keeping patients engaged in therapy sessions or consistent with medication regimes is notoriously difficult. Many patients discontinue treatment prematurely. For example, adherence to antidepressant medication is low because a large proportion of patients stop taking their medication within the first 3 months. Likewise, psychotherapy dropout rates are substantial; it's estimated that roughly

20–40% of patients drop out of therapy early, and for digital mental health interventions (like mental health apps), user retention can be as low as 3–4% after 2 weeks.[16] These adherence problems mean that even efficacious treatments often fail to realize their full benefits in real-world settings.

- **Right Treatment:** As hinted above, tailoring the treatment to the individual is often a trial-and-error endeavor. Clinicians currently rely on clinical judgment, patient preferences, and general guidelines, but the process can be slow. In depression treatment, for instance, if the first antidepressant does not work (which happens in about half of cases), the psychiatrist will try a second, possibly a third, which can take many months. The landmark STAR*D trial in depression found that only about one-third of patients achieved remission with the first medication, and after multiple treatment steps about two-thirds achieved remission, leaving a significant subset who did not get well.[17] This iterative approach prolongs suffering. Similarly, choosing an effective therapy modality or the optimal combination of treatments is not straightforward and may require adjustments over time. The need for *personalized or precision psychiatry* – matching patients to the treatments most likely to help them – is widely recognized but not yet fully realized in routine care.
- **Monitoring:** Regular outcome monitoring is crucial in treatment to gauge progress. Clinicians often rely on patient self-reports ("How are you feeling compared to last time?") or periodic rating scales in sessions. However, symptoms can fluctuate between appointments, and important information may be missed. If a patient's condition deteriorates between monthly visits, the clinician might only learn of it after a significant delay. There is a need for more continuous or objective monitoring tools to detect early warning signs of relapse or side effects of medication. Without good monitoring, opportunities to intervene early (for example, adjusting a medication dose when mild side effects start, before the patient decides to quit the medication on their own) can be lost.
- **Resource and Access Constraints:** Even when an ideal treatment plan is formulated, there are practical issues of access. As noted previously, there is a shortage of mental health professionals in many regions – for instance, nearly *half of the U.S. population lives in a mental health professional shortage area.*[18] Long wait times for psychotherapy or psychiatric consultations are common, especially for pediatric services and in rural areas. The COVID-19 pandemic further strained resources; surveys indicated that about 46% of providers felt unable to meet the demand, with many having to turn away new patients or put them on a long waitlist.[19] Such access issues mean that even after diagnosis, initiating and maintaining appropriate treatment can be difficult.

TECHNOLOGY APPLICATION AREAS IN MENTAL HEALTHCARE

We now have a foundation to discuss how technology and specifically AI come into play. In the next section, we identify a few TAA within each phase. We then move on to detailed AI use cases, showing how these technologies can help bridge gaps and overcome limitations identified in our journey overview. This is not meant to be comprehensive. Our aim is to illustrate a few AI use cases.

Tech has become interwoven with mental healthcare across all phases of the patient journey. In this section, we define several specific TAA for each phase (Prevention, Diagnosis, Treatment). These are conceptual categories that group similar uses of technology, providing a structured way to consider where digital tools are applied in mental health. We ensure that each area is well-defined and non-overlapping with the others, meaning each category addresses a unique aspect of mental healthcare without encroaching on another category's scope. For each area, we give a clear definition, explain how it differs from other categories, and describe what kinds of tools or solutions it includes.

Prevention phase – Technology application areas

In the Prevention Phase, technology is leveraged to promote mental well-being and to catch problems early. We identify three major application areas for technology in prevention:

Mental Health Promotion and Education Platforms: This category covers anything that educates or fosters helpful attitudes regarding mental healthcare and mental illness. Examples include public-facing websites (like government mental health portals or NGO sites) that contain articles, videos, and FAQs about mental health conditions and how to maintain wellness. Social media campaigns also fall here. A campaign on Twitter or Instagram using hashtags to normalize conversations about depression, or YouTube channels featuring psychologists sharing self-care tips. Another example is *e-learning mental health modules* in workplaces. Many companies now offer online training for employees on mental health awareness and how to support colleagues in distress. The defining characteristic of this category is that the technology is used in a one-to-many fashion (broadcasting information to a wide audience), and the content is primarily educational or motivational rather than diagnostic or therapeutic. The rationale for having this as a separate category is that awareness and education underpin all other mental health efforts: if people do not recognize symptoms or know that effective help exists, they will not engage with screening or treatment tools. This category does not overlap with others because it does not entail personalized assessment or direct intervention – it's about knowledge and attitude change at the population level.

Challenge	*AI Solution*
Conventional platforms provide identical content to all users and rely on individuals to seek out information. A state website cannot tailor advice to a person's unique situation, stressors, and knowledge gaps. Moreover, a website is a passive digital asset and cannot contact people who aren't already looking for help.	AI can enable personalized interactive mental health education. For example, a website or chatbot enhanced by NLP can converse with a user to answer specific questions. This addresses the one-size-fits-all issue: the AI can gauge the user's current understanding and emotional state (through their questions or tone) and adapt the educational content accordingly. Studies have shown that people often prefer asking sensitive questions to an AI anonymously rather than to a human, due to reduced fear of judgment.[20]

Risk Detection & Early Warning Systems: Here, technology's role is to act as a sentinel – *spotting trouble signs early*. One common example is online mental health screening tests. Numerous websites and apps provide clinically validated questionnaires for depression, anxiety, PTSD, etc., which users can take voluntarily. For instance, an online screening for depression might use the PHQ-9 questions and instantly give the user a score with interpretation (e.g., "Your answers suggest you may be experiencing moderate depression; consider reaching out to a professional"). Some national mental health organizations host such tools publicly. Beyond self-screening, this category also includes systematic screening initiatives: for example, tablets in the waiting room of a primary care clinic asking patients to answer mental health questions, or a university that emails students a link to a mental health check-in survey each semester. In workplace wellness programs, employees might periodically answer stress and burnout inventories via an app, triggering HR or counselor outreach if the scores are high (with privacy safeguards). Another angle of early warning is passive surveillance at the population level – researchers and public health experts have experimented with monitoring social media posts or Google search trends to detect spikes in suicide-related content or anxiety levels in a community, functioning as an early warning for public health response.[21]

Challenge	*AI Solution*
Digital screening tools for mental health are typically digitized static questionnaires. These rely on user honesty and self-awareness. Furthermore, they only provide a snapshot based only on self-reports at a single point in time. Many individuals with emerging mental illness may not take	AI can greatly enhance early detection by analyzing *richer data sources and patterns over time*, beyond what a single self-report can capture. One use case is AI analyzing social media content to identify users at risk for mental health issues such as depression or suicidal ideation. AI algorithms have demonstrated the ability to predict depression risk from social media posts months before formal diagnosis by finding subtle linguistic markers and changes in posting behavior. In one study, an AI model scanning Facebook posts could predict a future depression diagnosis with significant accuracy, highlighting phrases about loneliness and emotional pain that human friends might overlook.

Self-Help and Resilience-Building Tools: This category represents the plethora of apps and digital programs that individuals can use autonomously to maintain their mental health and handle minor issues. These tools often draw from established therapeutic techniques but package them in a lightweight, accessible format. For example, a meditation app guides users through daily mindfulness exercises to reduce stress and improve emotional regulation. A mood-tracking app might let users log how they feel each day, perhaps prompting them with questions about factors like sleep, diet, or activities; over time it can show patterns and even give gentle suggestions ("You often feel anxious on days you skip lunch – consider keeping a regular meal schedule"). Other tools might include interactive cognitive-behavioral self-help modules, where a user can learn to challenge negative thoughts – these are typically less comprehensive than formal CBT but can help with mild symptoms. There are also virtual peer support communities (forums or chat groups moderated on apps), which provide a space to talk and receive encouragement, serving as a preventative measure by combating isolation. What unites these examples is the focus on user-driven well-being practice. People use these tools to *build resilience skills, track their mental states, and implement positive behavior changes*. They are considered part of prevention because they are usually used *before* or *without* a formal clinical intervention – for instance, someone feeling "a bit down" might use a self-help app to try to improve their mood, potentially preventing worsening into major depression. This category is distinct from treatment delivery tools (like therapy apps with clinician oversight or prescription digital therapeutics for diagnosed conditions). It's also different from risk detection: while some self-help apps might incidentally flag if a user's inputs indicate severe distress, their primary purpose is to help the individual help themselves, not to identify them to authorities or professionals. And unlike promotion platforms, these tools are individualized and interactive, not just educational media.

Challenge	*AI Solution*
Traditional self-help apps are generally rule-based and inflexible. They offer a fixed set of exercises or tips, and if the user's motivation wanes or if the suggestions aren't quite fitting their situation, the app doesn't adjust. Many users report that generic wellness apps feel impersonal or irrelevant after the initial novelty wears off. This contributes to the notoriously high dropout rates for mental health apps (often, >90% stop using after a couple of weeks).[22]	AI can make self-help more engaging and personalized. The form of an app is becoming outdated with the rise of AI agents for this particular reason. A chatbot or agent can ask the user questions about their emotions and personalize lifestyle interventions or education to the user. Over time, this chatbot can learn the user's patterns. For example, the user tends to feel anxious on Sunday nights and then proactively suggests targeted strategies to prevent an anxiety spiral ("Hey I know the week ahead often stresses you out, shall we do a relaxation exercise tonight?"). The adaptive capabilities of AI far exceed static approaches. NLP allows the AI to understand free-text input form the user so the user is not limited to structured inputs. Journal entries and rants are useful for the AI in this context.

DIAGNOSIS PHASE – TECHNOLOGY APPLICATION AREAS

- In the Diagnosis Phase, technology can assist in assessing and determining a person's mental health condition. We propose four distinct application areas in which technology is applied for mental health diagnosis

Digital Assessment and Triage Tools: In traditional practice, diagnosing a mental health condition starts with an interview and paper questionnaires. At the end, the system might generate a summary for the clinician highlighting positive symptoms. Another example is a symptom-checker chatbot on a mental health service website – a user can chat with a bot that asks "What brings you here today? Can you describe your mood? How is your sleep?" and based on the answers it might triage the person: "Your responses suggest you might be experiencing moderate depression. It would be beneficial to schedule an appointment with a therapist. Would you like to see available appointment times?" These tools often use validated screening instruments behind the scenes. Triage is a key aspect: given workforce shortages, digital tools can prioritize who needs to be seen urgently versus who might benefit from self-help or watchful waiting. For instance, an online intake form might automatically flag if someone indicates suicidal ideation, alerting staff to respond immediately.

Challenges	*AI Solution*
Most existing digital assessments are essentially electronic versions of standard questionnaires or simple branching logic trees. They can certainly speed up data collection (e.g., a patient filling an intake on a tablet), but they don't fundamentally change the diagnostic process. A key limitation is that they are not very flexible or intelligent. For example, a typical computerized interview might ask a fixed set of DSM-based questions. If a patient gives a slightly ambiguous answer, the system might not know how to probe deeper the way a human would. Rule-based triage can also be brittle: e.g., if a patient endorses suicidal thoughts, trigger "high risk" flag – but such systems can't differentiate fleeting passive thoughts from an imminent plan with nuance. Additionally, traditional tools treat each question in isolation and often don't integrate other context (like the person's tone or hesitations).	AI (particularly NLP and machine learning) can make digital assessments conversational, adaptive, and context-aware. Psychiatric history interviews present a good use case. Instead of following a script or decision tree that a static technology would follow, AI can be incredibly dynamic. For instance, if the patient mentions "I haven't been sleeping much," a rule-based system might just note insomnia, but an AI could follow up: "You said your sleep is poor. Are you finding it hard to fall asleep, or do you wake up during the night?" – basically, imitating a skilled clinician's approach to clarify symptoms. Research prototypes of such systems exist; one study created an AI interviewer that could reliably identify symptoms of depression and PTSD by learning which follow-up questions to ask, yielding an assessment that correlated well with clinician evaluations. AI can use predictive models to determine urgency more accurately than simple rule triggers. For instance, rather than flagging everyone who endorses "yes" to suicidal ideation, an AI model could consider a combination of factors (history, severity of other symptoms, even linguistic markers of hopelessness) to predict which patients are at genuine acute risk.[23]

Neurobiological and Physiological Data: Although routine psychiatric diagnosis doesn't yet include blood tests or brain scans in most cases, technology is able to find patterns in such data that correlate with mental disorders. This category covers tools that analyze any biological measurement for diagnostic clues. For instance, in research settings, MRI scans have been analyzed with machine learning to distinguish patients with schizophrenia from healthy controls by identifying distributed patterns of brain volume or connectivity differences.[24] There are prototypes of algorithms that, given a brain scan, output a probability of a certain diagnosis. Electroencephalogram (EEG, brain wave recordings) is another area: algorithms can detect certain neural signatures (like specific event-related potentials) that might indicate risk for disorders (e.g., a reduced P300 wave linked to schizophrenia). Genetic analysis falls here too – polygenic risk scores for mental illness can be calculated from genetic tests, and tools can integrate that to estimate someone's predisposition to, say, depression or autism.

Challenges	*AI Solution*
When it comes to using biomarkers or neuroimaging for mental health, the challenge has been that any single biological measure is often too nonspecific or subtle for humans to interpret diagnostically. A psychiatrist might order an MRI mostly to rule out tumors, not to diagnose depression. EEGs are used for research or to rule out seizures, but not typically to confirm a psychiatric diagnosis. There's a massive amount of data in a brain scan or genomic profile, and historically we lacked tools to derive diagnostic classifiers from them. Standard radiology might note gross abnormalities, but micro-patterns in functional connectivity or cortical thickness associated with disorders were beyond reach. Also, mental illnesses likely involve complex combinations of markers (a bit like polygenic risk – many small contributions), which humans can't compute holistically in their heads or with simple linear tools.	Deep learning is incredibly good at pattern detection in images (like MRI scans) and high-dimensional data (like genomics). AI-based MRI diagnosis is a concrete use case. Researchers have developed ML models that take in an fMRI scan (showing functional connectivity between hundreds of brain regions) and output a probability that the subject has schizophrenia vs is healthy.[25] In trials, some models reached around 70–80% accuracy differentiating patients from controls – not perfect, but far above chance and beyond human capability which is essentially 0% since humans can't see those connectivity patterns with naked eye. Similarly, in autism, models analyzing brain network synchrony have shown promise in identifying autistic vs neurotypical individuals or predicting symptom severity. The common theme is that AI can detect and interpret complex, high-dimensional patterns that defy traditional analysis, thus finally unlocking some potential of "biological psychiatry" that has long been promised but elusive.[26]

Clinical Decision Support Systems (CDSS) for Diagnosis: This area is about helping human clinicians (or clinical teams) make better diagnostic decisions by using software intelligence. A CDSS for mental health diagnosis might be implemented as a module in an Electronic Health Record system that, when a clinician enters patient symptoms or questionnaire scores, provides diagnostic suggestions ("Consider generalized anxiety disorder; criteria seem met based on entered symptoms"). Or it might cross-reference the patient's data with thousands of past cases to find similar profiles and what diagnoses they received, essentially doing a pattern match to suggest what diagnoses are likely

Challenge	*AI Solution*
Clinicians currently rely on their training, experience, and guidelines like DSM criteria to diagnose. Traditional digital tools (like EHR templates or simple alert systems) provide minimal decision support. At best, an EHR might have hard stops ("patient answered yes to suicide question, do something") or perhaps a diagnostic checklist. But no tailored, patient-specific guidance arises from typical systems. This means diagnostic accuracy is variable – some studies find primary care doctors miss up to half of depression cases, or conversely over-diagnose in some instances. Human biases and knowledge limits play a role: a clinician might anchor on the first impression, or might not be aware of rarer conditions. Traditional computing can't improve this much beyond giving static.[27]	AI-driven decision support can synthesize all available patient data – including possibly the outputs of the AI analysis – to provide *probabilistic diagnostic suggestions or risk assessments* that aid clinicians. One example is an AI system that reads through a patient's entire electronic health record (EHR) history (structured and unstructured data) to flag potential overlooked diagnoses. There was a famous case where IBM's Watson (in the early days of Watson for medicine) read doctors' notes and suggested a rare leukemia subtype diagnosis that doctors had missed, because it matched the pattern in literature. Similarly, for psychiatry, an AI could parse years of notes, pick up mentions like "mood swings," "periods of high energy," "family history of bipolar" that are scattered and then suggest "Bipolar II disorder" even if the current physician was leaning toward unipolar depression. Essentially, AI can serve as a second pair of eyes (or a second brain) that *never forgets any detail* in the records and compares it to millions of cases or data in literature.

Treatment phase – Technology application areas

In the Treatment Phase, technology is employed to deliver or enhance therapeutic interventions and to support patients in adhering to and benefiting from treatment. We identify four key application areas for technology in mental health treatment:

Digital Therapeutics and Intervention Delivery: This is one of the most visible areas of tech in mental health treatment. It encompasses everything from smartphone apps that deliver a structured therapy program, to AI-driven conversational agents that talk patients through their problems, to VR systems that enable therapeutic experiences.

Traditional digital therapeutics like apps or telehealth platforms are often scripted or static. For example, a CBT app might have preset modules that the user works through. While useful, these lack the real-time adaptability and empathy of a human therapist. AI can elevate digital therapeutics to be more interactive, personalized, and human-like. A prime example is the AI therapy chatbot. Early therapy bots (like ELIZA in the 1960s) were rule-based and easily hit their limits in understanding. Modern AI, especially with large language models (LLMs) akin to GPT, has dramatically improved the conversational quality and coherence of chatbots. Now, an AI-powered chatbot can carry on a nuanced discussion, remember what the user said earlier, and steer the conversation in therapeutic directions. For instance, if a user expressing anxiety about work talks to an AI therapist, the AI can detect cognitive distortions in the user's statements (like "I'm sure everyone thinks I'm a failure") and respond with a gentle challenge or Socratic question (a CBT technique: "What makes you think they all see you as a failure? Can we identify evidence for and against that?"). This requires understanding context and subtlety – something feasible with NLP advances. A recent landmark randomized trial demonstrated the effectiveness of a generative AI-driven therapy chatbot: patients with depression or anxiety who engaged with an AI "therapist" saw significant symptom reductions (e.g., ~50% reduction in depression severity on average). These outcomes were comparable to traditional face-to-face therapy in magnitude, which is astonishing and suggests AI can deliver meaningful therapeutic benefit:[28]

Personalized Treatment Planning and Optimization: Traditional mental health treatment often follows a guideline-driven but trial-and-error approach – for example, first-line SSRI for depression, if that fails switch or add augmenting agent, etc. This category represents technology's role in making this process smarter and more tailored to the individual from the start. One major component is predictive analytics for medication response. With the accumulation of large clinical datasets (e.g., from electronic health records of patients with depression and their medication outcomes), machine learning models have been developed to predict which patients will respond to which antidepressant.[29] Factors like symptom profile, demographic data, medical comorbidities, and even genetic markers can be input, and the model outputs a recommendation (e.g., patient A has a 75% predicted chance to respond to SSRI X vs 40% to SSRI Y, suggesting try X first). Some companies and research consortia have created such tools, and while not yet common in practice, they illustrate how AI can reduce guesswork.

One of the hardest tasks in psychiatry is predicting which treatment will work for whom. As noted, without AI, it's trial-and-error guided by population-level probabilities. AI can analyze high-dimensional patient data (symptom patterns, history, genetic markers, etc.) to make *individual-level predictions*. A salient use case: AI guided medication selection for depression. Researchers have developed ML models (sometimes called "AI psychiatrists") that input a patient's profile (demographics, specific symptom items, comorbid conditions, maybe even brain or EEG data) and output which antidepressant (or none) is likely to lead to remission. In clinical trials, some of these models have outperformed psychiatrists' choices. For example, one study found that a machine learning model predicted which patients would not respond to an

SSRI with about 80% accuracy. If a doctor knew upfront that a patient has only 10% chance to respond to SSRI A but 60% to SNRI B, they would choose B first, thus saving months of ineffective treatment. AI can capture subtle nonlinear relationships (like that a particular cluster of symptoms plus the presence of childhood trauma might favor one medication's mechanism over another) which a human might not internalize from guidelines. A clinician might have bias or limited experience, whereas an AI trained on thousands of similar cases might rank options (like lithium augmentation vs switch to MAOI vs electroconvulsive therapy (ECT) vs ketamine) by likely benefit for that particular patient. This helps navigate complexity. Even choosing parameters for brain stimulation treatments (like TMS or ECT) could be aided by AI, but that's a niche. Still, some work uses functional magnetic resonance imaging (fMRI) and AI to target TMS to the right brain network per individual, boosting remission rates. A real-world demonstration of this: The U.S. Department of Veterans Affairs has deployed a predictive model that identifies patients with PTSD who are likely to benefit from adding an antipsychotic to their regimen vs not, helping psychiatrists there make that call. It learned from thousands of Veterans Affairs (VA) patients' outcomes. Such use cases show AI moving from academic promise to a clinical tool.

Patient Engagement and Adherence Support Tools: This category addresses the human element of treatment adherence – getting patients to actually do what is recommended and to stay motivated. Technology here can be surprisingly simple yet effective. SMS text reminders to take medication have shown in studies to modestly improve adherence for chronic illnesses. For mental health, a daily text saying "Don't forget to take your antidepressant this morning!" or a push notification from an app can help patients stick to their regimen. Beyond reminders, there are engagement strategies like gamification: for instance, an app might reward patients with points or badges for every day they complete their therapy homework or every week they attend their session, making it a bit like a game (some mental health apps do this to encourage habit formation).

While earlier we described how AI in diagnosis can detect relapse risk via phenotyping, in the treatment context it's about using those detections to actively manage ongoing care. Traditional remote monitoring might just collect data and perhaps set simple rules (like "if mood score < X, alert clinician"). AI makes monitoring *predictive and preventive* rather than reactive. One use case: preventing suicide during treatment. Patients in treatment for depression might still have suicidal thoughts that ebb and flow. An AI system might continuously gauge suicide risk based on digital phenotype and patient self-reports. If it predicts risk rising, it can autonomously trigger an intervention – perhaps sending an urgent alert to a crisis team or even initiating a chatbot that engages the patient in that critical moment ("I notice you seem to be in a lot of pain right now. Do you want to talk? Or I can connect you with help."). This is an active way to prevent relapse or crises by not waiting for the patient to reach out (since many won't in a crisis due to cognitive constriction).

Bringing it all together, AI in the Treatment Phase is enabling what we might call "precision support" – each patient gets the support they need, when they need it, how they need it, to stay on the path to recovery. Traditional technology provided tools, but those tools were only as effective as the patient's motivation to use them. AI is like the glue or the catalyst that makes these tools far more effective by *personalizing the treatment experience* and ensuring problems in the treatment process (lack of efficacy, side effects, dropout) are addressed promptly and intelligently.

While there are many other use cases for AI within the field of mental healthcare, we have highlighted a few salient examples in the domains of prevention, diagnosis, and treatment in this chapter.

NOTES

1 Colizzi, Marco et al. "Prevention and early intervention in youth mental health: is it time for a multidisciplinary and trans-diagnostic model for care?" *International Journal of Mental Health Systems*, vol. 14, no. 23, 24 Mar. 2020. https://doi.org/10.1186/s13033-020-00356-9.

2 Colizzi, Marco et al. "Prevention and early intervention in youth mental health: is it time for a multidisciplinary and trans-diagnostic model for care?" *International Journal of Mental Health Systems*, vol. 14, no. 23, 24 Mar. 2020. https://doi.org/10.1186/s13033-020-00356-9.

3 Colizzi, Marco et al. "Prevention and early intervention in youth mental health: is it time for a multidisciplinary and trans-diagnostic model for care?" *International Journal of Mental Health Systems*, vol. 14, no. 23, 24 Mar. 2020. https://doi.org/10.1186/s13033-020-00356-9.

4 Colizzi, Marco et al. "Prevention and early intervention in youth mental health: is it time for a multidisciplinary and trans-diagnostic model for care?" *International Journal of Mental Health Systems*, vol. 14, no. 23, 24 Mar. 2020. https://doi.org/10.1186/s13033-020-00356-9.

5 Ettman, Catherine K, and Sandro Galea. "The Potential Influence of AI on Population Mental Health." *JMIR Mental Health*, vol. 10, e49936, 16 Nov. 2023. https://doi.org/10.2196/49936.

6 National Alliance on Mental Illness (NAMI). *Mental Health By the Numbers*. NAMI, Apr. 2023. https://www.nami.org/About-Mental-Illness/Mental-Health-by-the-Numbers.

7 Meleiro, Alexandrina, et al. "Understanding the Journey of Patients with Depression in Brazil: A Systematic Review." *Clinics*, vol. 78, 2023, article 100192. https://doi.org/10.1016/j.clinsp.2023.100192.

8 Yang, Yihong, et al. "Brain Imaging Identifies Biomarkers of Mental Illness." *Biological Psychiatry*, vol. 95, no. 6, 26 Sept. 2023, pp. 466–476. https://doi.org/10.1016/j.biopsych.2023.08.028.

9 Abi-Dargham, Anissa et al. "Candidate biomarkers in psychiatric disorders: state of the field." *World Psychiatry: Official Journal of the World Psychiatric Association (WPA)*, vol. 22, no. 2, 2023, pp. 236–262. https://doi.org/10.1002/wps.21078.

10 Yang, Yihong, et al. "Brain Imaging Identifies Biomarkers of Mental Illness." *Biological Psychiatry*, vol. 95, no. 6, 26 Sept. 2023, pp. 466–476. https://doi.org/10.1016/j.biopsych.2023.08.028.
11 Berger, Michele W. "Linguistic Red Flags from Facebook Posts Can Predict Future Depression Diagnoses." *Penn Today*, University of Pennsylvania, 15 Oct. 2018. https://penntoday.upenn.edu/news/linguistic-red-flags-facebook-posts-can-predict-future-depression-diagnoses.
12 Salib, Veronica. "Understanding Gaps in Mental Health Treatment Amidst National Crisis." *TechTarget*, 28 Aug. 2023. https://www.techtarget.com/healthtech/news/Understanding-gaps-in-mental-health-treatment-amidst-national-crisis.
13 Wang, Philip S., et al. "Failure and Delay in Initial Treatment Contact After First Onset of Mental Disorders in the National Comorbidity Survey Replication." *Archives of General Psychiatry*, vol. 62, no. 6, 2005, pp. 603–613. https://doi.org/10.1001/archpsyc.62.6.603.
14 Nunez, John-Jose, et al. "Replication of Machine Learning Methods to Predict Treatment Outcome with Antidepressant Medications in Patients with Major Depressive Disorder from STAR*D and CAN-BIND-1." *PLOS ONE*, vol. 16, no. 6, 28 June 2021, e0253023. https://doi.org/10.1371/journal.pone.0253023.
15 Rivlin, Adrienne. *Mind-Altering Metamorphosis: Transforming the Patient Journey in Mental Health*. L.E.K. Consulting, 13 Oct. 2023. https://www.lek.com/insights/mind-altering-metamorphosis-transforming-patient-journey-mental-health.
16 "Thousands of Mental Health Apps Available: Supporting Evidence Not So Plentiful." *American Psychiatric Association*, 22 July 2019. https://www.psychiatry.org/news-room/apa-blogs/apa-blog/2019/07/thousands-of-mental-health-apps-available-supporting-evidence-not-so-plentiful.
17 Nunez, John-Jose, et al. "Replication of Machine Learning Methods to Predict Treatment Outcome with Antidepressant Medications in Patients with Major Depressive Disorder from STAR*D and CAN-BIND-1." *PLOS ONE*, vol. 16, no. 6, 28 June 2021, e0253023. https://doi.org/10.1371/journal.pone.0253023.
18 *The Behavioral Health Care Workforce*. NIHCM Foundation, 8 June 2023. https://nihcm.org/publications/the-behavioral-health-care-workforce. Accessed 25 May 2025.
19 Salib, Veronica. "Understanding Gaps in Mental Health Treatment Amidst National Crisis." *TechTarget*, 28 Aug. 2023. https://www.techtarget.com/healthtechAnalytics/news/Understanding-Gaps-in-Mental-Health-Treatment-Amidst-National-Crisis. Accessed 25 May 2025.
20 "Mental Health Chatbots: The Future of Therapy?" *Kommunicate Blog*, 14 Sept. 2022. https://www.kommunicate.io/blog/mental-health-chatbots/#:~:text=mental%20health%20concerns%20often%20find,mainstream%20solution%20in%20this%20field. Accessed 25 May 2025.
21 Ettman, Catherine K., and Sandro Galea. "The Potential Influence of AI on Population Mental Health." *JMIR Mental Health*, vol. 10, 16 Nov. 2023, e49936. https://doi.org/10.2196/49936. Accessed 25 May 2025.
22 Baumel, Amit, et al. "Objective User Engagement With Mental Health Apps: Systematic Search and Panel-Based Usage Analysis." *JMIR Mental Health*, vol. 6, no. 9, Sept. 2019, e14567. https://doi.org/10.2196/14567. Accessed 25 May 2025.
23 Ben-Zeev, Dror et al. "Next-generation psychiatric assessment: Using smartphone sensors to monitor behavior and mental health." *Psychiatric Rehabilitation Journal* vol. 38, no. 3, 2015, pp. 218–226. https://doi.org/10.1037/prj0000130.

24 "Brain Imaging Identifies Biomarkers of Mental Illness." *EurekAlert!*, American Association for the Advancement of Science (AAAS), 9 Nov. 2023. https://www.elsevier.com/about/press-releases/brain-imaging-identifies-biomarkers-of-mental-illness. Accessed 25 May 2025.

25 Yang, Yihong, et al. "Brain Functional Connectome Defines a Transdiagnostic Dimension Shared by Cognitive Function and Psychopathology in Preadolescents." *Biological Psychiatry*, vol. 95, no. 10, 2023, pp. 740–749. https://doi.org/10.1016/j.biopsych.2023.08.028. Accessed 25 May 2025.

26 Elsevier. "Brain Imaging Identifies Biomarkers of Mental Illness." *EurekAlert!*, 9 Nov. 2023. https://www.elsevier.com/about/press-releases/brain-imaging-identifies-biomarkers-of-mental-illness. Accessed 25 May 2025.

27 Salib, Veronica. "Understanding Gaps in Mental Health Treatment Amidst National Crisis." *TechTarget*, 28 Aug. 2023. https://www.techtarget.com/healthtech/news/Understanding-Gaps-in-Mental-Health-Treatment-Amidst-National-Crisis. Accessed 25 May 2025.

28 Kelly, Morgan. "First Therapy Chatbot Trial Yields Mental Health Benefits." *Dartmouth News*, 27 Mar. 2025. https://home.dartmouth.edu/news/2025/03/first-therapy-chatbot-trial-yields-mental-health-benefits. Accessed 25 May 2025.

29 Xu, Zhenxing, et al. "Using Machine Learning to Predict Antidepressant Treatment Outcome From Electronic Health Records." *Psychiatric Research and Clinical Practice*, vol. 5, no. 4, 2023. https://doi.org/10.1176/appi.prcp.20220015. Accessed 25 May 2025.

Chapter 3

Ethical challenges

PATIENT PRIVACY AND DATA SECURITY

One big challenge with using artificial intelligence (AI) in mental health care is ensuring vulnerable private data is protected and secure. There is a growing fear of potential breaches of protection as well as a potential misunderstanding of AI use by patients. There has been a researcher investigating these factors from the lens of physicians. Researchers found that physicians were uncomfortable with how AI might passively collect data. For example, data could be passively collected continuously or in ways that are not very obvious. The physicians in the study had issues that patients might not understand exactly what they are consenting to. They also had concerns about AI misinterpreting remarks (e.g., jokes), which could potentially lead to serious outcomes for the patient. For example, the patient could lose access to services and potentially be flagged a certain way in their records. There is a need for explicit consent that accounts for the complexity and the sensitivity of the data being collected. The relationship between clinician and patient is dependent on trust, so the AI efforts must take into account the broader implications of protecting vulnerable data.[1]

AI mental health tools are surrounded by sensitive personal data. There is an important need, then, to maintain strict privacy and data protection standards. Research has offered a framework to help understand the evolving role of the Health Insurance Portability and Accountability Act (HIPAA). Originally, HIPAA was designed for traditional healthcare systems; there is a new adaptation that aims to adapt AI tools into the framework. These tools have enormous volumes of personal health data, which is especially sensitive in mental health applications that frequently rely on real-time data collection, natural language input (such as chat transcripts), and behavioral patterns to function. These systems demand a level of data access that, if not properly secured, puts patient confidentiality at risk. Past research has highlighted key risks that AI poses in the mental healthcare field regarding privacy. For one, data breaches/ransomware are a potential risk which are only increasing in frequency and scale across the healthcare sector. Next, poor access controls where sensitive data is transmitted across different networks or stored in the cloud. There is also a challenge with auditability, where many AI models run

DOI: 10.1201/9781003565215-3

as black-box systems, which can obscure who accessed/changed data. Lastly, if there are insufficient or lacking consent protocols, it will violate traditional HIPAA's standard for transparency. If there is a breach of therapy notes, a misinterpreted AI recommendation or unauthorized data share could result in legal consequences, but also deep psychological harm and loss of trust. There are several strategies for mitigating these risks that will align AI-driven tools with HIPAA standards. The first strategy to prevent risks is to ensure there is robust encryption on all data. This will make sure that data is protected while stored and in transit, whether that is through the cloud or other networks. This protection of vulnerable data will also ensure personal information cannot be intercepted or read by unauthorized people. This takes us to the next strategy, which is making sure only authorized personnel, like the patient's therapist, have access to the mental health data. Beyond the data being protected and private, there is always the potential for data breaches or hacking of information. To prevent this, detailed logs should be created to log and monitor all access and changes to content. These logs are crucial to monitor compliance and respond to breaches in the system. The last strategy and important component to protect patients is that they must be informed in clear language about what sort of data is being collected. They also need to be made aware of how the data will be used and if and how they can revoke consent.

By adopting these security measures, it will ensure that the AI practices can be transparent enough for patients to feel protected and secure in their mental health care. The safeguards and measures put in place also help make sure that AI is used responsibly and ethically. HIPAA and other legal agreements around the world must evolve in tandem with AI adoption. In mental healthcare, trust and confidentiality are the foundation, so privacy and data protection are a must-have. As AI continues to reshape mental health treatment, HIPAA (and other legal health guidelines) must not be seen as a hurdle but as a guidepost for building systems that protect patient well-being.[2]

ALGORITHMIC BIAS AND FAIRNESS

A key issue in using AI for mental health care that is overlooked is the bias already embedded in the training data. The quality of the training data itself directly shapes how AI systems behave. A significant portion of the data being used is already flawed. Many data sets are often small and biased toward certain populations, usually ones who are easiest to sample/have access too. This sampling is problematic in all sectors and particularly in mental healthcare. Systems rely on highly personal input like voice tone or word choice, which can vary significantly across cultures and different backgrounds. If these variations that occur in all types of cultures and other sorts of factors are not accounted for, the resulting AI model will carry these biases moving forward. The further it goes and progresses, the more specific and, as a result, the more biased the data and results will be. In practice, this means that the AI tool could keep evolving based on specific demographic data and make it unable to be representative of other populations. For example, if an AI mental health data set was based on data from white males from western populations, the data and results will be perfectly suited for that group, but none others. AI will then have the potential to completely misinterpret and overlook signals in someone's mental health data simply because they do not match the original training data. For mental health, this is clearly a huge issue because it will reinforce inequality and reduce overall trust in care practices.[3]

Beyond the process of data collection, it is not just about having enough data, but about having the *right* data. Data that is collected in intentional, ethical, and contextually appropriate ways. One paper, *A Survey on Data Collection for Machine Learning*, outlines how data collection is becoming a major bottleneck in AI development, especially in emerging areas where large, high-quality datasets do not already exist. Mental health applications often start from scratch for data collection, unlike other fields that have years of data behind them. Mental health data is more subjective and ultimately tied to individuals' own lived experiences. This data includes information like emotional tone in speech or written expressions in therapy chat logs. All data that is highly sensitive and context-dependent. Bias in an AI diagnostic tool could mean that some patients receive incorrect assessments. An AI might rate non-white patients' risk of suicide as lower than it truly is because the training data underrepresented those patients' risk factors. Conversely, it might flag a higher rate of "false positives" for another group, subjecting them to unnecessary stress or interventions. These disparities have the potential to aggravate existing inequalities in mental healthcare outcomes.

The type of data collected and how it is handled at every step directly impact the ethical quality and technical performance of mental health AI. For example, if training data is mostly drawn from one demographic (white, English-speaking/digitally literate), the resulting model will work best for that group. This then fails to accurately recognize patterns or needs in others. In mental health, this is serious because biased or inaccurate predictions can and will shape clinical decisions. Current data collection methods are prioritizing scale and speed over nuance and diversity. For example, many public datasets are created from platforms where users did not give explicit consent for clinical use, or where metadata like gender, age, and cultural background are missing. Without this context, it becomes nearly impossible to identify how well the model generalizes across populations. AI systems in this space must be built on data that is representative and carefully interpreted. Otherwise, we risk building tools that work well on paper but fall short, or worse, cause harm when deployed in use.[4]

REPLACEMENT VS. AUGMENTATION

In the past few years, AI mental health tools have demonstrated their ability to augment clinical care. These tools that can offer 24/7 availability to conversational support can help reduce the burden on clinicians, especially those in underfunded and inaccessible areas. For example, the use of AI mental healthcare could have been incredibly beneficial during the height of the COVID-19 Pandemic. While human providers were scarce and spread incredibly thin, the onset of AI tools could be extremely helpful. In this sense, AI offers an aid to human providers, especially if they have limited access (social distancing/masks) to patients. Research has agreed with this concept of AI being a helpful tool to collaborate with human providers, but never replace them. The issues arise when replacement is in the discussion for AI in mental healthcare. If economic pressures or overall efficiency goals are prioritized, it might drive an over-reliance on AI systems. This has the potential to sideline human therapists as well as cause issues in the widespread use of the systems. For example, in some contexts like using AI in schools or in prisons, the AI has been implemented without human oversight, which raises alarms about neglectful care. Mental healthcare is fundamentally relational, and the therapeutic alliance is built on empathy and trust. These human factors cannot be replicated or replaced by AI. Even if AI can simulate conversation, it does not possess shared understanding or consciousness. If we reduce care to these one-sided interactions in assessment, it can lead to patients feeling misunderstood.

In order to navigate tensions in this context, a sensitive design approach can be useful. A framework that emphasizes designing technologies that preserve core human values such as dignity, empathy, and agency. When applied to AI in mental health, value-sensitive design insists that automation should not replace relational care but instead support and enhance it. Real-world applications show that these concerns are not hypothetical. In some institutional settings, automated mental health tools have been used to monitor behavior or flag emotional distress without integrating human review or follow-up. In these cases, users have reported feeling surveilled or unsupported, undermining trust in both the technology and the broader care system. Such examples highlight the need for guardrails. Institutions must avoid treating AI as a cost-saving substitute and instead commit to thoughtful integration, where AI supports but does not displace the clinician–patient relationship. The future of AI in mental healthcare should prioritize augmentation over automation.

A growing body of research reveals how providers are wrestling with fears of obsolescence and moral unease. Researchers who investigated these premises with physicians in general healthcare had findings connected to mental health care professionals. In both care settings, empathy and relational connection are central to the care itself. In a study, researchers found that professionals had expressed significant anxiety about job displacement, fearing their training could be undermined by AI systems. While AI can offer efficient tools (e.g., mood tracking), it can never replicate the affective presence of a real professional. If an AI system replaces, rather than supports, this alliance, both parties will experience loss. The provider will potentially lose their career, and the patient will face automated care that can be unhelpful for their treatment. There is an increasing burden healthcare officials feel when AI encroaches on roles that demand empathy and moral discretion. For many clinicians, there is fear of potential career loss and a shift in the entire field. They also have beliefs that AI lacks the moral framework needed to navigate these sensitive decisions in the mental healthcare field. AI, for its many strengths, cannot truly "care" – it may simulate empathy, but it cannot embody it. Technologies should be shaped not only by what is technically possible, but also by what supports clinician well-being and the patient-provider bond. In sum, while AI may promise to relieve burdens and improve access in mental health services, its deployment must avoid creating new forms of psychological distress among clinicians.[5]

In ongoing discussions about whether AI should replace or augment human providers, a critical insight emerging from consumer research is the role of framing. The way that AI is introduced as either an augmentation or replacement has a significant effect on whether users/patients accept this care delivery. Researchers found that framing AI as an augmentation to service was received with increased willingness to accept the AI-based service. In contrast, substitution framing led to more negative emotional reactions and lower acceptance rates. Although the study was conducted in hospitality, the core mechanisms of emotional response and relational expectations are applicable to mental health contexts, where human connections are central to care. For instance, in psychotherapy, framing a chatbot as a tool that assists the therapist (e.g., by tracking mood trends or offering after-hours support) is likely to be received far more positively than presenting it as a standalone replacement for human care. When users feel that AI is enhancing rather than undermining the therapeutic relationship, their openness to such tools increases. In mental healthcare, where feeling is as important as thinking, the way technology is framed can make the difference in resisting and trusting.[6]

TRUST AND THE THERAPEUTIC ALLIANCE

Continuing on the conversation of augmentation and AI disrupting the therapeutic alliance, there are questions about the extent to which humans can trust AI providers. Many other industries besides healthcare, and specifically mental healthcare, are using AI at an advanced rate. All of these industries see the success and increased productivity that AI can bring to different parts of work and care. The issue arises when human-specific skills or attributes like empathy and having strong interpersonal communication skills find themselves in the crossfire of whether they can actually be replaced or replicated by AI. Even though AI excels in things like data analysis and pattern recognition, it lacks the true interpersonal skills (e.g., active listening, emotional regulation) that are required for mental healthcare. This is especially concerning to the specific therapeutic alliance, which requires the moral presence and the actual two-sided relational aspect. Because again, AI does not have a moral presence or has any true internal convictions, making it an equal relationship.

To build a trusting relationship, there must be two sides contributing, and AI is a one-sided loop. This separation of skillset is crucial for mental health care success since the success of care is based on the strength of the therapeutic alliance. Patients are looking for solutions and treatment plans, but they are also looking to be validated and understood with compassion. These relational factors are not simply soft skills but are foundational to recovery.

Moreover, research proposes a vision of "high-tech, high-touch" care, in which AI augments decision-making while human providers maintain their core responsibilities in emotional and ethical domains. For mental healthcare practitioners, this means that when using AI they can leverage AI tools to enhance insight and help recognize patterns across different patient populations, but the end intervention and care is grounded and based in the clinical connection and evaluation. The goal is not just precision care, but compassionate precision. From a developmental standpoint, these concepts also speak to the need for educational reform. As AI transforms the skillsets required of future providers, medical and psychological education must evolve accordingly. While technical proficiency with digital tools is necessary, it must be balanced with deliberate cultivation of empathy and communication skills. These "critical human skills" are not replaceable and should be protected and prioritized as core competencies.[7]

Can machines be trusted?

Trust in mental health care is not transactional; rather, it is deeply relational. It arises from empathy and a shared sense of safety and understanding. These are not merely "nice to have" attributes-they are the psychological scaffolding of the therapeutic alliance. As AI tools begin to participate in mental health delivery, the question emerges: *can machines be trusted in the same way that human therapists are?*

Research has investigated this question, and one study gives a helpful framework for understanding trust. Researchers identified three distinct types of trust. The first type is inductive trust, which is based on prior experiences that are kept in memory. For example, in a past situation, one outcome occurred, and therefore, in future similar situations, you expect similar outcomes. The second type is social trust, which is based on general goals and behaviors. In this type of trust, humans interpret others' goal-oriented behavior and act accordingly in response. The last type of trust out of three is moral trust. Moral trust is based on shared values and a general sense of moral responsibility to do the right thing. This type of trust, when seen in "human-human" interactions, requires a shared obligation to respect moral beliefs that we project onto each other. This type of trust is also crucial for therapeutic alliances/relationships since it requires both parties to assess each other of having moral standards to create a positive working relationship. AI, however, meets only one of the three types of trust. AI only meets the standard for inductive trust. People have learned to trust AI from their own experiences as well as the experiences and vouching of others using it. When people see others in their social circle or network use AI, they find it more trustworthy and valid to use. AI, however, lacks the social and moral trust that humans have. AI has no internal goals or motivations other than its algorithm. It does not have moral standings that guide and control its behavior. It is impossible for AI to have true social trust since they have no internal convictions guiding them. AI also does not have any moral convictions since, again, AI has no internal guidance whatsoever, making it unable to be a moral agent in the world of healthcare. AI, however, mimics these types of trust and behavior, resulting in patients forming one-sided relationships with AI. Patients will most likely anthropomorphize AI tools (attribute human qualities/values to AI systems), but they are simply mimicking human-like conversations. The patients may perceive a sense of empathy from the AI, but it is a falsity. The relationship is one-sided and researchers warn that it is incredibly harmful to attribute AI to have social or moral capacities. Researchers find this harmful and worrisome since it can lead to patients over-trusting this technology as well as tarnishing the well-established therapeutic bond. The bond is built on factors with a moral presence which cannot be replaced by AI, no matter how fluent or realistic it may seem.

Additionally, trust is socially and contextually propagated. People often trust AI not because of firsthand experience, but because others in their network do. This social diffusion can lead to rapid adoption, but also to sudden, widespread disillusionment if trust is violated. One flawed interaction, especially if not transparently addressed, can trigger a broader collapse of confidence in the system or platform. To foster appropriate trust in AI-based mental health tools, there are several mechanisms rooted in explainable AI and value-sensitive design. AI systems must be transparent and honest – this means they need to clearly share and identify themselves as non-human. If there is any chance for deception, and to try to convince patients they are talking to a sentient being would be incredibly violating to patients' autonomy by trying to convince them of something false. It is unhelpful to encourage them to communicate and attempt to relate to a system in ways it cannot reciprocate. The capabilities and limitations need to be integrated in both the design of the AI when in use and at the introduction. Next, patients need explanations for all outputs from the AI. If, on some random occasion, the AI produces an unexpected or inappropriate response, there needs to be a clear rationale provided to help mediate. This communication will make AI transparent as well as give reassurance to the user. The AI system created in whatever specific context should also allow patients and providers to flag harmful or unhelpful responses. These inputs need to be reported and, in use, should meaningfully inform the system to refine it. AI also needs to avoid overreach because trust is proportional to capability. AI systems should not make therapeutic promises they cannot keep, nor should they handle high-risk disclosures (such as suicidal ideation or trauma processing) without immediate human involvement. When trust exceeds competence, the system becomes dangerous.[8]

Building on the foundational idea that trust in mental healthcare is relational and emotionally grounded, recent research adds further complexity by showing that how individuals relate to AI may vary based on their attachment styles. Recent research has explored this concept through attachment theory, which helps reveal that trust in AI is not uniformly distributed. The trust people have in AI can also be understood through relational models. People with different attachment styles can and will vary in how much trust they have toward AI systems. For example, people with secure attachments are actually more likely to have trust in AI systems. They are trusted, especially if the AI is framed in a way that evokes a sense of support or familiarity. For this type of person, if AI is catered to them and used as a tool, they will be more open to trusting the system. On the other hand, people who have anxious or avoidant attachment will have greater skepticism and less trust in the AI system. Overall, trust in AI is beyond judgment; it is also an emotional stance toward something that feels relational even when it is not. This is where the human sense to anthropomorphize things because of an increasing concern that people are being misled by AI. Patients and users may interpret the human adjacent language or expressions as a genuine version of empathy or emotional response. This can be incredibly misleading to all users, and especially those who might have unmet relational needs or insecure forms of attachment. What appears on the surface as "trust" may, in some cases, be more accurately described as projection.

Users are relating not to the AI's actual capacity for care, but to their own psychological needs. This creates a vulnerable situation in which emotional reliance is placed on a system that, by design, cannot reciprocate or repair relational ruptures the way a human therapist can. When AI tools inevitably fail to respond with nuance or attunement in sensitive moments, the emotional fallout for the user (particularly those with fragile trust) can be significant. Trust in AI is essential for therapeutic engagement, but it is not guaranteed, nor is it evenly distributed. It depends not only on system performance but also on individual histories, psychological dispositions, and emotional needs. In order for AI to support the genuine therapeutic alliance, the role must be transparently communicated and its limits must be clearly defined and understood. The design of the AI itself must also be embedded to take into account the relational complexities that shape the extent to which people interact with AI. Trust is foundational for mental healthcare, and trust is key to helping a patient heal. For AI to play a meaningful role in mental healthcare, it must do so in a way that respects emotional depth, avoids deception, and supports a spectrum of different relational experiences.[9]

RESPONSIBILITY WHEN AI MAKES MISTAKES

There are a lot of technological advances when integrating AI systems into mental healthcare that can increase accessibility and accuracy. However, in the event AI makes a mistake like incorrectly assessing a mood behavior or pushing the wrong treatment plan, a big question arises. One that introduces new ethical as well as legal dilemmas in how to assess mistakes. *Who is responsible when things go wrong?*

Suppose an AI scheduling system fails to flag a severely depressed patient who then attempts suicide, or an AI chatbot gives advice that a patient feels worsens their anxiety. Who is legally and ethically at fault? This is a complex issue. If a clinician was in the loop, was it their responsibility to catch the issue? Or did the tool's developer bear responsibility for a flaw in the algorithm? Currently, malpractice law does *not* have clear precedents for AI. Ethically, it suggests that we need clarity: healthcare providers and institutions might be reluctant to use AI if they fear being sued for its mistakes. Some researchers have suggested we treat AI tools like medical devices. If a device (e.g., a faulty pacemaker) causes harm, liability can fall on the manufacturer. But if a clinician contributed to the decision, liability might be shared. In any case, the uncertainty around liability itself is a barrier and ethical concern, because unclear responsibility is risky for patients.

Drawing on previous research, it must be recognized that the more AI systems are entrusted with critical judgment, and the more they outperform or replace human decision-making, the greater the moral obligation to ensure that these systems are safe and accountable. Failure to do so leaves us with responsibility gaps, zones of moral and practical uncertainty where harmful outcomes may occur without clear avenues for blame or reform. Responsibility becomes particularly murky in cases involving multiple stakeholders. Is it the AI developer who should be held accountable for flawed logic or inadequate training data? The healthcare provider who used the AI system as a clinical support tool? The hospital or institution that approved its deployment? What if a clinician follows the AI's recommendation in good faith, believing it to be a trustworthy guide? Here we face a distribution of responsibility that resists traditional liability models. One study identifies this challenge as an "R-gap" – a situation in which no individual actor may be blameworthy, even though something has clearly gone wrong. The ethical danger lies in a diffusion of responsibility that makes it easier to disavow accountability altogether.

Current malpractice laws were not designed to accommodate the layered, distributed nature of AI decision-making. Legal frameworks typically presume a clear causal chain between human action and harm. In contrast, AI technologies are co-constructed and co-deployed: developers build them, institutions implement them, and clinicians use them in practice. This shared structure blurs the line of blame assignment, revealing a legal gap on how to divide responsibility and determine how accountability is enforced. While no actor may be individually culpable, someone must still be responsible. In mental healthcare, where users are especially vulnerable and trust is paramount, this kind of ethical supervision is not optional. The risks of miscommunication, misdiagnosis, or emotional harm are amplified when interacting with AI.[10]

If we cannot eliminate responsibility gaps entirely, we must at least ensure that those gaps are bridged with deliberate, accountable action or a shared moral responsibility, especially given the high-stakes nature of healthcare, where such errors can mean the difference between life and death. Other research also challenges the assumption of responsibility gaps because it argues that human clinicians still make the final decisions. Due to this, the concept of a gap is overemphasized since the existing practice is grounded in the hands of the physician. In these scenarios, clinicians are not passive recipients of AI outputs. Instead, clinicians are expected to interpret AI insights into the broader clinical picture.

Research also explores a more complex ethical situation. Researchers pose a future in which AI takes on full clinical responsibility. In this future, the human role becomes passive, with little or no control over the AI's decisions once activated. If the doctors are no longer in the loop for decision-making, are they still accountable for outcomes? Does responsibility shift to the developers or institutions that build and put out the AI? Current research does not have a precise answer for this future; however, as long as clinicians are still involved, the responsibility still lies with the human practitioners. Even if AI is enhancing insight, it does not eliminate the physician's responsibility to critically evaluate each case as well as interpret the AI tool in the process. These factors help reinforce that AI must be integrated, not substituted, within medical practice. As such, claims of responsibility gaps may be premature or misplaced in current contexts. What remains ethically essential is the continued expectation of human oversight, and the development of AI tools that support clinical judgment. Responsibility must therefore be distributed with human practitioners maintaining the final say in patient care. Simultaneously, greater accountability must be demanded of developers and institutions that create and implement these technologies. Responsibility does not emerge from filling so-called "gaps," but from the direct and foreseeable role people play in shaping and acting upon AI-generated information. Clinicians, developers, and institutions are not morally removed from harm simply because the AI functioned autonomously. Mistakes made by AI are not ethically suspended in a void; they are embedded in human choices. Until AI achieves a level of autonomy that society deems trustworthy for full clinical control, mixed responsibility remains the only morally and professionally sound approach.[11]

LONG-TERM IMPACTS

AI and the use of AI in the mental health care world are in infancy, so there is a lack of long-term evidence and research of prolonged use of AI in this field (and many others). For mental healthcare, it is imperative to look beyond the immediate fixes AI can bring to the field, but also look into the future to identify potential issues or outcomes. This is also especially important since this AI is specifically for mental health, a vulnerable population facing personal struggles, as well as the chance for other vulnerable populations going through development (adolescents/teens, etc.). The long-term consequences could have a detrimental impact on the human psyche that research has not had the proper time to thoughtfully analyze the greater risks. This section will examine a couple of risks that research has identified to be a potential impact of long usage. The three risks are desocialization, altered self-perception and dependency, and changing their emotional regulation. This portion will also examine vulnerable populations like children/teens, as well as those struggling with psychosis.

DESOCIALIZATION

Prolonged reliance on AI-based mental health tools may, over time, erode users' motivation to seek real human contact. Some individuals may come to prefer the 24/7 availability and neutral tone of AI interactions (never judges or fatigues). However, this can foster a pattern of increased social withdrawal, especially if and when users begin to substitute AI tools (e.g., chatbot) for real-world emotional connections. Research has emphasized that "relationships" with AI lack reciprocity and any emotional depth, and over time can contribute to isolation. This self-isolation can potentially diminish a person's ability to successfully navigate social situations. This desocialization is especially concerning in regards to children/young adults who need social interaction to learn important social skills.

ALTERED SELF-PERCEPTION

Another emerging concern with prolonged AI use is the negative effects of being perceived through a data-driven lens. If patients are being seen through behavior prediction/automated mood tracking, it has the potential to reshape how individuals understand themselves. These patients may interpret their internal states into categories and can seemingly flatten the complexity of human emotion and life into simple metrics or labeling. In adolescents, whose identities are still forming, this can be extremely distorting. There is also an increased risk of therapeutic misconception, where users overestimate AI's insight or support, leading them to view it as a complete substitute for other people.

DEPENDENCY AND EMOTIONAL REGULATION

Conversational AI tools are marketed as emotional companions who are capable of helping users manage stress, anxiety, or sadness. While in moderation, this can be helpful, an overreliance (particularly among adolescents) raises risks of emotional dependency. Instead of developing coping strategies over time, users may turn to AI for immediate remediation in forming one-sided emotional bonds with the chatbot. These "relationships" simulate empathy, but ultimately lack the real nuance and responsiveness of a human. The 24/7 access and consistent feedback also have the potential to undermine a person's ability to tolerate emotional discomfort. If they are unable to delay gratification, it will prevent them from seeking real interpersonal help.

CHILDREN AND VULNERABLE POPULATIONS

For children and adolescents, the risk of AI-based mental health tools is magnified. Already, the widespread use of AI chatbots on the internet has proven to be incredibly harmful when in the hands of children and other young people still developing. To have access to a program at all hours can greatly reduce efforts to seek real relationships and care. Many chat sites (e.g., Character AI) offer "therapist" tools even though they are completely separate to an AI embedded into mental healthcare. However, for children or young people, they might not see a reasonable difference, making them have increased risks of deception and emotional misunderstanding. AI tools, especially chat ones, personalize over time with use and can create new behaviors and attitudes in children by steering them toward certain responses or habits. This is especially concerning if there are no guardrails in place that provide informed consent and transparency that they are talking to AI, as well as consent for parents/guardians. In specifically using AI for mental healthcare, where hopefully guardrails and security are embedded in the system, it still poses risks for vulnerable populations who misunderstand the system.

Beyond this developmental population, another overlooked group includes those who experience symptoms of psychosis. These are patients or people (undiagnosed) who may experience delusions, hallucinations, or similar symptoms. These types of people are especially at risk of using AI in such a way that can be extremely detrimental to their health. For these users, the boundary of one-sided conversation and human interaction is blurred, and many can view these chat experiences as real relationships. AI, as well as chatbot versions, often support and play into what people say, and in this case, can be extremely dangerous if the AI plays into being conscious or sentient. These users might be convinced that the AI is a conscious being, which will deepen their symptoms and push them away from real human care. The AI might reinforce psychosis like thinking patterns and validate narratives that are disconnected from reality. Even in an embedded system, AI makes mistakes and could misread delusions as something else and not flag them for the real clinician. There is an urgent need for frameworks that recognize beyond the "average" user, but also those who can be susceptible to harm in AI environments.

FORESIGHT AND RESEARCH GAPS

There is a significant lack of longitudinal research examining the psychological effects of using AI in mental healthcare over time. Few studies are tracking emotional development and interpersonal functioning in users who rely heavily on AI and less so with those during critical developmental stages. This is why there must be long-term assessments that are included in the approval and monitoring processes for mental health AI tools. These assessments included evaluating risks related to privacy, autonomy, emotional development, and therapeutic misunderstanding. Furthermore, AI use should not be viewed as a replacement for human therapists or clinicians. Instead, AI can be a supplementary tool, embedded within systems of human care with clear boundaries and safeguards in place.[12]

ACKNOWLEDGMENTS

The author wishes to express profound gratitude to Zoe Shapiro, whose extensive insights, detailed research, and thoughtful analysis were instrumental in shaping this chapter.

NOTES

1 Song, Shichao, et al. "Multimodal Transformer for Depression Detection: Integration of Resting-State EEG and Facial Video Data." *Proceedings of the 31st ACM International Conference on Multimedia (MM '23)*, 29 Oct.–3 Nov. 2023, Ottawa, Canada, pp. 4743–4751, https://www.sciencedirect.com/science/article/pii/S1746809425015502. Accessed 5 June 2025.

2 ABM Kamrul Islam Riad, Md Abdul Barek, Md Mostafizur Rahman, Mst Shapna Akter, Tahia Islam, and Md Abdur Rahman. "Enhancing HIPAA Compliance in AI-driven mHealth Devices Security and Privacy." *2024 IEEE 48th Annual Computers, Software, and Applications Conference (COMPSAC)*, 2–4 July 2024, Osaka, Japan. IEEE, 26 Aug. 2024. https://doi.org/10.1109/COMPSAC61105.2024.00390.

3 Whang, Steven Euijong, Yuji Roh, Hwanjun Song, and Jae-Gil Lee. "Data Collection and Quality Challenges in Deep Learning: A Data-Centric AI Perspective." *The VLDB Journal*, vol. 32, 2023, pp. 791–813. Springer. https://doi.org/10.1007/s00778-022-00775-9.

4 Roh, Yuji, Geon Heo, and Steven Euijong Whang. "A Survey on Data Collection for Machine Learning: A Big Data–AI Integration Perspective." *IEEE Transactions on Knowledge and Data Engineering*, vol. 33, no. 4, Apr. 2021, pp. 1328–1347. IEEE. https://doi.org/10.1109/TKDE.2019.2946162.

5 Roh, Yuji, Geon Heo, and Steven Euijong Whang. "A Survey on Data Collection for Machine Learning: A Big Data–AI Integration Perspective." *IEEE Transactions on Knowledge and Data Engineering*, vol. 33, no. 4, 1 Apr. 2021, pp. 1328–1347. IEEE. https://doi.org/10.1109/TKDE.2019.2946162.

6 *Current Issues in Tourism*. Taylor & Francis Online, https://www.tandfonline.com/journals/rcit20?src=pdf. Accessed 1 June 2025.

7 Alrassi, James, Peter J. Katsufrakis, and Latha Chandran. "Technology Can Augment, But Not Replace, Critical Human Skills Needed for Patient Care." *Academic Medicine*, vol. 96, no. 1, Jan. 2021, pp. 37–43. https://doi.org/10.1097/ACM.0000000000003733. Accessed 5 June 2025.

8 Andras, Peter, et al. "Trusting Intelligent Machines: Deepening Trust Within Socio-Technical Systems." *IEEE Technology and Society Magazine*, vol. 37, no. 4, Dec. 2018, pp. 76–83. https://doi.org/10.1109/MTS.2018.2876107. Accessed 5 June 2025.

9 illath, Omri, et al. "Attachment and Trust in Artificial Intelligence." *Computers in Human Behavior*, vol. 115, Feb. 2021, article 106607. Elsevier. https://doi.org/10.1016/j.chb.2020.106607.

10 Gillath, Omri, Ting Ai, Michael S. Branicky, Shawn Keshmiri, Robert B. Davison, and Ryan Spaulding. "Attachment and Trust in Artificial Intelligence." *Computers in Human Behavior*, vol. 115, Feb. 2021, article no. 106607. Elsevier. https://doi.org/10.1016/j.chb.2020.106607.

11 Naik, Nithesh, et al. "Legal and Ethical Consideration in Artificial Intelligence in Healthcare: Who Takes Responsibility?" *Frontiers in Surgery*, vol. 9, 13 Mar. 2022, article no. 862322. Section: Genitourinary Surgery and Interventions. Frontiers Media. https://doi.org/10.3389/fsurg.2022.862322.

12 Naik, Nithesh, et al. "Legal and Ethical Consideration in Artificial Intelligence in Healthcare: Who Takes Responsibility?" *Frontiers in Surgery*, vol. 9, 13 Mar. 2022. doi:10.3389/fsurg.2022.862322.

Chapter 4

Opportunities in prevention

INTRODUCTION

According to the World Health Organization (WHO), mental health disorders are now a substantial contributor to the global disease burden, with depression alone representing the leading cause of disability globally. With prominent mental illnesses such as depression and anxiety costing the global economy about 1 trillion USD annually in lost productivity, there is an urgency for effective solutions.[1]

In the context of mental healthcare, prevention refers to the strategies and interventions aimed at reducing the incidence, prevalence, and recurrence of mental health disorders, as well as minimizing risk factors and strengthening protective factors. The goal is to prevent not only those at-risk, but to prevent communities at large from developing a mental health condition.

Although the concepts of early intervention and prevention in mental health have been discussed for several decades, evaluation of empirically supported prevention programs has lagged far behind that of treatment. Much of the focus on addressing this burden has been on improving the lives of those who have already been diagnosed, and the prevention programs that do exist have largely focused on intervention with high-risk patient populations and problem behaviors, such as child abuse and teenage pregnancy to list a few, with research into prevention of some mental disorders only just beginning to emerge. In large measure, this has been due to the heterogeneity of the clinical phenotypes of mental health problems – including the blurred boundaries distinguishing one from the other and challenges with being able to identify specific etiological risk factors which may be prevented or mitigated. However, this is a misplaced assumption for, no matter what the phenotype in adulthood may look like, we do have specific targets for prevention of a range of mental health problems. Importantly, these are clustered in the early years of life, from birth through young adulthood, emphasizing the importance of early screening at a young age.

DOI: 10.1201/9781003565215-4

PREVENTION

Three sets of observations underlie the prevention of mental health. The first is that regardless of the clinical phenotype of the mental health problem, childhood neglect and deprivation – ranging from adverse family circumstances, effects of poverty and social determinants of health, to exposure to abuse and violence, are all strong risk factors.[2–3] The second observation is that the majority of mental health problems encountered in adulthood have their origins before the age of twenty-four years. Both these observations highlight the critically important role of the developmental phase stretching from early childhood through young adulthood in the etiology of mental health problems, and the responsibility in turn of the system to implement measures in these early years[4] to prevent the onset of a mental illness into adulthood. The third observation, which triangulates with these findings, is that of the growing evidence base on interventions, which target the social environments and psychological capabilities of children and young people in preventing mental health problems.

Despite the substantial body of evidence from epidemiological, clinical, and developmental research reporting the percentage of mental illness beginning in childhood and continuing into adulthood, structural, political, economic, and cultural barriers continue to be barriers in the implementation of effective preventative programs for mental health.

Emerging awareness of mental illness, globally, continues to unveil the scale of the mental health crisis that plagues societies worldwide. The surge in the prevalence of mental health disorders has placed an unprecedented demand on healthcare systems, revealing the inadequacies of traditional models of mental healthcare and highlighting the need for better and more innovative approaches.[4,5]

Conventional approaches continue to heavily rely on in-person consultations and therapies, which continue to fall short of addressing the increasing demand for accessible, affordable, and easily expandable mental health services.[5] More importantly, however, conventional approaches undermine the aforementioned existing evidence of 50% of mental disorders start by the age of 14. Recent research suggests that poor mental health during childhood can not only persist into adulthood but is associated with adverse health (e.g., substance use and abuse), social (e.g., delinquency), academic (e.g., school failure), and economic (high risk of poverty) adverse outcomes in adulthood.[6] Childhood and adolescence are critical periods for setting the ground for physical growth and mental well-being,[7] therefore, preventative interventions – identifying the individual, social and structural determinants of mental health, and then intervening to reduce risks, build resilience and establish supportive environments for mental health, should be a critical area of focus in the context of mental healthcare, however at present, conventional preventative approaches are rendered largely ineffective.

EXISTING PROBLEMS

Mental healthcare systems worldwide currently face several challenges that hinder prevention efforts.

The first issue with prevention in mental healthcare is of sustainability, availability and access. Though the challenge of geographical barriers has in some ways been overcome with the increased use of technology, technological limitations continue to be a barrier in seeking out early screening and preventative services. While telehealth services have expanded, technological barriers such as poor internet connectivity and a lack of digital literacy can impede access, especially among older adults and certain marginalized groups.[8]

Financial constraints also continue to hinder preventative efforts, as insurance coverage comes into play only once a diagnosis is made – if there is any place. Moreover, even in publicly funded healthcare systems, costs associated with transportation or time off work without any medical confirmation of an existing mental illness, can post as significant barriers.

Stigma and self-stigma – whereby negative attitudes and stereotypes surrounding mental illness can deter individuals from seeking help, leading to a delayed diagnosis and/or incomplete treatment. Stigma can impact preventative efforts, as individuals may internalize societal stigma, leading to feelings of shame and reluctance to seek out preventive mental health supports. In many cases, stigma can also create a fear of diagnosis, deterring individuals from participating in screenings.[9–10] Stigma can also contribute to issues around timing and implementation. Conducting screenings during periods of acute physical illness or stress may not yield accurate assessments, and individuals may not be receptive to mental health evaluations at that time.

A significant barrier is also that of transferability. However, a large number of excellent prevention programs are developed and conducted within a research framework. In most cases, once the research is completed these programs seize to exist (Headey et al., 2006). As such, the continuity and availability of programs for the prevention of mental disorders are probably the greatest barriers to successful implementation. Issues of transferability also impact timing and implementation challenges. In many cases, even when screenings identify mental health concerns, systemic issues such as provider shortages and inadequate referral processes can lead to insufficient follow-up care. This reinforces the idea that preventative programs need more than a screening mechanism, but an associated system that ensures results from a screening are not disjointed from the healthcare system at large. Although the issue of a fragmented system – integrating mental health care into the general medical system has in some ways improved, the U.S. mental health system remains largely separate from the general medical system, and there are multiple barriers to integrating care across systems.[11,12] Prevention requires collaboration across sectors up to and including education, health, housing, and social services – which is currently lacking integration. The fragmented mental health system is predominantly a treatment system. The "public mental health system" refers not to publicly funded mental health treatment, but to a system designed to address mental health from a public health perspective. The WHO defines optimal mental health as not simply an absence of illness but as a state of well-being in which an individual can realize their own abilities, cope with typical life stressors, work fruitfully, and contribute to their community.[13] Public mental health, therefore, entails a population approach to mental health, encompassing widespread promotion of mental well-being across all segments of society, prevention of mental illness, and prevention of the adverse impacts of mental illness when such illness occurs.

Another systemic and structural barrier is related to sociopolitical imperatives. In some cases, empirically validated prevention programs may not be supported due to clashes with government policy. Perhaps the best example of this situation can be found among condom distribution programs that are not supported by some governments, despite their demonstrated efficacy in reducing the spread of HIV. Efficacy and cost-effectiveness may not be ultimately supported by some governments because of their high individual cost. In essence, demonstration of efficacy is not sufficient. Sustainable prevention programs will require social advocacy in order to become a part of the political agenda.

Lastly, and most notably is the issue with shortages in mental health providers. In 2021, the U.S. psychiatry workforce met only 28% of population treatment needs, with an estimate 6600 additional psychiatrists required to fill the gap.[14] Workforce shortages are not limited to psychiatrists; psychologists, counselors, and peer support specialists are also in short supply.[15,16] This shortage can cause delays in screening due to long wait times and delays in early detection. These delays can be exacerbated by missed opportunities in primary care, given that primary care providers are typically the first contact for mental health concerns. As such, a shortage of mental health specialists makes primary care providers less likely to screen routinely due to a lack of time, training, or referral options.[17] With the short supply of providers, working providers often experience burnout, which reduces time spent on prevention and proactive care, as reactive crisis management takes precedence. Crisis services often result in higher costs and system strains, impacting any financial room for preventative care; however, without prevention, individuals are more likely to continue experiencing an acute mental crisis. A continued pattern of crisis intervention increases the long-term burden on public health systems, schools, and employers – a cycle that continues to persist. Preventative service like psychosocial education, early interventions, and screening are then sidelines when providers are overextended. Moreover, preventative mental health relies on outreach in schools, workplaces, and community centers; however, staff shortages mean these programs are either underfunded or not prioritized. This shortage of mental health providers impacts vulnerable populations profoundly. It not only compromises early screening in schools and pediatric settings, but also leads to a delay in diagnosis for older adults and reduces access to early intervention for BIPOC and immigrant communities.

CURRENT CONVENTIONAL APPROACHES USED FOR THE PREVENTION OF MENTAL HEALTHCARE

One conventional approach in the prevention of mental health care is integrating mental healthcare into primary care – moving toward community mental health care. A series of articles in World Psychiatry describes the successes and challenges that regions around the world have faced in integrating community mental health services in primary care.[18,19,20] Many countries have made significant strides in legislating mental health reform and in moving toward de-institutionalization. However, generally, mental health services in the community have not been prepared to face the resulting mental health care needs. Challenges with integrating mental health care into primary health care include limited infrastructure, shortages of human resources, limited community awareness of mental health, poverty and social deprivation, high rates of comorbidity with physical health problems, high levels of stigma and discrimination against people living with mental illnesses, and different explanatory models for mental health conditions, which influence the acceptability and uptake of services.[21,22,23]

Another conventional approach, focused on prevention has been addressing adverse childhood experiences (ACEs), like trauma, abuse, and neglect, through interventions like early childhood education programs and mental health support with the goal of reducing the risk of mental illness later in life. However, not all individuals with ACEs will develop mental illness; the impact of ACEs can vary greatly depending on individual factors, and identifying and addressing ACEs can be stigmatizing for individuals and their families, especially if they are not actively seeking help. Implementing and sustaining early intervention programs requires significant resources and can be challenging in resource-constrained settings – specifically in school settings where funding is limited. The effect sizes of the school-based prevention and intervention programs in terms of strengthening mental health, reducing psychological pressures/stress, reducing bullying/mobbing, and promoting prosocial behavior have been reported as low to moderate. This is notably higher when the prevention and intervention method targets students with an increased risk for mental health problems, such as anxiety or depression, or targets groups of students who display violent behaviors. It should be emphasized that only a sustained implementation of programs with quality assurance, qualified advanced and extended training for those conducting the programs, and an improvement of a school's atmosphere/climate will lead to sustained success in prevention and intervention in schools.[24]

A third conventional and perceivably innovative approach used in the prevention of mental healthcare is internet- and mobile-based interventions (IMIs). IMIs are designed to monitor health behavior as a form of mental health prevention. Despite its once hopeful outlook with its low-threshold, potentially flexible access, and bridging of wait times, Dederichs et al. [2021][25] found that users listed the main disadvantages as difficulties to find or decide on suitable IMIs based on clear quality criteria, fear of a misdiagnosis, lack of personalization and human interaction, recurrent technical problems, requirement of internet access, high time expenditure, financial barriers, and lack of anonymity.

ARTIFICIAL INTELLIGENCE AND PREVENTION OF MENTAL HEALTHCARE

To overcome many of the aforementioned problems with the prevention of mental healthcare, artificial intelligence (AI) is being employed within healthcare fields. AI possesses remarkable capabilities, such as efficiently handling extensive datasets and facilitating the examination of complex patterns and relationships.[26] In the context of mental healthcare, where understanding complex human behaviors and emotions is paramount, AI offers the potential to revolutionize mental healthcare by providing insights and solutions that were previously beyond the reach of conventional methods.[27,28]

Given the high morbidity and mortality in people with psychiatric disorders, coupled with a worsening shortage of mental healthcare providers, there is an urgent need for AI to help identify high-risk individuals and provide interventions to prevent mental illnesses. While published research on AI in neuropsychiatry is rather limited, there is a growing number of successful examples of AI's use with electronic health records (EHRs), brain imaging, sensor-based monitoring systems, and social media platforms to screen, predict, classify, or subgroup mental illnesses.

In terms of accessibility, AI-driven tools also have the potential to improve the accessibility of mental health therapy by helping with therapeutic exercises or providing supportive therapy sessions. For example, advancements in LLMs have enhanced the therapeutic potential of virtual reality. In a paper published in NPJ Digital Medicine in 2024, Spiegel and colleagues developed an extended-reality AI assistant that merged virtual reality and AI for precision mental health assistance based on cognitive behavioral therapy. After recording conversations with people with mild-to-moderate depression or anxiety, the assistant transcribed the speech into text, responded via Generative Pretrained Transformer 4, and played the output to the person together with a sentiment analysis of metadata controlling expressions. Although the assistant still needs to be optimized for a deeper engagement with users, it has potential advantages over traditional therapy for people who feel uncomfortable talking to therapists and provides a supplementary approach to meet the increasing need of psychological intervention.[29]

Another observational study published in Nature Medicine in 2024 suggested that AI could reduce the accessibility gap for people of minoritized ethnicities in the UK. The authors assessed the influence of a personalized, AI-enabled chatbot on self-referral efficiency in the National Health Service and found that implementation of the self-referral chatbot promoted more referrals by people of minoritized ethnicity compared with control services. Feedback provided by 42,332 individuals who completed the self-referral through the chatbot suggested that the chatbot could have removed potential barriers that people of minoritized ethnicity usually experience when seeking mental health treatment, suggesting that AI could contribute to overcoming the pervasive inequality in mental health care.

EXPLORING AI APPLICATIONS – DATA-DRIVEN APPROACHES

The advancement of AI in the field of mental healthcare is reliant on the availability and accessibility of diverse and high-quality datasets. These datasets are essential for training and validating AI models that are designed to understand, diagnose, and treat psychiatric disorders more effectively. As AI continues to permeate various aspects of research in mental healthcare, the need for open access to relevant data becomes paramount. This ensures that the development of AI tools remains transparent, reproducible, and ethical while also facilitating global collaboration among researchers.[30]

HEALTH/CLINICAL

AI has emerged as a valuable tool in the early detection and prediction of mental health disorders. These technologies, whether analyzing speech, text, facial expressions, or EHRs, are transforming how mental health is diagnosed and managed. With the aid of predictive models, AI can enhance early intervention using a data-driven approach to indicate those at risk.

In terms of healthcare/clinical data, AI has shown potential and promise in analyzing EHRs to aid in the early diagnosis of mental health disorders. The underpinning assumption is that there are historical patterns that predict future mental health crises and that such patterns can be identified in real-world EHR data. Machine learning algorithms can sift through large amounts of patient data, including medical histories, diagnostic tests, and clinical notes, to identify patterns suggesting a mental health condition. These algorithms can flag patients at risk, ensuring that healthcare providers pay closer attention to their mental well-being during routine care.

Additionally, AI can facilitate the integration of mental health data into a patient's overall health profile, enabling a more holistic approach to healthcare. One study published in Nature Medicine developed a machine learning model that uses EHRs to continuously monitor patients for risk of a mental health crisis over a period of 28 days. The model achieves an area under the receiver operating characteristic curve of 0.797 and an area under the precision-recall curve of 0.159, predicting crises with a sensitivity of 58% at a specificity of 85%. A follow-up 6-month prospective study evaluated the algorithm's use in clinical practice and observed predictions to be clinically valuable in terms of either managing caseloads or mitigating the risk of crisis in 64% of cases. Among the machine learning models evaluated, XGBoost demonstrated the best overall performance. This study was the first to continuously predict the risk of a wide range of mental health crises using EHRs to explore the added value of such predictions in clinical practice.[31]

GENETIC

Machine learning methods have been employed to make predictions in mental healthcare from genotypes, with the potential to bring improved prediction of outcomes in psychiatric genetics.

The integration of AI in the analysis of blood-based biomarkers has revolutionized the understanding of the biological underpinnings of psychiatric disorders.[32,33] By processing complex and multidimensional data from blood samples, AI-based models can identify patterns linked to mental health conditions, such as depression, schizophrenia, and bipolar disorder, which are not discernible through traditional diagnostic methods.[34,35] These models utilize Machine Learning (ML) algorithms to analyze various biological markers, including inflammatory proteins, genetic expressions, and metabolic indicators, to classify and predict psychiatric disorders with enhanced precision.[36,37] One significant advancement is the use of multi-domain integration models that combine biomarkers from multiple sources, such as immune-inflammatory proteins and cognitive metrics, to improve the diagnostic differentiation between related psychiatric conditions.[38] Additionally, unsupervised clustering methods have enabled the discovery of subtypes within psychiatric disorders, offering more personalized treatment pathways.[39,40] The application of neural networks and advanced imaging of blood samples, such as scattergram images, has also emerged as a cost-effective method for detecting psychiatric conditions like schizophrenia with high classification accuracy.[41,42]

LANGUAGE

The utilization of large language models (LLMs) in the analysis of social media data for research in mental healthcare has emerged as a transformative approach, enabling more nuanced assessments of mental health conditions.

AI algorithms can process large amounts of data including demographic information, lifestyle factors, and psychological parameters, to develop predictive models with high accuracy and reliability. Several studies have explored the use of AI in predicting mental health problems among college students.[43–44] These studies have shown favorable results, with AI algorithms achieving relatively high levels of accuracy in identifying individuals at high risk for mental issues, such as negative mental well-being traits, mental health problems, severe depressive symptoms, suicidal ideation, and perceived stress. The key predictors of poor mental well-being included the frequency of sports activities per week, body mass index, grade point average, sedentary hours, and ageLastly, in the study, "An artificial intelligence tool to assess the risk of severe mental distress among college students in terms of demographics, eating habits, lifestyles, and sport habits: an externally validated study using machine learning" by Zhang et al. (2024) a subgroup analysis revealed that participants with severe mental distress, likely to go on to develop a mental illness exhibited certain distinct characteristics. They tended to be older ($P=0.008$) and in higher grades ($P=0.016$) compared to those without severe mental distress. Additionally, they had a higher rate of smoking ($P=0.044$), a higher preference for consuming fat food ($P=0.037$), a higher monthly expense ($P<0.001$), a higher rate of chronic disease ($P=0.043$), and a higher PSQI score ($P<0.001$).[45]

SLEEP PATTERNS

In one study, Duke researchers have unveiled a groundbreaking AI model that predicts mental health declines in children with 84% accuracy, emphasizing the significant role of sleep disturbances over traditional factors like ACEs.[46] The researchers pulled existing data from the ongoing ABCD study, which is currently tracking biological and behavioral development of more than 11,800 children from age 9-adulthood, and used psychosocial and brain development assessments from that study to train an AI model to try and predict which children would develop worsening mental health in the next year. The Duke study found the AI model was 84% accurate in predicting which children would experience worsening mental illness in the next year. The model determined a child's risk score by looking at questionnaire responses to things involving their environment, behavior, social interactions, and sleep patterns.

Regarding potential prevention targets, sleep disturbances stood out as a robust predictor of high psychiatric illness risk. Their predictive influence surpassed variables such as ACEs, family mental health history, and socioeconomic status. Approximately 29% of the ABCD cohort had sleep disturbance scores exceeding clinical thresholds.[47] The importance of sleep disturbance in predicting mental illness is consistent with earlier research. A meta-analysis[48] found sleep disturbances to be a precursor for several psychiatric disorders, including depression, anxiety, and bipolar disorder. Other studies have associated sleep disturbances with subsequent substance use disorders, suicide attempts, and suicide completion.[49] Sleep is vital for healthy neurodevelopment, and sleep disturbances, particularly in adolescence, are implicated as contributors to mental illness across diagnoses.[50–51] Although further research is needed, sleep disturbances were clearly an influential predictor of high psychiatric illness risk, as sleep disturbances are modifiable with evidence-based behavioral interventions.[52]

LIFESTYLE

The increasing use of social media platforms has introduced novel methods for understanding, potentially preventing, and addressing mental health. Social media platforms such as Twitter, Facebook, and Reddit serve as rich sources of user-generated content, reflecting real-time emotional expressions, opinions, and health-related narratives.[53–54] These digital interactions provide valuable insights into public sentiment regarding psychiatric treatments and the lived experiences of individuals with mental disorders.[55–56] Studies leveraging ML and natural language processing (NLP) have demonstrated that social media data can be used to predict and classify mental health outcomes, including depression, anxiety, and suicidality.[57–58] For example, ML models trained on social media conversations have achieved high levels of accuracy in detecting suicide risk factors and depressive narratives.[59–60]

CASE STUDY

California-based AI startup Kintsugi was founded in 2019 by technologist Grace Chang and machine learning scientist Rima Seiilova-Olson. Kintsugi is focused on quickly and accurately identifying, triaging, and treating mental health conditions. With the advent of machine learning, Kintsugi harnesses the power of AI to analyze biomarkers in people's voices to quantify mental health conditions. The voice biomarker technology works to score clinical depression and anxiety from 20 seconds of free-form speech in any language. Its application programming interface (API) platform integrates into call centers, telehealth visits, and remote patient monitoring applications, enabling clinicians to deliver timely, evidence-based mental health care while improving outcomes for patients.[61]

What makes Kintsugi unique is that Kintsugi Voice does not require specific questions or text to product a result in real time, its flexible API enables hundreds of workflows from retrospective live in-call scoring, it can detect voice biomarkers for depression and anxiety based on how a patient speaks (not NLP) and their AI model represents over 40k patients verified by Psychiatrics with over 7 years of experience. The benefits include assisting clinicals with picking up subtle cues of voice to quantify conditions, its non-invasive, it can predict results in under a minute, it reduces bias by using language agnostics where scores are based on how you speak, not what you say, it can predict severity of conditions from low to severe, it can track mental health scores overtime and it can boost patient outcomes and profitability for healthcare organizations.

A recent study, by Mazur et al. [2025][67], aimed to evaluate the efficacy of machine learning technology (Kintsugi Voice, v1, Kintsugi Mindful Wellness, Inc) to detect and analyze voice biomarkers consistent with moderate to severe depression, potentially allowing for greater compliance with this critical primary care public health need. They performed a cross-sectional study from February 1, 2021 to July 31, 2022 to examine ≥25 seconds of free-form speech content from English-speaking samples captured from 14,898 unique adults in the United States and Canada where their voice biomarker results were compared with a self-reported Patient Health Questionnaire-9 (PHQ-9) at a cut-off score of 10 (moderate to severe depression).

In terms of model and architecture, a feed-forward deep neural network comprised of four algorithmic layers was "trained in a supervised manner using PHQ-9 scores as labels to detect the presence of vocal characteristics consistent with a moderate to severe acute depressive episode in a single binary output. Training and validation datasets were then split in a 70:30 ratio to ensure sufficient data were available in the validation set. The sets were balanced to include equal proportions of demographic features and PHQ-9 scores without sample overlap. Training was performed in batches of 32 audio files introduced in a minibatch gradient descent to conserve memory and increase output speed, with a learning rate of 7.5e–4 and using the AdamW optimizer.5 Weights and biases were initialized randomly, and fine-tuning was performed between batches. Fifty epochs through all batches of training data were performed. The training objective was binary cross-entropy weighted so that the depressed and nondepressed classes carried the same weight."[62]

Results of the study indicated that from as few as 25 seconds of free-form speech, machine learning technology was able to detect vocal characteristics consistent with an increased PHQ-9 ≥10, with a sensitivity of 71.3 (95% CI, 69.0–73.5) and a specificity of 73.5 (95% CI, 71.5–75.5). Together, these results highlight the potential of Kintsugu's voice biomarker technology.[63]

Moreover, in one case study, Kintsugi partnered with Dreavita – a mental health practice, to improve the success rate of screening patients for depression, which at the time was hindering their ability to adequately identify at-risk patients due to the low compliance rates of patient completion of standard self-administered assessments like the PHQ-9. Dreavita's existing process involved care coordinators to spend 20 minutes per patient on follow-ups and clinicals to conduct assessments in real-time – which inevitably extended the length of each visit. To overcome these challenges, Kintsugi's Voice API was integrated into Zoom – to reduce manpower and time, to collect audio samples from the consultation session, and return depression analysis to the provider in real time. It was also integrated directly into Healthie, the patient's health record – to ensure seamless functionality, highlighting Kintsugi's ability to integrate with any virtual platform. In fact, the tool can be integrated into clinical call centers, telehealth platforms, remote patient monitoring, apps, and more use cases. The results from this specific case study demonstrate that in the first 6 weeks of use, 96% of Dreavita's patients opted to use the Kintsugi technology to help assess and stratify their depression level, and 100% of patients noted increased engagement and satisfaction with their care, particularly with a preference for voice analysis over the PHQ-9.

In addition to patients, care providers also reported high levels of satisfaction with the ease of use and analysis. In terms of cost, roughly 1900 minutes were saved per month for every 100 patients.[64]

Some inherent challenges and limitations include accuracy and validity. The possibility of false positives or negatives with voice biomarker technology may misclassify emotional states, thereby masking true emotions. There is the possibility of limited generalizability, where models trained on specific populations may not perform well across all groups. In terms of ethical and privacy concerns, given the possible use in call centers, this could raise issues around consent and surveillance. That said, given that only 4% of primary care patients are screened for depression, Kintsugi's machine learning model shows great promise in identifying at-risk patients for depression and anxiety.

ACKNOWLEDGMENTS

The author wishes to express profound gratitude to Salina Pirzada, whose extensive insights, detailed research, and thoughtful analysis were instrumental in shaping this chapter.

NOTES

1 Mental Health Matters." *The Lancet Global Health*, vol. 8, no. 11, Nov. 2020, p. e1352. *ScienceDirect*. https://doi.org/10.1016/S2214-109X(20)30432-0.
2 Bick, Johanna, and Charles A. Nelson. "Early Adverse Experiences and the Developing Brain." *Neuropsychopharmacology*, vol. 41, 2016, pp. 177–196. https://doi.org/10.1038/npp.2015.252. Accessed 24 May 2025.
3 Bick, Johanna, and Charles A. Nelson. "Early Adverse Experiences and the Developing Brain." *Neuropsychopharmacology*, vol. 41, 2016, pp. 177–196. https://doi.org/10.1038/npp.2015.252. Accessed 24 May 2025.
4 Jones, Peter B. "Adult Mental Health Disorders and Their Age at Onset." *The British Journal of Psychiatry Supplement*, vol. 54, 2013, pp. s5–s10. https://doi.org/10.1192/bjp.bp.112.119164. Accessed 24 May 2025.
5 "Healthcare." *ScienceDirect*, https://www.sciencedirect.com/topics/psychology/healthcare. Accessed 24 May 2025.
6 Jenkins, Rachel, F. Baingana, R. Ahmad, D. McDaid, and Rifat Atun. "Social, Economic, Human Rights and Political Challenges to Global Mental Health." *Mental Health in Family Medicine*, vol. 8, 2011, pp. 87–96. https://www.ncbi.nlm.nih.gov/pmc/articles/PMC3178190/. Accessed 24 May 2025.
7 Kieling, Christian, Helen Baker-Henningham, Myron Belfer, Gabriella Conti, Ilgi Ertem, Olayinka Omigbodun, et al. "Child and Adolescent Mental Health Worldwide: Evidence for Action." *The Lancet*, vol. 378, 2011, pp. 1515–1525. https://doi.org/10.1016/S0140-6736(11)60827-1. Accessed 30 May 2025.
8 Cavanagh, Bianca E., et al. "A Scoping Review of the Barriers and Facilitators to Accessing and Utilising Mental Health Services across Regional, Rural, and Remote Australia." *BMC Health Services Research*, vol. 23, no. 1, 4 Oct. 2023, p. 1060. https://doi.org/10.1186/s12913-023-10034-4.

9 Radovic, Ana, et al. "Perceived Facilitators of and Barriers to Implementation of a Decision Support Tool for Adolescent Depression and Suicidality Screening: Focus Group and Interview Study." *JMIR Mental Health*, vol. 8, no. 9, 15 Sept. 2021, p. e26035. https://doi.org/10.2196/26035.
10 lshaikh, Usra, et al. "Barriers and Facilitators of Older Adults for Professional Mental Health Help-Seeking: A Systematic Review." *BMC Geriatrics*, vol. 23, no. 1, 25 Aug. 2023, p. 516. https://doi.org/10.1186/s12877-023-04229-x.
11 Hoge, Michael A., et al. "Mental Health and Addiction Workforce Development: Federal Leadership Is Needed to Address the Growing Crisis." *Health Affairs*, vol. 32, no. 11, 2013, pp. 2005–2012. https://doi.org/10.1377/hlthaff.2013.0541. Accessed 24 May 2025.
12 Bishop, Tara F., Michael J. Press, Stella Keyhani, and Harold A. Pincus. "Acceptance of Insurance by Psychiatrists and the Implications for Access to Mental Health Care." *JAMA Psychiatry*, vol. 71, no. 2, 2014, pp. 176–181. https://doi.org/10.1001/jamapsychiatry.2013.2862. Accessed 24 May 2025.
13 Galderisi, Silvana, Andreas Heinz, Marisa Kastrup, Joe Beezhold, and Norman Sartorius. "Toward a New Definition of Mental Health." *World Psychiatry*, vol. 14, no. 2, 2015, pp. 231–233. https://doi.org/10.1002/wps.20231. Accessed 24 May 2025.
14 Anji, Usha. "State Abortion Policies Affect Care for Pregnancy Loss." *KFF Health News*, 12 Sep. 2024, www.kff.org/quick-takes/state-abortion-policies-affect-care-for-pregnancy-loss/. Accessed 25 May 2025.
15 Olfson, Mark. "Building the Mental Health Workforce Capacity Needed to Treat Adults with Serious Mental Illnesses." *Health Affairs*, vol. 35, no. 6, 2016, pp. 983–990. https://doi.org/10.1377/hlthaff.2015.1619. Accessed 24 May 2025.
16 Covino, Nicholas A. "Developing the Behavioral Health Workforce: Lessons from the States." *Administration and Policy in Mental Health and Mental Health Services Research*, vol. 46, no. 6, 2019, pp. 689–695. https://doi.org/10.1007/s10488-019-00963-w. Accessed 24 May 2025.
17 Cavanagh, Bianca E., et al. "A Scoping Review of the Barriers and Facilitators to Accessing and Utilising Mental Health Services across Regional, Rural, and Remote Australia." *BMC Health Services Research*, vol. 23, no. 1, 4 Oct. 2023, p. 1060. https://doi.org/10.1186/s12913-023-10034-4.
18 Hanlon, Charlotte, Dawit Wondimagegn, and Atalay Alem. "Lessons Learned in Developing Community Mental Health Care in Africa." *World Psychiatry*, vol. 9, no. 3, 2010, pp. 185–189. https://doi.org/10.1002/j.2051-5545.2010.tb00308.x. Accessed 24 May 2025.
19 Semrau, Maya, Emily A. Barley, Alexandra Law, and Graham Thornicroft. "Lessons Learned in Developing Community Mental Health Care in Europe." *World Psychiatry*, vol. 10, no. 3, 2011, pp. 217–225. https://doi.org/10.1002/j.2051-5545.2011.tb00060.x. Accessed 24 May 2025.
20 Drake, Robert E., and Eric Latimer. "Lessons Learned in Developing Community Mental Health Care in North America." *World Psychiatry*, vol. 11, no. 1, 2012, pp. 47–51. https://doi.org/10.1016/j.wpsyc.2012.01.007. Accessed 24 May 2025.
21 Eaton, Julian, Laura McCay, Maya Semrau, Sudipto Chatterjee, Florence Baingana, Ricardo Araya, et al. "Scale Up of Services for Mental Health in Low-Income and Middle-Income Countries." *The Lancet*, vol. 378, no. 9802, 2011, pp. 1592–1603. https://doi.org/10.1016/S0140-6736(11)60891-X. Accessed 24 May 2025.
22 Hanlon, Charlotte, Nagendra P. Luitel, Tamara Kathree, Vishal Murhar, Sushil Shrivastava, Girmay Medhin, et al. "Challenges and Opportunities for Implementing Integrated Mental Health Care: A District Level Situation

Analysis from Five Low- and Middle-Income Countries." *PLoS ONE*, vol. 9, no. 2, 2014, e88437. https://doi.org/10.1371/journal.pone.0088437. Accessed 24 May 2025.

23 Collins, Pamela Y., Vikram Patel, Sarah S. Joestl, Deborah March, Thomas R. Insel, Abdallah S. Daar, et al. "Grand Challenges in Global Mental Health." *Nature*, vol. 475, no. 7354, 2011, pp. 27–30. https://doi.org/10.1038/475027a. Accessed 24 May 2025.

24 Schulte-Körne, Gerd. "Mental Health Problems in a School Setting in Children and Adolescents." *Deutsches Ärzteblatt International*, vol. 113, no. 11, Mar. 2016, pp. 183–90. https://doi.org/10.3238/arztebl.2016.0183.

25 Dederichs, Marion, Julia Weber, Claudia R. Pischke, Peter Angerer, and Jana Apolinário-Hagen. "Exploring Medical Students' Views on Digital Mental Health Interventions: A Qualitative Study." *Internet Interventions*, vol. 25, 2021, article 100398. https://doi.org/10.1016/j.invent.2021.100398. Accessed 24 May 2025.

26 Bajwa, Umer, Munir A. Nori, and Bryan Williams. "Artificial Intelligence in Healthcare: Transforming the Practice of Medicine." *Future Healthcare Journal*, vol. 8, no. 2, 2021, pp. e188–e194. https://doi.org/10.7861/fhj.2021-0095. Accessed 24 May 2025.

27 Oscar Esteban et al. "MRIQC: Advancing the Automatic Prediction of Image Quality in MRI from Unseen Sites." *PLoS ONE*, vol. 12, no. 9, 2017, p. e0184661. https://doi.org/10.1371/journal.pone.0184661.

28 Langarizadeh, Mostafa, Maryam Tabatabaei, Kamran Tavakol, Mohsen Naghipour, and Fatemeh Moghbeli. "Telemental Health Care, an Effective Alternative to Conventional Mental Care: A Systematic Review." *Acta Informatica Medica*, vol. 25, no. 4, 2017, pp. 240–246. https://doi.org/10.5455/aim.2017.25.240-246. Accessed 24 May 2025.

29 Shinohara, Rintaro, et al. "Digital Mental Health Interventions for Depression, Anxiety, and Enhancement of Psychological Well-Being Among College Students: Systematic Review and Meta-Analysis." *PLOS Digital Health*, vol. 3, no. 5, 2024, article e0000305. https://www.ncbi.nlm.nih.gov/pmc/articles/PMC11784658/. Accessed 24 May 2025.

30 Wasil, Akash R., et al. "Artificial Intelligence for Global Mental Health: Potentials and Pitfalls." *JMIR Mental Health*, vol. 11, no. 1, 2024, article e51893. https://www.ncbi.nlm.nih.gov/pmc/articles/PMC11854694/. Accessed 24 May 2025.

31 Roger Garriga et al., "Machine Learning Model to Predict Mental Health Crises from Electronic Health Records," *Nature Medicine*, vol. 28, no. 5, 2022, pp. 1240–1248.

32 Fernandes, B.S., C. Karmakar, R. Tamouza, T. Tran, J. Yearwood, N. Hamdani, H. Laouamri, J.-R. Richard, R. Yolken, and M. Berk. "Precision Psychiatry with Immunological and Cognitive Biomarkers: A Multi-Domain Prediction for the Diagnosis of Bipolar Disorder or Schizophrenia Using Machine Learning." *Translational Psychiatry*, vol. 10, 2020, article 162. https://doi.org/10.1038/s41398-020-0836-4. Accessed 24 May 2025.

33 Karaglani, M., A. Agorastos, M. Panagopoulou, E. Parlapani, P. Athanasis, P. Bitsios, K. Tzitzikou, T. Theodosiou, I. Iliopoulos, and V.-P. Bozikas. "A Novel Blood-Based Epigenetic Biosignature in First-Episode Schizophrenia Patients Through Automated Machine Learning." *Translational Psychiatry*, vol. 14, 2024, article 257. https://doi.org/10.1038/s41398-024-02946-1. Accessed 24 May 2025.

34 Sánchez-Carro, Yolanda, Andres de la Torre-Luque, Itziar Leal-Leturia, Núria Salvat-Pujol, Carles Massaneda, Ana de Arriba-Arnau, Mikel Urretavizcaya, Víctor Pérez-Solà, Alba Toll, and Antonio Martínez-Ruiz. "Importance of

Immunometabolic Markers for the Classification of Patients with Major Depressive Disorder Using Machine Learning." *Progress in Neuro-Psychopharmacology and Biological Psychiatry*, vol. 121, 2023, article 110674. https://doi.org/10.1016/j.pnpbp.2022.110674. Accessed 24 May 2025.

35 Wollenhaupt-Aguiar, Beatriz, Daniel Librenza-Garcia, Guilherme Bristot, Leticia Przybylski, Lucio Stertz, Rafael Kubiachi Burque, Kamilla M. Cereser, Larissa Spanemberg, Márcio A. Caldieraro, and Bruno N. Frey. "Differential Biomarker Signatures in Unipolar and Bipolar Depression: A Machine Learning Approach." *Australian & New Zealand Journal of Psychiatry*, vol. 54, 2020, pp. 393–401. https://doi.org/10.1177/0004867419888027. Accessed 24 May 2025.

36 Mürner-Lavanchy, Isabelle, Julian Koenig, Corina Reichl, Julia Josi, Miriam Cavelti, and Michael Kaess. "The Quest for a Biological Phenotype of Adolescent Non-Suicidal Self-Injury: A Machine-Learning Approach." *Translational Psychiatry*, vol. 14, 2024, article 56. https://doi.org/10.1038/s41398-024-02776-4. Accessed 24 May 2025.

37 Chen, Shuai, Guozheng Chen, Yajing Li, Yiming Yue, Zhen Zhu, Ling Li, Wen Jiang, Zhenzhen Shen, Ting Wang, and Zhiqiang Hou. "Predicting the Diagnosis of Various Mental Disorders in a Mixed Cohort Using Blood-Based Multi-Protein Model: A Machine Learning Approach." *European Archives of Psychiatry and Clinical Neuroscience*, vol. 273, 2023, pp. 1267–1277. https://doi.org/10.1007/s00406-022-01540-3. Accessed 24 May 2025.

38 Fernandes, B.S., C. Karmakar, R. Tamouza, T. Tran, J. Yearwood, N. Hamdani, H. Laouamri, J.-R. Richard, R. Yolken, and M. Berk. "Precision Psychiatry with Immunological and Cognitive Biomarkers: A Multi-Domain Prediction for the Diagnosis of Bipolar Disorder or Schizophrenia Using Machine Learning." *Translational Psychiatry*, vol. 10, 2020, article 162. https://doi.org/10.1038/s41398-020-0836-4. Accessed 24 May 2025.

39 Siegel, C.E., E.M. Laska, Z. Lin, M. Xu, D. Abu-Amara, M.K. Jeffers, M. Qian, N. Milton, J.D. Flory, and R. Hammamieh. "Utilization of Machine Learning for Identifying Symptom Severity Military-Related PTSD Subtypes and Their Biological Correlates." *Translational Psychiatry*, vol. 11, 2021, article 227. https://doi.org/10.1038/s41398-021-01324-8. Accessed 24 May 2025.

40 Marriott, H., R. Kabiljo, G.P. Hunt, A.A. Khleifat, A. Jones, C. Troakes, the PMAS Consortium, the ST Consortium, A.L. Pfaff, and J.P. Quinn. "Unsupervised Machine Learning Identifies Distinct ALS Molecular Subtypes in Post-Mortem Motor Cortex and Blood Expression Data." *Acta Neuropathologica Communications*, vol. 11, 2023, article 208. https://doi.org/10.1186/s40478-023-01686-8. Accessed 24 May 2025.

41 Zhu, X., C.-l. Wang, J.-f. Yu, J. Weng, B. Han, Y. Liu, X. Tang, and B. Pan. "Identification of Immune-Related Biomarkers in Peripheral Blood of Schizophrenia Using Bioinformatic Methods and Machine Learning Algorithms." *Frontiers in Cellular Neuroscience*, vol. 17, 2023, article 1256184. https://doi.org/10.3389/fncel.2023.1256184. Accessed 24 May 2025.

42 Tasci, B., G. Tasci, H. Ayyildiz, A.P. Kamath, P.D. Barua, T. Tuncer, S. Dogan, E.J. Ciaccio, S. Chakraborty, and U.R. Acharya. "Automated Schizophrenia Detection Model Using Blood Sample Scattergram Images and Local Binary Pattern." *Multimedia Tools and Applications*, vol. 83, 2024, pp. 42735–42763. https://doi.org/10.1007/s11042-023-16676-0. Accessed 24 May 2025.

43 Anbarasi, L.J., M. Jawahar, V. Ravi, S.M. Cherian, S. Shreenidhi, and H. Sharen. "Machine Learning Approach for Anxiety and Sleep Disorders Analysis During COVID-19 Lockdown." *Health Technology (Berlin)*, vol. 12, no. 4, 2022, pp. 825–838. https://doi.org/10.1007/s12553-022-00674-7. Accessed 24 May 2025.

44 Calegar, Deiviane A., et al. "A Community-Based, Cross-Sectional Study to Assess Interactions between Income, Nutritional Status and Enteric Parasitism in Two Brazilian Cities: Are We Moving Positively Towards 2030?" *Journal of Health, Population and Nutrition*, vol. 40, article no. 26, 2021. https://doi.org/10.1186/s41043-021-00252-z. Accessed 25 May 2025.
45 Zhang, Lirong, et al. "An Artificial Intelligence Tool to Assess the Risk of Severe Mental Distress among College Students in Terms of Demographics, Eating Habits, Lifestyles, and Sport Habits: An Externally Validated Study Using Machine Learning." *BMC Psychiatry*, vol. 24, no. 581, 2024. https://doi.org/10.1186/s12888-024-06017-2. Accessed 25 May 2025.
46 Hill, Elliot D., et al. "Prediction of Mental Health Risk in Adolescents." *Nature Medicine*, 5 Mar. 2025. https://doi.org/10.1038/s41591-025-03560-7. Accessed 25 May 2025.
47 Mossaheb, Nilufar, et al. "The Community Assessment of Psychic Experience (CAPE) Questionnaire as a Screening-Instrument in the Detection of Individuals at Ultra-High Risk for Psychosis." *Schizophrenia Research*, vol. 141, no. 2–3, Nov. 2012, pp. 210–214. https://doi.org/10.1016/j.schres.2012.08.008. Accessed 25 May 2025.
48 Bruni, O., et al. "The Sleep Disturbance Scale for Children (SDSC): Construction and Validation of an Instrument to Evaluate Sleep Disturbances in Childhood and Adolescence." *Journal of Sleep Research*, vol. 5, 1996, pp. 251–261. https://doi.org/10.1111/j.1365-2869.1996.00251.x. Accessed 24 May 2025.
49 Pigeon, W. R., T. M. Bishop, and K. M. Krueger. "Insomnia as a Precipitating Factor in New Onset Mental Illness: A Systematic Review of Recent Findings." *Current Psychiatry Reports*, vol. 19, no. 44, 2017. https://doi.org/10.1007/s11920-017-0802-x. Accessed 24 May 2025.
50 Telzer, Eva H., Dana Goldenberg, Andrew J. Fuligni, Matthew D. Lieberman, and Adriana Gálvan. "Sleep Variability in Adolescence Is Associated with Altered Brain Development." *Developmental Cognitive Neuroscience*, vol. 14, 2015, pp. 16–22. https://doi.org/10.1016/j.dcn.2015.05.007. Accessed 24 May 2025.
51 Freeman, Daniel, Bryony Sheaves, Felicity Waite, Allison G. Harvey, and Philip J. Harrison. "Sleep Disturbance and Psychiatric Disorders." *The Lancet Psychiatry*, vol. 7, no. 7, 2020, pp. 628–637. https://doi.org/10.1016/S2215-0366(20)30136-X. Accessed 24 May 2025.
52 Harvey, Allison G., Greg Murray, Rachel A. Chandler, and Adriane Soehner. "Sleep Disturbance as Transdiagnostic: Consideration of Neurobiological Mechanisms." *Clinical Psychology Review*, vol. 31, no. 2, 2011, pp. 225–235. https://doi.org/10.1016/j.cpr.2010.04.003. Accessed 24 May 2025.
53 Chekroud, A.M., J. Bondar, J. Delgadillo, G. Doherty, A. Wasil, M. Fokkema, Z. Cohen, D. Belgrave, R. DeRubeis, and R. Iniesta. "The Promise of Machine Learning in Predicting Treatment Outcomes in Psychiatry." *World Psychiatry*, vol. 20, 2021, pp. 154–170. https://doi.org/10.1002/wps.20882. Accessed 24 May 2025.
54 Le Glaz, Arnaud, Yannis Haralambous, Delphine-Harriet Kim-Dufor, Philippe Lenca, Rémi Billot, T.C. Ryan, J. Marsh, J. Devylder, Michel Walter, and Sylvain Berrouiguet. "Machine Learning and Natural Language Processing in Mental Health: Systematic Review." *Journal of Medical Internet Research*, vol. 23, 2021, article e15708. https://doi.org/10.2196/15708. Accessed 24 May 2025.
55 Alvarez-Mon, M.A., C. Donat-Vargas, J. Santoma-Vilaclara, L. de Anta, J. Goena, R. Sanchez-Bayona, F. Mora, M.A. Ortega, G. Lahera, and R. Rodriguez-Jimenez. "Assessment of Antipsychotic Medications on Social

Media: Machine Learning Study." *Frontiers in Psychiatry*, vol. 12, 2021, article 737684. https://doi.org/10.3389/fpsyt.2021.737684. Accessed 24 May 2025.

56 Lin, S.-Y., X. Cheng, J. Zhang, J.S. Yannam, A.J. Barnes, J.R. Koch, R. Hayes, G. Gimm, X. Zhao, and H. Purohit. "Social Media Data Mining of Antitobacco Campaign Messages: Machine Learning Analysis of Facebook Posts." *Journal of Medical Internet Research*, vol. 25, 2023, article e42863. https://doi.org/10.2196/42863. Accessed 24 May 2025.

57 Kim, D., L. Quan, M. Seo, K. Kim, J.W. Kim, and Y. Zhu. "Interpretable Machine Learning-Based Approaches for Understanding Suicide Risk and Protective Factors Among South Korean Females Using Survey and Social Media Data." *Suicide and Life-Threatening Behavior*, vol. 53, 2023, pp. 484–498. https://doi.org/10.1111/sltb.12959. Accessed 24 May 2025.

58 Bernert, Rebecca A., Amanda M. Hilberg, Ryan Melia, Jin P. Kim, Nigam H. Shah, and Farzaneh Abnousi. "Artificial Intelligence and Suicide Prevention: A Systematic Review of Machine Learning Investigations." *International Journal of Environmental Research and Public Health*, vol. 17, no. 16, 2020, article 5929. https://doi.org/10.3390/ijerph17165929. Accessed 24 May 2025.

59 Kaminsky, Zachary, R. J. McQuaid, K. G. Hellemans, Z. R. Patterson, M. Saad, R. L. Gabrys, T. Kendzerska, A. Abizaid, and R. Robillard. "Machine Learning–Based Suicide Risk Prediction Model for Suicidal Trajectory on Social Media Following Suicidal Mentions: Independent Algorithm Validation." *Journal of Medical Internet Research*, vol. 26, 2024, article e49927. https://doi.org/10.2196/49927. Accessed 24 May 2025.

60 Roy, Arunima, et al. "A Machine Learning Approach Predicts Future Risk to Suicidal Ideation from Social Media Data." *NPJ Digital Medicine*, vol. 3, 2020, article no. 78. https://doi.org/10.1038/s41746-020-0287-6. Accessed 25 May 2025.

61 Tom, Prentice, et al. "Evaluation of an AI-Based Voice Biomarker Tool to Detect Signals Consistent With Moderate to Severe Depression." *Annals of Family Medicine,* vol. 23, no. 1, Jan./Feb. 2025. https://www.annfammed.org/content/23/1/early-release. Accessed 25 May 2025.

62 Mazur, Alexander, Helen Costantino, Paul Tom, Michael P. Wilson, and Ronald G. Thompson. "Evaluation of an AI-Based Voice Biomarker Tool to Detect Signals Consistent with Moderate to Severe Depression." *Annals of Family Medicine*, vol. 23, no. 1, 2025, pp. 60–65.

63 Mazur, A., H. Costantino, P. Tom, M.P. Wilson, and R.G. Thompson. "Evaluation of an AI-Based Voice Biomarker Tool to Detect Signals Consistent with Moderate to Severe Depression." *Annals of Family Medicine*, vol. 23, no. 1, 2025, pp. 60–65.

64 "Case Study: Improving Patient Experience and Increasing Clinical Value." *Kintsugi Health.* https://www.kintsugihealth.com/blog/case-study-improving-patient-experience-and-increasing-clinical-value. Accessed 24 May 2025.

Chapter 5

Biological and neural approaches to diagnosis

NEUROIMAGING

Introduction

Neuroimaging is becoming a useful tool in the effort to diagnose mental health conditions quantitatively and objectively. Studies date back to 1976 when computer tomography (CT) was used to study enlarged ventricles in schizophrenia patients.[1] The field has only continued to grow as imaging technology has improved. While there exist neuroimaging diagnostic studies across multiple primary psychiatric disorders, there has been little translation and clinical adoption. Still, there do exist limitations. Many findings have not been replicated due to inconsistencies across methods. Also, small sample sizes make results that are difficult to broadly generalize. Despite the existing limitations, the current body of work suggests that neuroimaging will be pivotal in the field of mental health diagnostics. With improved computational resources and methods, as well as larger, standardized, and multimodal neuroimaging studies, the future of this field looks encouraging.

There exists evidence for its use in quantifying biomarkers for mental health across multiple techniques and disorders. Specifically, studies have been done using standard methods to assess the structure and function, both electrical and molecular, of the brain using methods such as magnetic resonance imaging (MRI) and diffusion tensor imaging (DTI) for structure and functional MRI (fMRI) and molecular imaging for function. Structural biomarkers relate to the anatomical and physical structure of the brain while functional relate to the brain's activity. MRI and DTI are structural measures where biomarkers studied include thickness, density, and volumes of brain regions in the case of MRI and structural connectivity within and between regions for DTI. Using fMRI, it is possible to indirectly assess the activity of the brain either at rest or in response to particular tasks. Molecular imaging enables measurements of biological processes within the brain at the molecular and cellular levels.

DOI: 10.1201/9781003565215-5

Structural neuroimaging

Structural magnetic resonance imaging

Structural neuroimaging studies emerged first with CT in 1976 but were quickly replaced with sMRI, which was first used for psychiatry in 1983 but is still heavily used today.[2] sMRI uses magnetic properties to visualize tissue contrast and therefore structures in the brain. Measurements commonly assessed include the volume, density, and thickness. Volumes include global brain volume, white and gray matter volume, as well as specific brain structure volumes – frequently hippocampus, amygdala, and cingulate cortex.[3] Density measures are done indirectly utilizing signal intensities for the same areas. Lastly, the whole cortex or specific cortical areas are used for thickness measurements. Structural abnormalities have been found in many psychiatric disorders, including schizophrenia and psychosis,[4,5,6,7,8,9,10,11,12,13] depressive disorders,[14,15,16,17] autism spectrum disorder (ASD),[18,19,20,21,22,23] attention deficit hyperactivity disorder (ADHD),[24,25,26] and post-traumatic stress disorder (PTSD).[27,28,29] Hippocampal volume is one of the most studied structural biomarkers, with notable trends such as volume reduction in schizophrenia,[30,31,32] major depressive disorder,[33,34,35,36,37] and PTSD[38,39,40] and volume enlargement in ASD.

Diffusion tensor imaging

DTI is another structural neuroimaging methodology that supplements sMRI by imaging white matter tracts in the brain. It was introduced after sMRI in the 1990s and has since been used to identify structural abnormalities in ASD,[41,42,43] bipolar disorder,[44,45,46,47] schizophrenia [van den Heuvel 2013, van den Heuvel 2010, Sun 2015], and addiction [Ersche 2012]. Typically, there exists degeneration in tracts compared to control cohorts. DTI is not as frequently studied in the context of mental health as other sMRI or functional methodologies.

Functional neuroimaging

Functional magnetic resonance imaging

fMRI measures oxygenated blood flow as a proxy for brain activity and was introduced in 1991 but first used for psychiatry in 1994.[48,49] Since its introduction, it has become the most popular neuroimaging method for analyzing mental health, with fMRI during a task condition first popularized in 1997 and finally resting-state fMRI in 2007.[50] It has been used to study all identified psychiatric disorders. These studies can either use the time series data directly or obtain functional connectivity, a derived measure relating the function of specific regions. Some of the highest cited studies utilizing task-based fMRI for mental health include a study that identified impaired prefrontal lobe and cingulate cortex function in schizophrenia,[51,52], impaired mirror neuron activity in children with ASD,[53] and impaired activity in multiple areas in adult patients with ASD.[54,55] ADHD and depressive disorders are frequently studied in resting state, with influential studies finding increased functional connectivity in select cortical and subcortical regions in depression[56,57] and spontaneous activation and decreased long-range connectivity in ADHD.[58,59]

Molecular imaging

Molecular imaging has multiple techniques that are used for the brain. Some examples include positron emission tomography (PET), single photon emission computed tomography (SPECT), and magnetic resonance spectroscopy (MRS). Both PET and SPECT use radiotracers to measure metabolic processes, neurotransmitter activity, or receptor binding with SPECT being lower resolution but more readily available than PET. Lastly, MRS is a non-invasive measurement of brain metabolites, typically neurotransmitters.[60] A study of patients with major depressive disorder (MDD) found reduced glutamate and gamma-aminobutyric acid (GABA).[61] In mental health, most studies have been published utilizing PET followed by SPECT then MRS.[62]

There are multiple common radiotracers used in PET studies. Oxygen-15 labeled water ($[^{15}O]$-H_2O) measures cerebral blood flow (CBF) and has been used to study the pathophysiology of depressive disorders, amongst others. In the seminal paper showing the efficacy of deep-brain stimulation in depression, regional CBF was used to compare depressed to non-depressed subjects.[63] Fluorodeoxyglucose (($[^{18}F]$-FDG) measures brain glucose metabolism with abnormal FDG uptake observed in mental disorders. Specifically, it was found that bipolar disorder and depression have decreased activity in the prefrontal cortex using both CBF and glucose metabolism via FDG.[64] Dopaminergic PET tracers, including $[^{11}C]$-raclopride and $[^{11}C]$-SCH23390, are used to study dopamine receptor occupancy. An example is the finding of decreased dopamine levels in the dorsal striatum during cravings with individuals with addictions.[65] Interestingly, using the same methods, increased striatal synaptic dopamine concentrations were found in schizophrenia.[66] Further study of dopamine has been done, such as assessment of dopamine transporter level using $[^{11}C]$-D-threo-methylphenidate and dopaminergic function using $[^{18}F]$-fluoro-L-DOPA. For example, decreased striatal dopamine transporters were also found in methamphetamine users.[67] Lastly, using PET with $[^{18}F]$-FEPPA or $[^{11}C]$-PBR28 assesses microglia activation, where increased microglial activity has been shown in patients with schizophrenia or at a high risk of psychosis.[68] Similarly, SPECT studies include multiple tracers, with an example being studies of SPECT to measure dopamine receptor occupancy using $[^{123}I]$-IBZM. This technique again found increased striatal dopamine in patients with schizophrenia.[69]

Trends

In line with the invention and popularization of modern neuroimaging technology, the majority of studies linking neuroimaging to mental health diagnostics and pathophysiology occurred after 1989. Most studies focus on one psychiatric condition and one imaging modality. According to an analysis of the most influential studies in this field, the most commonly studied psychiatric conditions were depressive disorders (30%), schizophrenia and other psychotic disorders (27%), and ASD (17%). Other disorders less frequently studied include PTSD (7%), substance-related and addictive disorders (7%), ADHD (5%), obsessive compulsive disorder (3%), bipolar disorder (3%), anxiety disorders (2%), specific learning disorders (2%), and antisocial personality disorder (1%).[70] A separate review found that 75% of neuroimaging studies on psychiatric conditions compare people with a diagnosis to health controls using matched cohorts.[71] Among the most cited studies, fMRI was the most common method used in 42% of cases. Of those, two-thirds focused on brain activity during tasks while the rest looked at resting-state activity. sMRI was the next most common (30%), followed by PET scans (22%). That said, many of these studies had very small sample sizes, ranging from just 3 to 1188 participants, with a median of only 21 and an average of 63.[72]

Limitations, challenges, and future directions

Even though there is growing support for using neuroimaging to diagnose mental health, there are still some major challenges. One is that many findings have not been replicated, which is critical before clinical adoption. Small sample sizes also make it difficult to draw broad conclusions, especially given how varied mental health disorders can be. Due to the inherent heterogeneity of such disorders, including comorbidities and time since onset, large cohorts and stringent inclusion criteria are necessary to obtain reliable results. Lastly, there are discrepancies in acquisition and analysis methods, making replication difficult. From the type of scanner to the preprocessing pipeline to data analysis, there exist many stages with different techniques resulting in further variability. In order to truly compare results, standardization of methods is vital.

Neuroimaging diagnostics hold great promise moving forward. There has been a marked increase in large and multimodal studies to account for cohort variability. Additionally, newer imaging techniques, such as 7T MRI with higher resolution and near-infrared spectroscopy (NIRS) as well as optogenetic imaging to name a few, all provide additional insight to the brain. Finally, with improved compute power and methods, including artificial intelligence (AI), it is easier than ever to derive insights from large and complex datasets.

TECHNICAL APPROACHES AND MODEL TYPES IN NEUROIMAGING

AI models applied to brain imaging for depression span various architectures. Key model types include:

- Convolutional Neural Networks (CNNs): CNNs excel at spatial feature extraction and have been used on all types of neuroimaging. They have also been combined with autoencoders for unsupervised feature learning of MRIs.

- Recurrent Neural Networks (RNNs): RNNs (including LSTM and GRU units) capture temporal dynamics and are thus useful for fMRI time-series data. They model how brain activity changes over time, potentially detecting aberrant neural dynamics in mental health, such as altered resting-state fluctuations or delayed recovery of activity in certain circuits. RNNs have also been used more recently on dynamic functional connectivity states.
- Transformers and Attention Models: Transformers use self-attention mechanisms to handle multimodal inputs and long-range dependencies. As such, they have recently been applied to neuroimaging.
- Autoencoders (AE) and Variational Autoencoders (VAEs): Autoencoders learn latent and lower-dimensional representations of data. Given the high dimensionality of neuroimaging data, these models have emerged to reduce dimensionality without supervision. They are also used to combine multimodal data by encoding each modality.
- Graph Neural Networks (GNNs): Brain connectivity data can naturally be represented as a graph where the nodes are anatomical or functional regions and edges represent structural or functional connectivity measures. From this, GNNs, including graph convolutional networks, can then be used to predict from the brain graph inputs.
- Hybrid and Other models: There are some deep learning (DL) frameworks that fuse spatiotemporal features or employ attention on top of existing features. Other methods focus on multimodal data encoding. Lastly, ensemble models and classical machine learning (ML) are sometimes combined with DL for prediction.

There are many different methods for modeling neuroimaging data using DL with varying complexity and interpretability. Often, the model type is determined by the task of interest.

AI IN NEUROIMAGE PREPROCESSING

Introduction

Preprocessing is the first step in neuroimaging analysis. Traditional pipelines perform a series of steps to clean and standardize images prior to analysis. Some steps include correcting for head motion, segmenting anatomical tissues, and normalizing images to a standard template. More recently, DL methods have emerged as alternative preprocessing techniques, which are becoming important with large datasets. Below is an overview of standard preprocessing methods and new DL approaches.

Overview of existing methods

There exist many well-established software tools for neuroimage preprocessing including FSL (Functional MRI Software Library), FreeSurfer, AFNI

(Analysis of Functional Neuroimaging), and ANTs (Advanced Normalization Tools). Each software provides a suite of tools for various preprocessing steps. For example, FSL has motion correction while FreeSurfer does 3D surface reconstruction.[73,74] These methods produce measures such as cortical thickness and brain volumes. fMRIPrep is a popular pipeline that integrates tools from all these packages for automated fMRI preprocessing with minimal intervention.[75]

These standard methods have been honed over decades and are considered the "gold standard" in many research settings. They are largely rule-based or optimization-based, requiring careful parameter tuning but offering interpretable outcomes. For example, using these steps, fMRIPrep was shown to produce high-quality results across diverse datasets with no manual intervention.[76] However, they can be time-consuming. For example, FreeSurfer's full segmentation process can take many hours per subject. They also may struggle on atypical data, such as scans with lesions, low resolution, or different MRI contrasts. In recent years, DL techniques have been applied to MRI preprocessing tasks, yielding new tools that complement or improve upon traditional approaches. DL models, typically CNNs, are trained on large datasets for tasks like brain extraction, segmentation, and denoising.

Preprocessing steps

Quality control

Structural and fMRI images are known to contain significant noise and are likely to have artifacts.[77] Low-quality images can result in inaccurate results reporting on image noise rather than signal[78,79,80,81] Traditionally, quality control is done by expert manual inspection, but this process is expensive, time-consuming, subjective, and prone to errors. There even exist artifacts and image degradations that cannot be detected by humans at all.[82] fMRIPrep creates visual reports for each subject to streamline quality control, but more automated methods are needed.[83] Initial efforts for automated quality control (QC) focused on the extraction and comparison of image-quality metrics (IQMs) with cutoff thresholds. Due to the variability that exists between studies and sites, it is challenging to find appropriate thresholds that generalize.[84,85,86,87] The first ML methods for quality used ML classifiers trained on structural image features, including existing IQMs, to predict quality scores of T1w MRI scans with improved performance over thresholding, but again there was a lack of generalization for multi-site datasets.[88] The state-of-the-art ML method used for automated MRI quality control is MRIQC from Stanford University, which was published in 2017. It performs well on intra-site quality prediction, but is susceptible to site effects resulting in an accuracy of 76%.[89]

In 2022, Trinity College Dublin published **BrainQCNet**, which uses ProtoPNet, an interpretable attention-based DL architecture, to classify scan quality achieving a maximum accuracy of 91% compared to manual QC annotations using the Adolescent Brain Cognitive Development Study quickly (1 min per scan).[90,91] The architecture used a convolutional neural network backbone, specifically ResNet152, pre-trained on MRI data. The additional ProtoPNet layer uses prototype learning, where many examples of artifacts (e.g., motion blur, ghosting) are stored during training paired with an attention mechanism that computes the similarity between the new input images and the prototypes.[92,93]

Head motion correction

In fMRI, head motion can severely impact the quality of signals acquired. As such, volumes are aligned to correct for head movements. In most methods, the 3D rigid-body motion is estimated and resampled across all volumes to the same orientation. This step seeks to prevent motion artifacts from confounding the signal and is often combined with flagging high-movement time points. These algorithms assume movement between volumes is small and use cost functions (e.g., normalized correlation or least squares) to optimize alignment. While this substantially reduces motion-induced image blurring or misregistration, it cannot fully correct subject movement during the acquisition of a single volume. Because slices are acquired sequentially, each slice may be offset differently if the head moves during the scan, violating the rigid-body assumption.[94] Residual motion artifacts can still remain after standard realignment. Additional techniques like slice-time correction or motion parameter regression help clean the data further, but it is often difficult to fully eliminate motion from MRI using traditional techniques.[95] Specifically, classic motion correction is relatively reliable for small and between-volume head movement but has limitations for larger and within-volume movements.

Alternatively, there are new approaches using DL to improve motion correction. One example treats motion degradation as a learnable transformation between images. MC-Net (Motion Correction Net) uses a CNN to remove motion artifacts from MRIs. It is trained on scans with synthetic motion and their clean targets. From this, the CNN learns to output a motion-corrected image in a single pass. It was found that these models can implicitly handle non-rigid and slice-wise motion. MC-Net is also fast. It is able to process a 3D volume in roughly 40 milliseconds on a GPU while traditional iterative realignment takes a few seconds per volume.[96] Another method predicts motion parameters directly using a DL model that has been trained to regress head motion estimates from image data. It does this by integrating MR physics to correct for motion during reconstruction. Specifically, Singh et al. combine a physics-informed model with DL to retrospectively correct for head motion in MRIs.[97] These methods mark just the beginning for motion correction in neuroimaging.

Brain extraction

Brain extraction, or skull stripping, removes non-brain tissues (like the skull) from sMRI to isolate the brain making subsequent steps more focused. The popular method, and the method implemented in fMRIPrep, is FSL's BET (Brain Extraction Tool), which estimates the brain outline and masks the skull. However, it is limited to high-resolution MRI.

Alternatively, DL models have been developed to perform brain extraction more robustly than classical algorithms. Utilizing a 3D CNN architecture in 2016, a research group from Heidelberg University Hospital was able to generalize brain extraction beyond standard T1 images. Their method handled T1 with contrast, T2, and FLAIR sequences as well as MRI with tumors, significantly outperforming six common skull-stripping tools on a clinical tumor dataset, including BET and AFNI's 3dSkullStrip tool. It achieved a mean Dice score of ~95% on tumor patients, whereas traditional methods struggled with the abnormal anatomy.[98]

More recently, SynthStrip was introduced from a research group at Massachusetts General Hospital (MGH). It uses synthetic training data with randomized image contrast, resolution, and artifacts. The benefit of this heterogeneous training is generalization to many datasets. As a result, SynthStrip produces highly accurate brain masks on everything from research-quality T1w scans to thick-slice clinical scans and even other modalities including CT and PET.[99] DeepBrain, another CNN-based brain extraction tool, has even been incorporated into clinical workflows, having received regulatory approval from the FDA as part of an automated volumetry software, indicating the maturity of such methods.[100]

Image enhancement and reconstruction

High-resolution images generated from low-resolution scans in a process called super-resolution can be done using generative adversarial networks (GANs) or CNNs. This can improve the quality of images before further analysis, which is particularly useful if only low-resolution or fast-acquisition scans are available.

SynthSR is one of the most significant breakthroughs in brain MRI enhancement to date. This tool can transform clinical brain MRI scans of any orientation, resolution, and contrast into high-resolution 1-mm isotropic T1-weighted images that are compatible with any downstream neuroimaging analysis tool. Validated on over 10,000 scans from health controls and patients with various pathologies including brain tumors, strokes, and Alzheimer's disease, SynthSR achieved morphometric measurements that strongly correlated with those obtained from actual high-resolution T1 scans making it possible to conduct large structural studies using existing clinical data. It is a 3D U-Net CNN that, similar to SynthStrip, is trained on randomized artificial brain scans making it robust to inputs. It also implicitly learns intensity normalization, removing the need for a separate bias field correction step. Furthermore, this work is from the same group as SynthStrip, so skull stripping is included.[101]

Enhanced Super-Resolution Generative Adversarial Network (ESRGAN) and its variant Real-ERSGAN have also been successfully adapted for brain MRI enhancement.[102, 103] These networks were originally developed for natural image super-resolution but have been modified for medical imaging. While CNNs work by training a single model to map low-resolution images to high-resolution, GANs for super-resolution use a generator to create a realistic high-resolution image and a discriminator to ensure the generated images closely match real high-resolution images. A study used a modified version for enhancing T2-FLAIR MRI images of brain tumors, and was able to improve the accuracy of brain tumor segmentation.[104]

More recently, transformer architectures are also being utilized for super-resolution of MRIs. For example, TransMRSR is a hybrid CNN-transformer architecture introduced in 2023. It functions using a two-stage framework with generative prior learning that encapsulates MRI priors via a GAN-trained decoder. Then it has a dual-branch enhancement with 3D CNNs to extract local slice-wise features and transformer blocks that model global inter-slice relationships. In this work, the transformer positional encodings are adapted for anisotropic MRI voxel spacing, and the multi-head attention is scaled to brain morphology. It was able to achieve better performance on multiple datasets compared to ESRGAN variants faster and with better hallucination control.[105]

Tissue segmentation

The structural MRI (usually T1-weighted) is segmented into different tissue types – gray matter (GM), white matter (WM), cerebral spinal fluid (CSF) – and often further in specific anatomical regions. SPM and FSL are able to classify tissues, while FreeSurfer is further able to label approximately 100 neuroanatomical structures using an atlas-based approach. This segmentation provides quantitative measures, such as tissue volumes, and helps define masks for later steps, including noise regression of WM and CSF.

The gold standard thus far has been manual delineation, which is again tedious and costly, thus limiting its utility for large-scale datasets. Software tools, such as FreeSurfer, exist and function by registering the brain to an existing atlas of manually labeled data, which is then automatically parcellated into different regions of interest (ROIs).[106,107,108] Despite its popularity, FreeSurfer does exhibit significant limitations. A primary example is its long processing times, which are on the order of hours for a single subject. This is in part due to the methods, but also because it cannot run processes in parallel or on GPUs. Quality control and correction are often necessary, but it is a manual process in FreeSurfer.[109] Furthermore, multiple studies have demonstrated that FreeSurfer consistently over or underestimates volumes compared to manual estimates leading to concerns about accuracy.[110,111,112] There even exist inconsistencies between software versions,[113] and it is limited to research-grade 1.0-mm T1w MRI images, meaning it is incompatible with CT, PET, and lower resolution scans. This is specifically an issue in clinical-grade MRIs, which tend to be thicker, often at lower resolution, and contain artifacts. A particular issue causing inaccurate volumes is the systematic biases in segmentation using FreeSurfer with the major limitation in this method being the atlases, which have limited population and contrast inclusion. This means subjects different from the atlases as well as scans with different acquisition protocols have limited reliability in their segmentations.[114,115,116,117,118,119] With the increase in large neuroimaging datasets, the limitations of FreeSurfer become a serious bottleneck.

MRI segmentation has particularly benefited from DL. These methods are not only faster but often more accurate and reliable. One architecture that stands out is U-Net, which is now commonly used for segmenting medical images, including MRIs. U-Nets are specially designed to learn and identify structure within an image, making them well-suited for segmenting brain scans. One of the original DL tools for segmentation was FastSurferCNN, which was developed in 2020. It uses multiple stacked CNNs to segment the brain into anatomical regions in under 1 minute. This significantly outpaces FreeSurfer. The segmentations are also better able to reproduce and maintain disease effects. Lastly, FreeSurferCNN has improved generalizability in its segmentations, with improved performance across datasets with disease states, various age groups, and differing imaging protocols. Its main limitation is that it only works with research-grade 1.0-mm resolution images.[120] The follow-up was FastSurferVINN, released in 2022. It introduced a Voxel-size Independent Neural Network (VINN) architecture that allows for segmentation across a range of voxel sizes, but it is still limited to high-quality inputs.[121]

SynthSeg+, released in 2023, is designed for robust segmentation of MRI scans, built specifically to handle heterogeneous clinical data. It employs a hierarchical architecture that combines segmentation and denoising neural networks with granular segmentations. To train SynthSeg+, synthetic MRIs were used with randomized contrast and resolution, enabling the model to generalize across diverse clinical scans. This work is from the same group that produced SynthSR and SynthStrip using synthetic data; therefore, brain extraction is included in SynthSeg+, so this step can be skipped. SynthSeg+ works to segment images from 1.5T T2w scans to 3T T1w to even CT scans. Additionally, it includes automated QC of faulty segmentations by attributing a score to each output.

Therefore, it is highly robust against clinical artifacts, changes in MRI contrast and resolution, and variations in subject populations making it suitable for analysis of heterogeneous datasets. In its validation, SynthSeg+ shows unparalleled generalization compared to other methods, achieving high accuracy on healthy, atrophied, and lesioned brains with output segmentations in 1-mm isotropic space regardless of the input resolution. It also segments images quickly, needing only mere seconds on a GPU. The resulting outputs are cortical and subcortical segmentations as well as anatomical volume estimates.[122,123] Overall, DL methods show significant promise for segmentation applications.

Bias field correction

Bias field correction is done to normalize intensities across the image due to MRI intensity inhomogeneities. In classical pipelines, this step is crucial to improve the performance of tissue segmentation and intensity-based registration. Recent DL methods perform this correction implicitly during segmentation. For example, SynthSeg+ uses synthetic images that have simulated random bias fields. As a result, SynthSeg+ can segment MRIs without additional bias correction.[124]

Coregistration (fMRI-sMRI alignment) and registration (spatial normalization)

A functional imaging scan is typically sampled at a lower resolution than a structural. These two images are aligned so that fMRI images can use segmentations and normalizations derived from the higher resolution sMRI images. Classical methods typically optimize an intensity-based cost function to find the rigid or affine transform that best overlaps the images. FSL and FreeSurfer are both frequently used for this step. Indeed, fMRIPrep utilizes FreeSurfer's Boundary-Based Registration (BBR) tool.[125] Traditional coregistration is generally fully automated; however, in difficult cases, manual initial alignment or re-running with different settings may be needed. Furthermore, the optimization needs to be done for each new image pair and adapted to new image types.

Similarly, spatial normalization or registration is a process where individual subjects' images are transformed into a standard reference space using atlases (such as MNI) to enable group analysis and comparison between subjects. Common steps are to first affine-align the subject's T1 image to the template, then apply a nonlinear transformation for finer alignment of brain structures. ANTs, FSL, and SPM provide high-quality nonlinear registration to achieve this.[126,127] SPM is more flexible but has a higher computation time compared to FSL. In fMRI preprocessing, the normalization transform computed on the structural image is then also applied to the functional data after coregistering the fMRI to the sMRI, thereby bringing the fMRI data into atlas space.

DL is also used for image registration by learning to predict deformation fields between fMRI and sMRI. An example is VoxelMorph, a 3D U-Net CNN that learns functions to map image pairs to a deformation field.[128,129] SynthMorph evolved from VoxelMorph using the same synthetic images used for training as in SynthSeg+, SynthSR, and SynthStrip. A large advantage of DL tools for registration is their speed. They take a few minutes compared to hours with traditional methods. Both methods are fully automated, however, DL models usually require only a one-time training phase which can be done on GPU clusters, and downstream inference is fast. Furthermore, robustness is a key consideration with DL trained on synthetic datasets being more robust. DL models can also potentially eliminate some sub-steps of preprocessing, including skull stripping or bias correction, because it can learn to ignore irrelevant parts of the image. Overall, DL-based normalization is highly scalable compared to classical methods.[130]

Cortical surface reconstruction

Cortical surface reconstruction entrails extracting the pial surface, or outer cortex boundary, and white matter surface from the structural MRI. This is classically done by following tissue segmentation with mesh generation. The most prominent tool is FreeSurfer's reconstruction pipeline, which performs intensity normalization (bias field correction), skull stripping, segmentation of white matter, iterative surface deformation, and topological corrections. While it is accurate for typical brains compared to manual tracing, it is limited to 1-mm T1-weighted images, which take roughly 5–8 hours for a single subject on a CPU (it does not have GPU compatibility).[131]

DL drastically speeds up surface generation. In addition to segmentation, FastSurfer also reconstructs surfaces by mapping the segmented labels onto an existing spherical mesh, rather than performing the lengthy deformable evaluation. It is able to obtain cortical thickness and surface maps in approximately 1 hour. Its reconstructions are similar to those of FreeSurfer, and cortical thickness measures show increased test-retest reliability.[132] Fast Cortical Surface Reconstruction (FastCSR) is a more recent 3D U-Net approach that directly learns to generalize surfaces. It trains a model to predict an implicit level-set representation of the cortical surfaces from the MRI. After prediction, a fast topology correction and marching-cubes-like extraction yields the white pial meshes. The surface reconstruction is obtained in ~5 minutes, which is significantly faster than both FreeSurfer and FastSurfer. While maintaining computational efficiency, FastCSR has comparable mesh quality and cortical metrics to FreeSurfer and also generalizes well, with tests showing robust performance on scans with different qualities and even in the presence of lesions.[133] Both FastSurfer and FastCSR are fully automated and require a GPU for inference.

Cortical surface registration

Once individual cortical surfaces are reconstructed, they are often registered to a template surface or aligned across subjects for comparison and further analysis. This registration aligns gyral and sulcal features so that functional and anatomical data can be compared vertex-to-vertex across brains. Surface registration is generally performed using FreeSurfer.[134] Its algorithm is accurate but computationally heavy, again taking on the order of hours per subject.

DL has recently been applied to cortical surface alignment to dramatically accelerate this process while maintaining or improving alignment quality. A cutting-edge example is SUGAR (Spherical Ultrafast Graph Attention Registration), an unsupervised DL framework for surface registration. SUGAR uses DL on two cortical surfaces and outputs a deformation field that aligns them leading to a model that can perform both rigid and non-rigid alignment. In evaluations on over 10,000 scans, SUGAR achieved equivalent or better accuracy than conventional methods in terms of matching cortical landmarks and test-retest reliability. Importantly, it did so with tremendous speed gains: on the order of 0.2–0.5 seconds per hemisphere, a 12,000 × speed-up.[135] Another approach, SphereMorph, uses an unsupervised CNN to predict spherical warp fields, also yielding fast runtime (seconds) and accuracy on par with FreeSurfer.[136] Some DL pipelines bypass explicit registration altogether by predicting standardized outputs. For example, FastSurfer directly segments cortical regions. Given their speed and performance, DL tools will likely replace or considerably augment traditional surface registration, especially for large datasets.

Denoising and artifact removal

Denoising includes a range of methods with the goal of removing noise and artifacts from images. Filtering is often applied as it is generally effective in boosting the signal-to-noise ratio. For sMRI, a common classical approach is non-local means (NLM) filtering, which averages intensities of similar image patches. Other filters like Gaussian smoothing or anisotropic diffusion are also used but tend to sacrifice some resolution; in contrast, NLM adapts to image content to retain structure. Traditional denoising can improve the quantitative accuracy of analyses, but these methods must be carefully parameterized (e.g., kernel size in NLM) to avoid removing clinically relevant details.

In fMRI, denoising often refers to artifact removal procedures. Classical fMRI pipelines address this at multiple stages: high-pass filtering is applied to remove scanner drift; retrospective physiological correction can be used if heartbeat and breathing signals were recorded, regressing out cyclic fluctuations. Additionally, steps are taken for spatial smoothing including smoothing with a Gaussian kernel, which improves the signal-to-noise ratio at the cost of spatial resolution. More advanced denoising and confound estimation exist using dimensionality reduction methods based on principal component analysis (PCA) or independent component analysis (ICA). For example, CompCor uses principal component analysis on WM and CSF regions to capture physiological noise components then regresses them out of the fMRI data.[137] ICA-based methods are popular for resting-state fMRI – FSL's ICA-AROMA and FIX are two notable examples. ICA-AROMA (Independent Component Analysis-based Automatic Removal Of Motion Artifacts) is a popular method that applied ICA to fMRI and automatically classifies components as "noise" (motion-related) or "signal" by extracting IC features and classifying using ML. The noise ICs are then removed from the data.[138] FIX (FMRIB's ICA-based X-noiseifier) works similarly. These are classical ML approaches and have proven effective when trained well – studies show ICA+FIX can remove motion artifacts and yield cleaner functional connectivity maps, improving sensitivity to true neural signals. SPM-based pipelines often use a simpler approach of multiple regression. Overall, classical denoising techniques are robust and well-understood yet they often involve manual intervention or conservative assumptions (linear regression, thresholding) and might not capture all complex noise patterns. They also treat denoising as a separate step, not necessarily optimized in conjunction with the final analysis.

DL is leveraged to perform denoising and artifact removal in MRI, often yielding superior performance by learning from large datasets of examples. In structural MRI, CNN-based denoisers have demonstrated higher noise suppression and detail preservation than conventional filters. For instance, unsupervised models like **noise2void** (a blind-spot network) and supervised models trained on clean and noisy image pairs have been applied to MRI.[139] A 2021 study compared two unsupervised deep denoisers against NLM on sMRI and found the networks outperformed NLM in most quantitative metrics.[140] The DL output was closer to the ground-truth clean images than the NLM-filter and tended to preserve fine textures better by learning to distinguish true anatomical edges from noise. These networks can also adapt to the MRI noise distribution by training on synthetic MRI noise, improving accuracy of denoising. Once trained, a CNN-based denoiser processes a 3D volume in a fraction of a second using a GPU while standard filters require minutes on CPUs.

DL has also been used for denoising fMRI and other functional data, although it is less common. One example is a CNN-LSTM model that takes in ICA components as inputs and learns to label them as "signal" or "noise."[141] This model achieved over 98% accuracy in classifying components on a testing set. Such performance is on par with or better than the traditional FIX classifier, essentially reaching human-level labeling accuracy in their dataset. The advantage is that a DL model can potentially generalize to new datasets better by capturing more abstract features of artifacts, though in practice it may still need some fine-tuning with new labeled data. Once identified, noise components can again be projected out of the data, effectively cleaning the fMRI signals.

Beyond classification, DL can directly denoise time-series data. Yang et al. (2020) introduced a DNN with a temporal convolution and LSTM to clean task-fMRI signals without any explicit artifact model. They trained the network in an unsupervised manner by maximizing the correlation of denoised fMRI time-courses with task design in gray matter while minimizing it in noise regions (white matter). This deep denoiser automatically learned to suppress physiological noise and other fluctuations, yielding more homogenous activation maps. In evaluations on a working memory fMRI dataset, the DNN reduced noise more effectively than common traditional methods, improving detection of task-related activation (e.g., higher contrast-to-noise in activation maps).[142] This illustrates how DL can leverage the structure in data (temporal correlations, known task design) to separate signal from noise in a way that linear regression approaches might not fully capture.

Holistic pipeline

Fully automated and standardized preprocessing pipelines for MRI have become essential in neuroimaging research. These tools handle sMRI and fMRI data with minimal user intervention, following standardized workflows which is crucial for reproducibility and scalability.

fMRIPrep (from the NiPreps ecosystem) is a robust, analysis-agnostic preprocessing pipeline for fMRI with accompanying sMRI processing. It combines multiple well-validated tools from FSL, ANTs, FreeSurfer, and AFNI. fMRIPrep performs the standard preprocessing steps, including skull-stripping, bias correction, spatial normalization (using ANTs for nonlinear registration), motion correction, and slice-timing correction (if needed). It has been validated on dozens of datasets to ensure it handles diverse acquisitions and data qualities.[143]

The classical pipeline prioritizes quality over speed, so it can be computationally intensive. It parallelizes internally where possible (i.e., segmentation and normalization) but processes each subject largely sequentially. On a typical workstation, a single subject's fMRIPrep run might take several hours (commonly 8–12 hours if doing cortical surface reconstruction, 2–3 hours without). Memory requirements can also be high. Scalability is achieved by processing subjects independently, although fMRIPrep itself does not have built-in distributed workflow management. Overall, it is high-quality with rich confound metrics and visual quality reports but is computationally intensive with high memory and CPU requirements.

DeepPrep is a newer pipeline that introduces DL to accelerate and enhance MRI preprocessing. It is an accelerated, scalable, and robust pipeline for anatomical and fMRI, engineered to handle large datasets efficiently. DeepPrep replaces several slow processing steps from traditional pipelines with fast deep-learning models mentioned above including FastSurferCNN, SynthMorph, and SUGAR. DeepPrep is both fast and accurate. Initial measures show it is approximately 10x faster than fMRIPrep, thus enabling large-scale studies and quick turnaround while maintaining high-quality results. It also requires less manual intervention, with automatic quality assessment.[144] Overall, DeepPrep highlights the need for automated, reliable, robust, and scalable pipelines for neuroimaging preprocessing, especially in the context of large-scale and multimodal datasets.

Comparison of standard and deep learning approaches

Advantages of deep learning methods

The approaches above illustrate several advantages of DL in neuroimaging preprocessing compared to classical methods. Efficiency and speed are major benefits of DL methods. Once trained, these models can process images in seconds to minutes rather than hours, which is crucial for large datasets and time-sensitive applications. It also allows for real-time or interactive uses. Furthermore, depending on the training data, some preprocessing steps can even be skipped by using DL. For example, SynthSeg+ automatically learns to extract the brain during tissue segmentation, bypassing the need for a separate skull stripping step. These methods are also more automated and require less manual intervention and explicit parameter tuning. Naturally, a more automated process results in higher preprocessing standardization.

Accuracy and standardization also tend to improve with DL methods, where models trained on large and robust datasets which allows them to capture subtle features and have less variability than human-trained methods or atlases based on small, homogeneous, and healthy subjects. For instance, DL often achieves higher scores for segmentation than traditional algorithms, especially on challenging scans (see SynthSeg+). Training using more diverse examples than atlases also allows for better image handling.

DL models can be particularly robust. By learning on diverse or augmented datasets, these models can better handle complex cases like disease states. A caveat is that robustness is still not necessarily guaranteed if a model encounters truly novel data. Flexibility and generalization have been key features of DL models, where traditional preprocessing was largely developed for a specific modality and each tool is usually tuned to those. A key example is segmentation limited to high-resolution T1 images. Therefore, using them outside those specific conditions might require custom adjustment, yield suboptimal results, or simply not work. By training on or simulating many conditions, DL can create more universal solutions (e.g., SynthSeg+). This flexibility is beneficial for heterogeneous and large-scale studies.

Challenges of deep learning

However, DL methods have their own challenges. A model is limited by the data it was trained on, so if it is confronted with a severely out-of-distribution image, it might fail unpredictably (e.g., producing an implausible segmentation). Traditional methods, while less flexible, are often grounded in physics or anatomy and might degrade more gracefully. Ensuring generalization is a key focus of current research, hence approaches like SynthSeg+'s domain randomization. Deep models can also sometimes "hallucinate" incorrect results (e.g., misidentifying tissue if the image quality is poor), so results validation is still critical. Computationally, applying a trained model is efficient, but training the model requires significant computation. Many models are supervised, which requires a large corpus of labeled datasets that can be difficult to curate or a barrier for developing new models for niche tasks. DL models typically require a GPU either to run at all or to achieve desired speed increases, while classic tools can run on standard CPU clusters. This is a consideration for labs or clinics without GPU resources. Additionally, classical methods often have an associated no-code user interface, making it easier for users compared to DL models which require programming knowledge to implement. Another key difference is interpretability. Traditional preprocessing involves clear-cut steps, whereas a deep model's internal workings can be a black box, although the outputs are usually designed to be the same kind of end products that are inspected just like traditional outputs. Lastly, due to their novelty, the existing literature using these methods is limited compared to classical techniques making inter-study result comparisons more difficult.

In summary, DL-based preprocessing methods tend to excel in speed once trained and often achieve equal or better accuracy and robustness on challenging data, with a high degree of automation. Traditional methods excel in their proven reliability on typical data, interpretability, and not requiring training data. The choice may depend on context. For a well-controlled research study with health, standard scans, classical pipelines are still very effective and widely used. In the case of large-scale or clinical applications where efficiency is paramount of data quality variations, DL methods offer compelling advantages. In practice, a combination might work best. For example, a physics-based distortion correction then a DL segmentation.

Comparing clinical and research applications

In research, the focus is generally on maximizing reproducibility and accuracy, often at the expense of speed or convenience. Thus, many researchers have continued using standard pipelines like fMRIPrep or FreeSurfer because they are well-validated, and their results are familiar and comparable across studies. Currently, there is a transition where DL methods, specifically those published with open-source code, are being incorporated into research workflows as they prove their accuracy relative to traditional techniques. For example, FreeSurfer's newest version integrates SynthSeg+ as an option for certain segmentation tasks, indicating even the classic tools are adopting AI improvements. In research settings, one must also consider that introducing a new method could confound results if not applied uniformly, so there is a desire to ensure consistency with previously published pipelines unless a clear benefit is demonstrated. DL's advantages in handling large, heterogeneous datasets make it especially useful for big neuroimaging consortia or population imaging studies where manual QC is not feasible and data come from different sites. Indeed, SynthSeg+ emphasized robust segmentation for large-scale heterogeneous clinical datasets, aligning with needs in big-data research.[145]

Clinically, the priorities are different. Speed, automation, and proven accuracy on individual cases are key. A radiologist or technician cannot spend hours running complex software for each patient. Instead, they need results quickly, ideally integrated with the scanner's workflow. Here, DL prevails by delivering nearly instant results. Indeed, there exist FDA-cleared AI tools for tasks like brain tumor segmentation or stroke detection on MRI. For volumetric analysis of the brain, products like Quantib ND or Cortechs NeuroQuant have been used, and newer AI-driven products like InBrain or DeepBrain are emerging. These tools output clinically interpretable metrics (e.g., hippocampal volume percentiles) in a report that a doctor can use. Traditional research tools were rarely used clinically because of their complexity and lack of regulatory approval. DL is helping bridge that gap by enabling fast, one-click solutions that can be validated on clinical populations and cleared by regulatory agencies. A caution in clinical use is the validation and trust. AI models must be thoroughly validated on the relevant patient population and scanning protocol. Clinicians also value transparency, where a surprise failure of a black-box algorithm can be problematic. Therefore, many clinical AI tools include checks or only operate within certain parameters. In practice, a clinical center might use a hybrid. For example, DL segmentation may be used to obtain an initial brain mask and tissues followed by a human double-checking boundaries in critical regions.

In summary, for research, standard methods have offered reliability and consistency, but DL is attractive for large studies and novel data where traditional methods falter. For clinical deployment, DL methods make advanced MRI analytics feasible during routine care due to their speed and automation.

Emerging trends and future directions

Hybrid pipelines are likely to emerge rather than DL completely replacing traditional methods. For example, bias correction is done using typical methods followed by DL-based skull stripping and tissue segmentation then a conventional spatial normalization. Conversely, DL registration could provide a good initial alignment that is further fine-tuned by a classical optimizer to save time while preserving accuracy. It is likely that there will continue to be AI-augmentation of popular tools, similar to FreeSurfer's integration of SynthSeg+. This hybrid approach leverages AI, where it offers clear benefits and keeps traditional methods where they are sufficient or where data is limited.

A more radical future direction is end-to-end preprocessing, where a single AI system could take raw images and output fully preprocessed data or even directly extract scientific measurements of interest. For instance, one could envision an autoencoder or transformer pipeline that outputs a cleaned, normalized fMRI time series in standard space, all in one go. Some research has taken steps in this direction, using cascades of neural networks that are trained jointly. End-to-end approaches might discover intermediate representations that are optimal for the final outcome (e.g., denoising that optimizes detection of brain networks). However, training such systems is complex, and they currently lack the transparency of defined intermediate results. Still, this could streamline preprocessing dramatically and potentially optimize for ultimate analysis metrics, such as improving reliability of a connectivity matrix directly.

A key limitation in developing DL preprocessing tools is the need for ground truth (e.g., manual segmentations for training). Future methods are turning to self-supervised learning to overcome this. For example, autoencoders can be trained to remove noise without explicit clean targets by using clever data splits like DeepCor using "noise-only" inputs. Another method is augmentation, where synthetic noise is added and the original image is predicted. Similarly, self-supervised MRI reconstruction techniques learn to produce artifact-free images from undersampled k-space data.[146] These could extend into preprocessing by learning from raw data alone. For example, a model that learns to enhance MRI quality by making the reconstruction consistent with known MRI physics and learned priors, effectively doing denoising and bias correction implicitly. Generative models (GANs, VAEs) are also being used to simulate data for training. It is likely there will be more use of synthetic data to train AI, including simulations of motion and artifacts. This will broaden the applicability of DL beyond scenarios where curated training datasets exist.

As AI becomes more prevalent, there is an increasing emphasis on built-in QC. Future deep models are likely to output uncertainty measures or flags when they encounter something unusual. Research in Bayesian DL or test-time augmentation is allowing models to state their confidence level. This could prompt a human to review or a fallback to a different method. Automated QC classifiers, which are often DL models as well, can be applied after preprocessing to detect bad outputs. For example, a network could examine a brain mask and decide if it is acceptable or if the skull strip failed. This meta-AI helps catch the small percentage of failures.

A key future goal is to ensure DL tools generalize across scanners, populations, and even modalities. Techniques like domain adaptation, domain invariant training, and federated learning will help create more universally reliable preprocessing tools. For instance, a federate learning setup could train a skull stripper on multiple hospitals' data, capturing a wide variety of MR image characteristics, resulting in a model that is robust to site differences without any single site having to share sensitive data. Transfer learning will also be important. Models trained specifically for adult brains could, for example, be fine-tuned on adolescent brains to specialize them.

As MRI technology evolves, preprocessing will face new challenges. AI is well-suited to adapt to these, often more so than rewriting traditional algorithms. For instance, in real-time fMRI or neurofeedback, a fast AI denoiser could clean data on the fly, something not feasible with iterative traditional methods. The future will likely see specialized AI preprocessing for these cutting-edge applications.

Traditionally, image reconstruction and preprocessing are separate. With AI, this boundary is blurring. We might see future MRI scanners with integrated AI that directly produce distortion-corrected, denoised images as they are reconstructed, effectively doing much of the preprocessing in-line. For fMRI, one could image the scanner's image reconstruction being aware of motion and correcting it in the raw data domain, or producing outputs in standard space immediately if the subject's anatomy is known. This convergence could drastically simplify the data flow with the scanner output being a ready-to-analyze dataset.

In conclusion, AI is profoundly shaping MRI preprocessing. The trend is toward pipelines that are faster, more autonomous, and more adaptive to different data, driven by DL advances. Traditional methods provided the foundation and are still indispensable in many cases, but select steps are slowly being replaced or augmented by AI. The likely scenario is a hybrid approach, combining domain knowledge from decades of MRI methods with the DL pattern learning. With careful validation and standardization, AI-enhanced preprocessing will improve both research and clinical workflows, enabling us to extract more information from MRI data with less effort.

AI IN NEUROIMAGING ANALYSIS: MENTAL HEALTH DIAGNOSTICS

Introduction

Advances in AI and ML have led to significant progress in using neuroimaging for mental health diagnostics. Over the past decade, researchers have applied AI to neuroimaging data, including sMRI, fMRI, and molecular imaging, to improve the detection and prediction of psychiatric and neurological conditions. Key areas of research include supervised diagnosis (distinguishing patient vs healthy controls using labeled imaging data), early risk detection (identifying individuals likely to develop a disorder before full onset), prediction of disease progression (forecasting how a patient's condition will evolve), and subtyping (identifying and characterizing distinct groups or subtypes within a broader psychiatric disorder). These AI-driven approaches aim to discover objective neuroimaging biomarkers that complement clinical assessments, addressing the heterogeneity and subjectivity in mental health diagnosis. This chapter seeks to summarize the most influential work across different modalities and disorders, and highlight broader trends, such as which conditions are most studied on each imaging modality, where AI has seen the greatest success, and which disorders remain challenging for neuroimaging-based AI diagnostics.

Recent years have seen a surge of interest in applying DL to neuroimaging data for objective and quantitative diagnosis of mental health disorders. Traditionally, psychiatric disorder diagnoses rely on subjective symptom assessments from the Diagnostics and Statistical Manual of Mental Disorders

(DSM) in the United States and the International Classification of Diseases (ICD) elsewhere. Neuroimaging modalities, including sMRI, fMRI, and PET, offer potential biomarkers of brain abnormalities. Classical ML has been used on crafter neuroimaging features, but it requires extensive feature engineering and has achieved limited success. In contrast, DL models can automatically learn complex, distributed patterns from high-dimensional brain scans, which is advantageous given the subtle changes in mental health. A 2021 review of 53 studies found that DL methods generally outperformed conventional ML for neuroimaging-based psychiatric classification.[147] Of note, there are different accuracies across different disorders, but the existing body of work in the space is promising.

Trends and challenges

Different modalities have proven more useful for certain conditions. Structural MRI (anatomical scans) is most valuable in disorders with clear brain morphology changes – for example, Alzheimer's and other dementias, where atrophy patterns are strong diagnostic clues.[148] MRI has also shown utility in schizophrenia (ventricular enlargement, gray matter loss) and in developmental disorders (e.g., cortical thickness delays in ADHD), but these changes are smaller in magnitude.[149] Diffusion MRI (DTI) has contributed to disorders like schizophrenia and autism by revealing connectivity differences. Some ML models incorporate DTI features which can improve classification modestly. fMRI (typically resting-state connectivity) is heavily used for mood disorders and neurodevelopmental disorders, where structural differences are subtle but network dysconnectivity can act as a fingerprint. fMRI has enabled the discovery of subtypes (as in depression biotypes) and provides markers for disorders like OCD and PTSD that revolve around circuit dysfunction. Molecular imaging (e.g., PET) is less common in psychiatric research due to its invasiveness and cost, but it has been transformative in neurodegenerative diseases. PET scans like glucose metabolism and amyloid/tau tracers combined with AI have given very high accuracy for early AD detection and even allowed prediction of future pathology, such as using MRI to predict PET biomarker status.[150] PET has also been used to study neurotransmitter systems in psychiatric conditions (e.g., dopamine receptor PET in schizophrenia), but applications of AI on those data are still limited in large part due to the lack of large datasets.

AI-driven imaging diagnostics have seen the greatest success in conditions with distinct, disease-specific brain changes. Alzheimer's disease stands out with numerous studies reporting 85–95% accuracy in distinguishing AD from healthy aging or mild impairment, and AI can even detect presymptomatic signs years in advance.[151,152,153] Schizophrenia is another disorder with strong results, showing multiple studies achieving ~80–85% accuracy using neuroimaging.[154,155,156] Some autism and OCD studies have also achieved ~70–80% accuracy, indicating moderate discriminative power in neuroimaging data.[157,158,159] AI has also proven capable of prognosis in prodromal states, such as predicting conversion from MCI to AD or psychosis development for risk stratification.[160,161]

The hardest disorders to classify via imaging tend to be those with heterogeneous presentations and minimal structural brain change. This is in part due to the challenges of fMRI analysis. Furthermore, mood disorders are strongly heterogeneous and comorbid, suggesting that they may exist as non-unique brain states, creating difficulties in classification due to probabilistic labeling. Major depression and generalized anxiety are prime examples as they likely consist of multiple biological subtypes and have no single biomarker. Imaging classifiers for these conditions tend to hover just above chance, with efforts focusing on subtyping rather than healthy vs control classification. ADHD has also been notably difficult with brain differences in ADHD being more subtle and age-dependent, so models and subsequent findings do not generalize well.[162] Bipolar disorder also presents difficulties, especially in distinguishing it from unipolar depression using scans alone. Mood disorders tend to share many neural features. Personality disorders and many childhood psychiatric disorders, such as conduct disorder, have seen little success in imaging-based AI, largely due to a lack of distinctive neuroimaging signatures as well as fMRI analysis bias toward adult cohorts. It is also worth noting that even in disorders with higher diagnostic accuracy, there exist caveats. Primarily, models that perform well in academic studies may not generalize to new scanners or populations. For example, an algorithm trained on one hospital's schizophrenia MRI data might see a performance drop on another's due to site differences (a well-known issue of batch effects in MRI). Thus, generalizability and robustness are key challenges going forward.

Another broad trend is the shift from using small, single-site datasets to large consortium datasets and data aggregations. Collaborative initiatives such as ENIGMA, ADNI, UK Biobank, and ABCD have greatly expanded sample sizes, allowing DL models to train without overfitting. Many highly cited papers in the last few years leverage such big data – e.g., the 51k-subject dementia study or multi-cohort schizophrenia analysis.[163,164] These large studies often appear as preprints before peer review, given the fast pace of AI research. Influential preprints have introduced novel techniques like GNNs for connectomes and transformer models on MRI sequences, which are quickly adopted by others even prior to journal publication. The field remains very active, with new methodologies (e.g., federated learning to train models across sites without sharing data) and a focus on explainable AI to interpret what brain features drive the models.

Specific disorders

DL for psychotic disorders

Psychotic disorders are a group of mental health conditions characterized by psychosis, or a disconnection from reality, leading to significant disturbances in thinking, perception, emotions, and behavior. The primary hallmarks of psychosis are hallucinations, perceiving things that are not present, and delusions, firmly held false beliefs. Other symptoms include disorganized thinking and speech and impaired functioning. Some examples of psychotic disorders include schizophrenia and schizoaffective disorder, although psychosis can be observed in certain mood disorders.[165] Psychotic disorders, specifically schizophrenia, have had relative success in diagnosis via neuroimaging DL. A large number of studies utilize the publicly available neuroimaging dataset from SchizConnect, which has 1400 subjects from 5 different datasets.[166]

DL on structural MRI

A 2020 study using 900 subjects from SchizConnect applied a 3D-CNN to diagnose schizophrenic patients using sMRI and achieved an AUC of 96%, but performance dropped to 71% when the algorithm was applied to a new dataset with younger patients. This indicates the model did not generalize across age groups. The network's predictive regions, which were identified via occlusion testing, were in the right temporal and temporoparietal areas aligning with known structural deficits in schizophrenia.[167] Zhang et al. published a study in 2023 that trained a 3D CNN architecture to differentiate schizophrenia using T1w sMRI on nearly 900 subjects with an ROC of 99%. This study had improved preprocessing and region analysis. By applying gradient class activation maps, it was possible to localize the brain regions related to schizophrenia identification. Corroborating previous findings, localized subcortical regions (including the basal ganglia) and ventricles were most predictive.[168,169,170] This study demonstrates near-perfect separation of patients using a single MRI scan using data from three different studies.

Another study used a 80 patient dataset from Northwestern and 1200 health controls from the Human Connectome Project (HCP). In an effort for more interpretable analyses, they used an autoencoder to create a normative model using the sMRI from the health subjects. Then they estimated the total and regional neuroanatomical deviation in individuals with schizophrenia. Despite the small sample size, the model generated different values of neuroanatomical deviation for schizophrenia relative to control than other disorders. It also revealed distinct neuroanatomical deviations that were consistent with existing literature, highlighting a DL framework with utility even with small patient samples.[171]

DL on functional MRI

DL has further been applied to fMRI and derived measures in schizophrenia. Combining data from multiple datasets, a study applied a deep discriminant autoencoder network to learn FC features. They achieved 85 and 81%

accuracies on multi-site pooling and leave-site-out transfer classification, respectively. The learned features showed dysregulation of the cortical-striatal-cerebellar circuit across default, salience, and control networks in schizophrenia.[172] Another study used GCN applied to whole-brain FC matrices from 1400 patients across 6 sites. It achieved higher accuracy (86%) than standard ML baselines (SVM 81%). Using a salience map, the found the most discriminative regions were located in a distributed network, including striatal areas (i.e., putamen, pallidum, and caudate) and the amygdala. This work concluded that functional topological deficits in the striatal areas may be the primary neural deficit leading to negative symptomatology in schizophrenia.[173] Similarly, a study used a GCN applied to 69 graph-theoretical measures computed from FC on 170 subjects with data augmentation and achieved an accuracy of 82%. Some of the discriminative biomarkers had previously been cited in literature (frontoparietal region, temporal gyrus) while some had not, emphasizing the ability of DL models to detect subtler single-subject differences.[174]

Studies are more recently looking into multi-class classification and subtyping in psychotic disorders. Specifically, a 2022 study out of Georgia Institute of Technology analyzed the rs-fMRI data from nearly 700 subjects using the B-SNIP (Bipolar-Schizophrenia Network on Intermediate Phenotypes) study.[175] Spatially constrained ICA time courses were obtained from rs-fMRI data using group information guided ICA (GIG-ICA) followed by a multi-scale recurrent neural network (MsRNN) model for multi-class classification. The four classes were schizophrenia, psychotic bipolar disorder, schizoaffective disorder (SD), and health controls. An accuracy of 46% was reached, which is significantly above chance. The network representations were clustered using tSNE succeeded by leave-one-feature-out to identify disorder-related biomarkers. From this, SD was separated into two subtypes where Subtype 1 has significantly higher Positive and Negative Syndrome Scale (PANSS) scores in emotional withdrawal, anxiety, guilt feelings, and tension.[176]

Multimodal

Recently, a 2025 study was published for schizophrenia diagnosis using multi-omics. They constructed multiple brain graphs, gut graphs, and brain-gut combined graphs for each individual and used a novel multi-omics graph convolutional network (MO-GCN) with an attention mechanism to classify schizophrenia patients with an accuracy of 84%. It was applied to data from 100 subjects from a single site. Furthermore, they identified important brain and gut features using the top-k pooling layers and analyzed their correlations with the patients' behavioral and cognitive scores. The top 10 brain features were primarily from the hippocampus, olfactory, fusiform, and pallidum which are involved in learning, memory, and emotion. Additionally, the top features from both the brain and gut significantly correlated with the patient's behavior scores. This emphasizes a general trend toward integrating multiple data types and explainable diagnostic systems.[177]

Trends

The majority of studies are on schizophrenia diagnostics, thanks to the development of large datasets like SchizConnect. sMRI achieves high diagnostic accuracy compared to other psychiatric disorders, with studies typically using 3D-CNNs or autoencoder methods. fMRI, while successful, does not reach accuracies as high as sMRI, but more advanced methods such as spatiotemporal modeling hold promise. Multimodal and interpretable studies are becoming more common in diagnostics. It appears there is less heterogeneity observed in schizophrenia, as there is high classification accuracy and little work on subtyping.

Mood disorders

Mood disorders, also known as affective disorders, are mental health conditions characterized by persistent disturbances in a person's emotional state that are considered disproportionate to external circumstances. These disorders significantly impact daily functioning and quality of life. Some examples of mood disorders include major depressive disorder (MDD) and bipolar disorder.[178]

DL on sMRI

DL on sMRI has picked up some anatomical differences associated with depression. Common findings include reduced volumetric or thickness measures in limbic and frontal regions for depressed patients. For example, a 3D-CNN model on sMRI of approximately 100 older adults with depression predicted certain symptom severities, including suicidality and found that the anterior cingulate cortex (ACC) and orbitofrontal cortex were among the most discriminative regions for depression symptom prediction.[179] This aligns with traditional neuroimaging studies linking ACC and frontal lobe alterations to mood regulation. Another study used a CNN to differentiate between bipolar disorder (BD) and MDD with 300 subjects and achieved an accuracy of 86%.[180] Another study from the ENIGMA BDs working group applied ML to 3000 individuals from 13 cohorts to differentiate BD from controls. They used support vector machines (SVM) and had an aggregate accuracy of 65%, although individual site accuracies ranged from 45% to 81%. Their findings were consistent with regions that have previously been implicated in BD, including the hippocampus, amygdala, and cortical regions, such as the inferior frontal gyrus and precentral gyrus.[181]

DL on fMRI

fMRI studies often highlight dysregulation in networks such as the default mode network (DMN), salience network, and fronto-limbic circuits in mood disorders. Deep models have reinforced some of these observations. In a multicenter study (>3300 subjects), a graph convolutional network (GCN) model identified whole-brain functional connectivity differences, especially a prominent thalamic hyperconnectivity in depressed patients. Thalamic over-connectivity with other regions emerged as a reproducible signature of depression across datasets, even though most other connections were slightly weaker in MDD than in controls. The relatively modest accuracy (61%) in the study underscores that depression is a diffuse and heterogeneous brain condition, making it challenging to classify.[182] It also emphasizes the importance of large samples as smaller studies may overestimate accuracy due to site-specific effects or limited heterogeneity. Another study used a Transformer-Encoder model on rs-fMRI to classify MDD and healthy controls (HC) on 1600 samples and reached a 69% accuracy. When focusing solely on recurrent MDD, the model accuracy improved to 78%. Abnormalities were found in the frontal gyri and cerebral cortex of MDD patients in both datasets.[183]

Multimodal

Recent research trends emphasize combining modalities to improve diagnostic power. Mood disorders appear to manifest in both brain structure and function, so fusing sMRI and fMRI data can provide a comprehensive picture. There is a substantial body of evidence in favor of multimodal studies for MDD diagnosis. A 2022 study combined FC from rs-fMRI and sMRI features to distinguish MDD. They used GCN for the fMRI data and CNN for sMRI with cross-modal feature adaptation and fusion. Their framework, adaptive multimodal neuroimage integration or AMNI, outperformed single-modality and standard ML baselines. An interesting aspect was their use of KNN graphs based on the densely connected FC matrix to maintain the top edges. Overall, they achieved a 67% AUC on 500 subjects.[184] Notably, they could not comment on top features overall. A related study also using rs-fMRI and sMRI developed feature-specific encoders for each modality. The brain function encoder (BFE) encoded both FC using an MLP and time courses using a transformer followed by an MLP. After encoding each modality, there was a combined attention mechanism, which learned to weight structural features higher than functional. This model achieved 75% accuracy in diagnosis on the REST-meta-MDD dataset.[185]

More recent studies have even better specificity in interpretable features. A 2024 study developed a novel evolutionary neural architecture search (M-ENAS) to find the top features using sMRI, DTI, and rs-fMRI. The method determines optimal weight and network architecture using a two-stage search strategy. First is supernet training using one-shot network architecture search (NAS) followed by a self-defined evolutionary search to optimize network structure. Afterwards, all the features from different modalities were concatenated and fed into fully connected layers. The best performance combined features from all three modalities (75% accuracy on 2000 subjects) and outperformed prior handcrafted models. Individually, the structural modalities slightly outperformed the functional measures. The most important features were determined using an occlusion study, which emphasized brain regions in the somatomotor network.[186] A follow-up study from the same lab looked at a contrastive learning framework with self-supervised pre-training on the REST-meta-MDD dataset, followed by hierarchical feature fusion. After fine-tuning on a separate dataset, they were able to achieve a 73% AUC on a small sample size with the default mode network (DMN) and cerebellum as key regions.[187]

Some studies are looking at other modalities entirely. In a 2025 study, the researchers combined regional brain volumes from sMRI with cerebral blood flow obtained from arterial spin leveling (ASL) in 260 subjects. They compare individual models to a fusion classifier, which uses a soft-voting ensemble combining multiple SVMs, random forest, and a fully connected neural network (FCNN). It outperformed the other single-modality and single-models with an accuracy of 91%. They also performed SHAP to identify the top individual features across modalities, which included 8 structural volumes and 6 CBF measures. Furthermore, they used FIMP (Feature Interaction based on Model Performance) to detect key feature interactions. From this, they identified 3 feature interactions amongst the top 14 features and 7 interactions between sMRI and CBF features. Despite the small sample size, this study highlights the importance of CBF in MDD diagnosis.[188]

Lastly, a study looked at diagnosing MDD and BD by integrating sMRI and whole-exome sequencing (WES) genetic data. The genetic data used included WES, extracted SNPs associated with MDD and BD from GWAS databases, and calculated unweighted polygenic risk scores (PRS). They tested a combination of different models for image and genetic feature extraction and found the best performance with a vision transformer for sMRI features and XGBoost for SNP and PRS. The features were summed element-wise, followed by softmax classification to obtain an 89% AUC. While this demonstrates promise for the integration of genetic and MRI features, the sample size was relatively small (321) and without a region-specific interpretation of their results.[189]

Subtyping

One of the most promising applications of AI in mood disorders is data-driven subtyping of mood disorders. Traditional diagnoses treat MDD as a single category, but patients vary widely in symptom profiles, etiologies, and treatment responses. DL and clustering methods applied to neuroimaging are uncovering biotypes of mood disorders, which are subgroups defined by distinct brain patterns rather than symptoms alone.

A landmark study identified six depression subtypes ("biotypes") using fMRI in both resting and task conditions. On a cohort of 800 subjects, multiple fMRI metrics were obtained, and unsupervised hierarchical clustering was applied to separate subtypes. The resulting biotypes displayed different symptomatology and behavioral performance. Furthermore, they showed differential likelihood of responding to specific treatments. For example, some biotypes were more responsive to medications while others responded better to psychotherapy.[190] These results validate the idea that "depression" actually comprises multiple neurobiological sub-conditions where diagnostics and treatment prediction may be improved by first identifying a patient's biotype. These subtyping efforts often use techniques like clustering algorithms, dimensionality reduction, or deep representation learning on brain features. For instance, graph autoencoders can embed individual brain networks into a latent space, and clustering in that space might reveal groupings corresponding to different mood disorder phenotypes.[191]

Beyond clustering, some studies use supervised approaches to identify subtypes related to known factors. For example, networks have been trained to classify depression with high anxiety compared to depression without anxiety, revealing distinct neural signatures for "anxious depression." Specifically, the study looked at 400 subjects using a random forest model on features extracted from sMRI and rs-fMRI, obtaining an AUC of 80%. Anxious MDD patients showed differences in gray matter volume and fMRI differences in multiple frontal cortical regions.[192]

It is important to note that there may not be a single "correct" number of subtypes. Six biotypes is one useful model, but depression likely exists on a spectrum with multiple dimensions. Nonetheless, the ability of AI to objectively parse heterogeneity is a major advancement over the one-size-fits-all diagnostic category. Future studies are likely to integrate not just imaging but also genetics, cognitive profiles, and symptom data into multimodal AI models to refine subtypes even further. The emerging consensus is that embracing this complexity, with help from AI, will lead to better-targeted interventions than the current trial-and-error approach in treating mood disorders.

Trends

There exists a range of success in diagnosing mood disorders using DL. Early, small-sample studies often reported artificially high accuracy in distinguishing mood disorder patients from health individuals using neuroimaging features.[193] Larger and more rigorous studies show more modest but still above-chance performance, reflecting the clinical heterogeneity of mood disorders. On average, ML and DL models can reasonably discriminate depression but with substantial variability across studies. Factors such as sample size, scanning protocol, and analytical methods contribute to differing results.[194] Furthermore, the data type used for diagnosis affects the outcome. Two of the larger datasets in this space include ENIGMA for bipolar disorder (BD), MDD, and suicidal thoughts; the other is REST-meta-MDD, which has fMRI from nearly 2500 subjects.[195,196]

sMRI measures continuously emerge as important features in mood disorder diagnosis with key regions being consistent with known neurobiology.

CNNs are particularly effective in sMRI analysis. fMRI highlights network dysregulation in key functional networks, but the results are generally noisier with less interpretability. Graph networks seem common in functional network analysis. Multimodal integration is a promising trend with fusion across modalities consistently improving diagnostic accuracy. Furthermore, model interpretability and feature attribution are gaining traction in an effort to develop more biologically meaningful models. Due to the development of large datasets, MDD is better studied than other mood disorders. Lastly, mood disorders are highly heterogeneous. Therefore, subtyping and careful consideration of both subject and control cohort selection need to be taken into account.

Neurodevelopmental disorders

Neurodevelopmental disorders are conditions that affect the growth and development of the brain and nervous system, leading to challenges in areas such as learning, behavior, and social interaction. These disorders typically emerge in early childhood and can persist into adulthood. Some examples of mental health conditions that are considered neurodevelopmental disorders include ASD and attention-deficit hyperactivity disorder (ADHD).[197]

Autism spectrum disorder

ASD is a neurodevelopmental condition that affects how individuals communicate, interact socially, and behave.[198] It encompasses a wide range of characteristics and abilities, including social communication challenges, repetitive behaviors, restricted interests, and sensory sensitivities.[199]

Neuroimaging research on autism diagnosis is aided by the Autism Brain Imaging Data Exchange (ABIDE) initiative that aggregates and shares both functional and structural neuroimaging data from individuals with ASD and neurotypical controls. The goal of the ABIDE program is to facilitate large-scale studies to understand the neural underpinnings of ASD. The initial data release (ABIDE I) had over 1000 subjects aged 7–64, and the follow-up doubled that number with data collected from over 24 international sites.[200] As such, much of the research on ASD utilizes this dataset.

DL on structural MRI

A landmark study on early ASD diagnosis predicted autism in infants between low-risk and high-risk groups with 88% sensitivity using a multi-layer perceptron (MLP) trained on sMRI, specifically cortical surface expansion. The results found accelerated brain growth in high-risk groups, where infants who developed ASD showed early cortical surface hyper-expansion and brain volume overgrowth. Of note, there were only 150 subjects, with a 2:1 ratio of high-risk to low-risk infants.[201] Using the ABIDE dataset, a 2024 study applied CNNs achieving 60% ROC AUC. They tested both standard and medical CNNs, where the CNN with medical image training overfit their training data. While modest in accuracy, the approach was fully interpretable. Using saliency mapping, the authors identified neuroanatomical regions that contributed most to autism predictions. The areas encompassed a left-lateralized network of regions that supports language processing, which is consistent with previous literature.[202] This study again highlights the importance of multi-site studies in training and testing.

DL on functional MRI

A 2018 study using ABIDE I achieved 70% accuracy in distinguishing ASD from health controls using functional connectivity (FC) derived from rs-fMRI. Stacked denoising autoencoders were used for unsupervised feature learning, followed by a fully-connected network for classification. This was in comparison to standard ML methods tested, including SVM, which achieved only 61% accuracy. The study found two distinct sets of areas that were underconnected (negatively correlated) and highly connected (positively correlated) in ASD. Specifically, there was a distributed network of anterior and posterior brain areas with negatively correlated activation in rs-fMRI and a posterior network of areas whose activation was highly correlated.[203] This is consistent with an existing data-driven theory of anterior-posterior underconnectivity in ASD.[204] Another similar study utilized a CNN to differentiate between ASD and controls in ABIDE I FC and achieved 70% accuracy, which was slightly above their ML baselines (SVM reached 69%). The FC was obtained using functional parcellation and four posterior brain regions were implicated.[205]

A 2018 study combined imaging and phenotypic data in sparse graphs where imaging-based features were nodes and phenotypic information (age, gender, site) acted as edge weights. Their graph convolutional network (GCN) model achieved 70% accuracy on the ABIDE dataset. Significantly, incorporating non-imaging data yielded better performance than imaging data alone.[206] More recently, a study used a spatiotemporal deep neural network (stDNN) on time-series data rather than static FC. Using preprocessed regional fMRI time-series from over 200 brain regions and one-hot encoding of site, sex, and age data, they trained the stDNN on the ABIDE dataset and tested it on a Stanford ASD dataset. 78% accuracy was achieved in validation and 73% on testing. The distinguishing features were all found to be in the default mode network (DMN). Notably, they tested their model on ADHD as well and did not perform higher than chance.[207]

Multimodal

In 2024, a study using ABIDE applied a joint fusion deep neural network with two feature-extractor sub-networks, one for sMRI and fMRI (FC) features respectively, with outputs concatenated for final classification. Multimodal data fusion significantly improved ASD detection, where solely sMRI features gave AUC 66%, fMRI gave 76% and combined achieved 78%. Using SHapley Additive exPlanations (SHAP), an explainable AI technique, feature importance could be analyzed. From this, the most influential features involved the DMN and "social brain" regions, suggesting that structural and functional abnormalities in these circuits together differentiate ASD.[208]

Subtyping

Subtyping ASD using DL is also an ongoing area of research due to its believed heterogeneity. A 2022 study looking at data derived from sMRI using the ABIDE dataset, applied HYDRA (Hierarchical Dense Representation of Subtypes) to find two neuroanatomical subtypes among men. This method is a semi-supervised clustering technique that separates patients into subgroups while using controls as a reference. Voxel-wise volume, clinical measures, and dynamic rs-fMRI measures were used for subtyping. The two subtypes displayed differing voxel-wise volumetric patterns. The total intracranial volume was correlated with performance IQ in Subtype 1, while it was correlated with communication and social scores in Subtype 2. Subtype 1 further showed lower dynamic rs-fMRI measures, lower dynamic functional architecture stability, and higher mean and lower standard deviation of concordance among dynamic rs-fMRI measures in the cerebellum. Classification accuracies improved when ASD neurosubtypes were included in differentiating against health controls.[209]

Another 2023 study found four reproducible ASD subtypes with distinct FC alterations in ASD-related networks. Using ABIDE and an NDA dataset, rs-FC was obtained, and the features were ranked by correlation with clinical symptoms. Then, regularized canonical correlation analysis (RCCA) was used to select the best linear combination of features. From this, three latent dimensions were identified that robustly predicted individual differences in ASD behaviors. Clustering along these dimensions produced four subtypes with genetic differences. Specifically, within each subgroup, ASB-related FC was explained by regional differences in the expression of distinct ASD-related gene sets, implicating molecular signaling mechanisms.[210]

Trends

ASD diagnosis seems to only reach moderate accuracies around 70%. Combined features seem to perform better than individual MRI modalities. Subtyping appears to be an important first step in ASD diagnostics, indicating the heterogeneity of the current ASD labels. Future work will likely focus on integrated modalities, including behavioral observations, for subtyping and diagnostics.

ADHD

Attention-Deficit/Hyperactivity Disorder (ADHD) is a neurodevelopmental disorder characterized by inattentiveness, hyperactivity, and impulsivity. Inattentiveness is difficulty with sustained focus or organizing tasks, hyperactivity refers to excessive movement or fidgeting, and impulsivity is characterized by hasty actions without forethought. These traits interfere with daily functioning and development. There are three main presentations of ADHD: predominantly inattentive, predominantly hyperactive-impulsive, and combined.

The largest dataset for ADHD neuroimaging is ADHD-200, which is a publicly available dataset of nearly 1000 subjects aged 7 to 21 across 8 collection sites. The data includes rs-fMRI, sMRI, and phenotypic information.[211]

DL on structural MRI

Subsequent studies on sMRI often employed deep networks on large datasets. Zhang-James et al. (2021) used a multilayer perceptron (MLP) on sMRI features from the ENIGMA consortium (a worldwide sample of ~4k subjects). Their deep model significantly separated ADHD from controls in children (AUC ~0.64) but performed poorly in adults (AUD ~0.56). This finding implies that anatomical differences associated with ADHD are pronounced in youth but attenuate with age.[212] Overall, sMRI-based DL tends to yield moderate accuracy (roughly 60–75% in most studies) for pediatric ADHD, and it struggles for adults. Key anatomical biomarkers identified by these models often include reduced volumes or altered surface area in frontal lobes, temporal lobes, insula, basal ganglia, and cerebellum.[213,214]

A few structural MRI studies have reported very high accuracy, although these often involve small samples or heavy preprocessing. For example, Cicek & Akan (2021) applied a transfer-learning CNN (pre-trained ResNet-50) to structural MRIs of children.[215] [They reported ~100% accuracy in classifying ADHD vs. control with 10-fold cross-validation. Such near-perfect results, also seen with some autoencoder-based models reaching ~99%, likely reflect overfitting or site-specific idiosyncrasies rather than a generalizable achievement.[216] In general, deep models on structural MRI outperform classical ML only when trained on sufficiently large datasets. For instance, an extreme learning machine (ELM) reached 90% accuracy using handcrafted MRI features in a sample of 110 children, showing that with limited data, simpler models can rival DL.[217] Thus, while structural MRI contains useful signals for ADHD, especially in children, robust diagnosis via DL remains challenging without large, diverse samples.

DL on functional MRI

fMRI, particularly resting-state fMRI, has been widely explored for ADHD given the disorder's association with altered brain connectivity. DL methods aim to automatically extract spatio-temporal patterns from fMRI that distinguish ADHD. A seminal effort was Riaz et al. (2020), who proposed DeepFMRI, an end-to-end CNN-based model to learn functional connectivity directly from resting-state data.[218] Their architecture included a CNN feature extractor for each brain region and a Siamese-like network to learn pairwise region similarity (functional connectivity), followed by a classifier. Using the multi-site ADHD-200 dataset of children and adolescents, DeepFMRI achieved 73% accuracy in classifying ADHD compared to typically developing controls at the site level. Notably, performance varied by site, reflecting how scanner and site differences impact generalization. This study highlighted the importance of modeling functional connections with deep nets as well as the need for methods to handle multi-site heterogeneity.

Graph-based DL has also been applied to fMRI. Jha et al. (2020) introduced HLGSNet, an end-to-end lightweight CNN architecture with hierarchical representation learning, to classify ADHD using resting fMRI graphs. Brain regions were nodes and their temporal correlations formed edges then a graph CNN with a Siamese (triplet-loss) architecture learned to distinguish ADHD from control connectivity patterns, reaching 68% accuracy on test data from ADHD-200. HLGSNet is comparable to CNN-based approaches but with the advantage of an interpretable graph representation of affected networks.[219] Similarly, other graph neural network models have identified aberrant network topology in ADHD. For example, one study found disrupted default mode (DMN) and frontoparietal network connectivity in combined-type vs. inattentive ADHD children.[220]

Another analysis method has been combining fMRI time-series analysis with temporal networks, such as recurrent networks or attention mechanisms. A recent study by Niu et al. (2022) used 3D-CNNs to extract spatial features from each fMRI time frame and a customized gated recurrent unit (GRU) to capture temporal dynamics.[221] This spatio-temporal model achieved 72% accuracy in ADHD vs control classification on ADHD-200. By explicitly modeling temporal information, it slightly improved generalization over static connectivity methods. Likewise, an attention-based autoencoder by Qiang et al. (2022) learned long-distance dependencies in fMRI sequences and attained 73% accuracy across multiple sites.[222] These results converge in the 70–75% accuracy range, indicating that resting-state fMRI alone provides a signal modestly above chance for diagnosing pediatric ADHD.

It is worth noting that some fMRI-based deep models report very high within-sample accuracy. Tang et al. (2022), for example, combined a convolutional autoencoder with a binary hypothesis testing framework and reported 97.6% accuracy on an ADHD-200 subset.[223] However, such results have not been replicated in independent cohorts and likely reflect overfitting or optimistic evaluation. In contrast, a systematic review of 27 studies of both sMRI and fMRI for ADHD diagnosis found pooled sensitivity of 74% and specificity of 75%, corresponding to an AUC of 0.81.[224] This suggests that when averaged across many studies, the true performance of MRI-based classifiers for ADHD is in the 75–80% range. DL models have matched or exceeded this benchmark by leveraging more data and complex features, but they still face generalization challenges. In practice, careful cross-site validation and augmentation (e.g., using techniques to mitigate head motion and other confounds) are needed. Indeed, motion is a strong confounder in ADHD fMRI, where children with ADHD tend to move more, and models must ensure they are capturing neural signatures rather than motion artifacts.

MULTIMODAL

Zou et al. (2017) developed one of the first 3D CNNs to automatically classify ADHD using both structural MRI and resting-state fMRI. They extracted 3 fMRI features and 3 sMRI features for each subject. Their multimodal 3D-CNN achieved 69% accuracy in distinguishing children with ADHD from controls. The joint modalities outperformed each single-modality CNNs, which were closer to change. Important brain features included gray matter volume patterns in frontal-striatal regions.[225] This pioneering work demonstrated the feasibility of end-to-end ADHD classification but performance was modest.

Molecular and emerging imaging modalities

Beyond MRI, other neuroimaging modalities have seen limited DL research due to smaller sample sizes. Molecular imaging like PET can probe neurochemical differences in ADHD (e.g., dopamine or serotonin function), but DL models are rare. A noteworthy study by Kautzky et al. (2020) used a traditional ML random forest model on PET scans of the serotonin transported in adults, combined with genetic SNP features.[226] They achieved 82% accuracy distinguishing ADHD from controls with PET-based biomarkers. While not a deep network, this result suggests molecular imaging carries discriminatory signals, though integrating such data with DL is constrained by very small sample sizes. For example, Kautzky only had 16 ADHD patients. At this point, there exist no published DL models on PET for ADHD, highlighting an opportunity for future research as datasets grow.

Diffusion MRI (DTI) and MR spectroscopy (MRS) are other modalities that could provide microstructural or metabolic markers. Thus far, most ML on DTI in ADHD has used classical approaches, and DL is virtually unexplored. An example of this is fractional anisotropy differences which have been shown to predict impulsivity.[227] Similarly, functional near-infrared spectroscopy (fNIRS), a portable imaging modality, has been tested with ML for ADHD, finding prefrontal activation patterns as strong measures to classify children, but deep models are not yet common.[228] A few studies have started combining modalities. For instance, one study fused structural MRI features with fNIRS signals in a hybrid model, finding that shape features of the caudate nucleus plus fNIRS-derived metrics improved classification accuracy, reaching 87%.[229] Overall, novel imaging modalities remain an emerging frontier with current DL efforts overwhelmingly focusing on MRI-based features. As more multimodal data becomes available, deep networks that integrate across modalities may unveil more powerful ADHD biomarkers.

Subtyping

In addition to diagnosis, researchers have applied DL to differentiate ADHD subtypes or discover new "biotypes" of ADHD. The DSM defines 3 subtypes: ADHD inattentive (ADHD-I), hyperactive-impulsive (ADHD-HI), and combined (ADHD-C). These have subtle neurological differences that are hard to detect.

A breakthrough came from Firouzi et al. (2024), who introduced Skip-Vote-Net, which is a CNN with skip connections and a majority-voting scheme on dynamic functional connectivity segments. Using 176 rs-fMRI scans of children (NYU subset of ADHD-200), Skip-Vote-Net achieved remarkable accuracy for subtype classification, reaching 99% accuracy for distinguishing ADHD-I vs ADHD-C and classifying these two subtypes against controls. For binary ADHD vs. control classification, it reached 97%. These results are suspiciously high, but the authors attribute the success to modeling time-varying connectivity (splitting each scan into segments and ensembling predictions) and to architectural innovations (skip connections to preserve multiscale features, and majority voting to stabilize predictions). If generalizable, this approach suggests that ADHD subtypes do have distinct neural signatures that a sufficiently powerful model can extract. However, independent replication is needed as other attempts have not seen such clear separability. It is possible that the constrained sample (one site, excluding ADHD-HI) and segment-level training boosted performance in this study. Nonetheless, Skip-Vote-Net provides proof-of-concept that DL might aid in objective subtype diagnosis, which is traditionally based solely on clinical observation.[230]

Going beyond predefined subtypes, deep clustering methods have been used to uncover data-driven ADHD biotypes. A recent study applied a graph convolutional network-based deep clustering (GCN-BSD) on functional connectivity data to identify natural groupings of ADHD patients. Analyzing two large pediatric cohorts – the ABCD study and a Chinese dataset – they consistently found two robust ADHD biotypes. Biotype 1 comprised a majority of patients and exhibited milder symptoms. These children showed well-known ADHD brain anomalies such as frontal gyrus and cerebellar dysregulation, which aligns with the "classic" ADHD profile. Biotype 2 was a smaller subgroup with more severe symptoms, especially hyperactivity and impulsivity, and showed atypical connectivity patterns, including greater disruptions in sensorimotor-to-default mode network connections and cerebellum-fusiform circuits. Importantly, these biotypes replicated across independent datasets and correlated with cognitive measures and medication response differences. This suggests that DL can detect novel subtypes within ADHD beyond the

DSM labels. Such biotypes might eventually guide personalized treatment (e.g., patients in cluster 2 might need different interventions than cluster 1). Deep clustering thus represents a promising direction to embrace ADHD's heterogeneity, though it requires large samples and careful validation.[231]

Trends

Earlier DL studies used smaller sample sizes, which yielded overly optimized accuracies and failed to generalize. Large-scale datasets, like ADHD-200, are improving study robustness. Typical accuracy for ADHD is in the 60–75% range, reflecting the disorder's heterogeneity. The larger studies report lower accuracies, suggesting the early results were inflated by overfitting or size effects. Model advancements and multimodality show promise to detect and subtype subtler distinctions in ADHD. Lastly, due to the heterogeneous nature of the disorder, subtyping and biotyping are an increasing area of research.

Anxiety disorders

There are a number of studies utilizing DL on sMRI for anxiety disorders spanning raw MRI data to derived features. The results are mixed, with large consortial studies showing modest accuracy, whereas smaller studies again tend to report higher performance. In general, functional or multimodal data types are studied with less emphasis on structural imaging in these disorders.

DL using sMRI

One of the largest datasets in this space comes from the ENIGMA (Enhancing NeuroImaging Genetics through Meta Analysis) Study.[232] Specifically, the ENIGMA-Anxiety Consortium which has data from over 3000 subjects across 32 sites with ages ranging from 10 to 25 years old with Panic Disorder (PD), Generalized Anxiety Disorder (GAD), and Social Anxiety Disorder (SAD). A 2024 study specifically used ML models to diagnose subjects using neuroanatomical features, such as cortical thickness, cortical surface area, and subcortical volumes. Classification only surpassed chance for PD with an AUC of 62%. The key features were in the fronto-striato-limbic and temporo-parietal regions. Of note, better transdiagnostic classification was achieved when subgrouping was done, taking into account sex, medication, and anxiety severity (AUC 59%–63%).[233] Studies focusing solely on structural MRI for anxiety disorder diagnosis using DL are limited with the majority of studies being traditional ML and often with small sample sizes. Use of sMRI has been combined with other modalities, though, and is covered in more detail in the multimodal section.

DL using fMRI

fMRI is a key area of study for anxiety disorders in both rest and task states, although there are few studies using DL. One of the largest studies looks at fear-induced brain activation in 300 subjects (ages 18–65). The study examined task-specific activation of 10 brain regions commonly activated during fear conditioning and extinction. Subjects were either anxiety patients (combined GAD, PD, SAD, and specific phobia SP) or trauma-exposed (PTSD). After training, their CNN model reached a mean AUC of 84% with similar performance in both males and females. Performance ranged from 79% to 85% when a specific disorder was left-out, suggesting strong generalizability between anxiety disorders. Feature contribution was assessed by removing different features then re-running the classification. The result from the feature ranking analyses suggested that activations from the fear conditioning phase of the task and the ventromedial prefrontal cortex (vmPFC) had the strongest contribution when distinguishing anxious brains. This is in line with previous understanding of the role of the vmPFC in emotion regulation and fear extinction. Notably, performance significantly decreased when using activations from task-irrelevant brain regions or from networks irrelevant to fear.[234]

Two other smaller studies focused on PTSD specifically. The first looked at 80 matched pediatric PTSD and control subjects, analyzing FC determined from an anatomical atlas and partial correlation. Graph theory was used to analyze the topological properties of the functional connectome, and then DL was used to distinguish between the two groups. Specifically, a multi-layer neural network was used for dimensionality reduction, followed by a traditional support vector machine (SVM) for classification, reaching an accuracy of 71%. The weights and hidden layers were analyzed to find that the frontoparietal areas (central executive network), cingulate cortex, and amygdala contributed most to the model performance.[235] While this study had a small sample, it highlights the importance of dimensionality reduction in classification. Lastly, a recent study assessed rs-fMRI in 40 male subjects to diagnose PTSD. They focused on the 11 most studied regions in trauma and applied ICA for dimensionality reduction, followed by traditional ML and a 3D-CNN. While the ML models did not have good results, the 3D-CNN achieved a 98% accuracy. This strong result is likely due to overfitting on the small dataset, but it can still provide meaningful insights. Again, the amygdala and insula regions were determined to be the most activated ROIs in PTSD subjects.[236]

Multimodal

Naturally, the ENIGMA dataset provides a source for multimodal analyses. Utilizing the sMRI, rs-fMRI, and DTI data from the PTSD Working group, a 2023 study classified PTSD from controls across over 20 collection sites. Combining sites leads to lower results than previous single-site datasets, emphasizing the tendency for single-site models to overfit on data. When analyzing each modality, sMRI achieved the highest AUC of 60%, followed by rs-fMRI (59%) and DTI (56%). When controls with any trauma history were excluded, performance in each modality increased to 75% AUC. This suggests that models are picking up some neural signature associated with trauma. The analysis was done with traditional ML as well as a denoising variational autoencoder (DVAE). DVAE used fewer features and required less feature engineering but achieved similar performance and better generalization compared to traditional ML. This work emphasizes the importance of multi-site studies and proper selection of control groups.[237]

Another group proposed a particularly novel method called subspace-enhanced hypergraph neural network (seHGNN) for classifying anxiety disorders. The model is an extension of a standard hypergraph neural network (HGNN) with additional feature extraction to strengthen the influence of particular hyperedges in the graphs. The dataset contained nearly 300 subjects and data analyzed included voxel-based multimodal features, including ALFF, ReHo, and VBM. Only features from the 18 regions within the limbic system were utilized. First, regional SVM Recursive Feature Elimination (SVM-RFE) was used to identify the top 10 most informative regions. Afterwards, the seHGNN model built hypergraphs from those regions where each node is a brain region and the hyperedge is a shared similarity across modalities. The seHGNN learns a subspace representation, which is then clustered to classify. Overall, the model achieved an AUC of 92%, which significantly outperformed all other DL models tested, including other binary hypothesis testing frameworks. The identified biomarkers matched with previously published literature for anxiety disorders.[238]

Trends

Most studies focus on particular areas rather than the whole brain. Specifically, the limbic regions are studied with amygdala, insula, cortex, and hippocampus generally emerging as key discriminative features. DL models that explicitly constrain their inputs to these regions tend to perform better than whole-brain inputs, emphasizing the need for neurobiological priors for accuracy and interpretability in diagnosing anxiety disorders. CNNs are particularly popular, although newer work tends to focus on graph-based models for fMRI with the goal of capturing inter-regional dependencies beyond standard FC. This reflects a shift from handcrafted features and ML to data-driven, high-dimensional pattern learning. The range of accuracies is quite large, from near chance to 99%. This variability can be attributed to sample size variation, study design, methods used, and fMRI preprocessing differences. Studies look at both task and resting-state, with fear paradigms providing key insights for task-fMRI. There are fewer studies of DL for anxiety disorder diagnosis than all of the other categories, with most studies still focusing on ML or traditional analysis methods. Not much work has been done in subtyping anxiety. Even those that are published generally have small sample sizes. The recent ENIGMA-Anxiety project may lead to more studies in this space given the size and multimodality of their dataset.

Population differences and demographic considerations

DL is applied to neuroimaging data for diagnosing mental health conditions; however, population and demographic differences can significantly influence model performance and fairness. Recent research reveals that factors such as age, sex, race, and socioeconomic status (SES) can significantly affect accuracy. Below, key findings and trends are summarized, highlighting which groups are more easily diagnosed by these models and the implications for generalizability and fairness.

Age differences: Pediatric vs. adult diagnoses

Neurodevelopmental disorders often show age-dependent differences in brain features, impacting diagnostic modeling. For example, children with ADHD often have clear brain structure and function deviations, such as delayed cortical maturation, smaller subcortical volumes, and hyper- or hypo-connectivity in attention networks.[239,240,241,242]. In adulthood, many of these differences are less pronounced. It was found using DL applied to sMRI that classification accuracy and effect sizes were higher for children than adults. Structural differences associated with ADHD, such as reduced cortical volumes, are clear in childhood but may attenuate in adulthood suggesting childhood ADHD is easier to detect from neuroimaging.[243] Similarly, the ENIGMA-ADHD consortium reported significant cortical and subcortical anomalies in children with ADHD, yet virtually no detectable structural differences in adults.[244,245] Experts hypothesize that this may be due to developmental normalization or compensatory changes with age. Further, adults have more confounds of lifelong experiences and treatments or developed coping mechanisms. In general, adolescence is a critical period for all mental disorder development, not just neurodevelopmental disorders.

As such, models trained on adolescent or child brains might not directly generalize to adults, as brain connectivity patterns evolve with age. Thus, if possible, age stratification can be important. A model may need to be age-specific or include age as an input to maintain accuracy across the lifespan. Another issue is that many tools, databases, and atlases have been developed using adult data. Given the prevalent age differences observed in mental disorders, this may provide serious limitations. It is important moving forward to collect more data from children and adolescents, as well as longitudinal data, as is being done in the Adolescent Brain Cognitive Development (ABCD) Study.[246]

Sex differences

Sex is a major source of heterogeneity in mental health, affecting both structure and function. Female brains differ from males, and in many disorders, females are historically underdiagnosed.[247] ASD has a well-known male bias in prevalence, somewhere between 2:1 and 5:1.[248] A DL study in 2022 identified robust gender-specific brain organization differences in ASD. Specifically, their spatiotemporal DNN could distinguish autistic females from males with high accuracy, but the same model could not distinguish neurotypical females from males. This indicates that ASD manifests differently in female brains than males, beyond normal sex dimorphism. They found features in motor, language, and attention networks that differed between the two. The motor cortex connectivity in particular correlated with symptom severity in females but not in males. It is therefore key to have sex-specific diagnostic models or at least incorporate sex as a factor to improve accuracy for females to ensure they are not overlooked due to male-centric patterns.[249]

Many mental health conditions show sex differences in prevalence and neurobiology. Depression and anxiety are more common in females, whereas impulse-control and substance disorders are more common in males, and brain connectivity predictors reflect this. In the ABCD study, it was found that FC could predict externalizing behaviors (e.g., aggression) in both boys and girls but could only predict internalizing symptoms (e.g., anxiety/depression) only in girls. A model trained to predict internalizing problems in females did not work for males and vice versa, underlining sex-specific brain-behavior links.[250] Prior work also shows that predictions of cognitive and personality traits fail to generalize across sexes.[251,252]

A practical challenge is that female patients are underrepresented in some neuroimaging datasets.[253] This imbalance can yield biased classifiers that perform better on males than females. A 2020 PNAS study noted that sex imbalance in imaging datasets produces biased models that underdiagnosed females.[254] Ensuring adequate female samples or using data augmentation is critical to avoid biased outcomes.

Racial and ethnic differences

Race and ethnicity can also influence neuroimaging diagnostics in two distinct ways: through biological and cultural effects on the brain and from data biases. Recent work suggests that DL models do not generalize across racial and ethnic groups if the groups are underrepresented or if there are unmodeled confounds. A 2022 study provided strong examples of racial bias in brain-based predictive models. Researchers trained ML models to predict behavioral and cognitive phenotypes from rs-fMRI data. When models were trained on a dataset dominated by White American (WA) participants, their accuracy dropped significantly for African American (AA) participants. Specifically, out-of-sample prediction errors were higher for AAs than WAs demonstrating that the model learned patterns that reflected the majority WA brain-behavior relationships, failing to capture minority-specific patterns. Even when the models were retrained only on AA data, performance improved for the group but did not reach the accuracy levels seen in WAs. This suggests that current brain-based models may inherently favor the majority group's brain features and struggle with minority populations. Even an equal training mix left a performance gap, implying there may be distinct brain-behavior relationships by groups or unmeasured confounders correlated with race.[255]

One reason for such disparities is the historical underrepresentation and under-reporting of race and ethnicity in neuroimaging research. A review of over 400 U.S.-based MRI studies (2010–2020) found that only 10% reported participants' race and 4% reported ethnicity. Most studies also primarily sampled white populations. This limited diversity means many published ML/DL models might be trained on narrow populations.[256] The field is emphasizing inclusive datasets and reportings, such as in the ABCD study.[257] Ensuring diversity in training data and validating models on independent sets with different demographic makeup is seen as an essential step for generalizability.

Socioeconomic status

Socioeconomic status (SES) often correlates with brain development and could affect diagnostic algorithms. Children growing up in low SES environments show subtle differences in brain structure and function. Studies have found lower SES associated with reduced gray matter in regions like the hippocampus, orbitofrontal cortex, and anterior cingulate as well as differences in cortical thickness and surface area. Functional studies report that FC and activity can vary by SES, especially in regions supporting language, executive function, and emotion regulation. It is noted that low SES and non-Western subjects are, in general, underrepresented.[258] These are clear confounding factors to neuroimaging studies.

Mitigating bias

There is a growing body of research that one-size-fits-all models may fail, and, instead, personalized or subgroup-specific approaches could yield better results for marginalized groups. In general, models need testing across different groups to censure generalizability and avoid perpetuating health disparities. Techniques to reduce bias in models include dataset balancing, subgroup-specific modeling, and fairness constraints. Simple balancing can help but is likely not enough. Advanced approaches may be better, such as transfer learning or adversarial debiasing. These techniques are still being explored to make models focus on disorder-specific signals rather than demographic proxies. The goal is a fair neurodiagnostic model that maintains high accuracy across all groups, so that one population is not systemically misdiagnosed or missed.

ACKNOWLEDGMENTS

The author wishes to express profound gratitude to Margot Wagner, whose extensive insights, detailed research, and thoughtful analysis were instrumental in shaping this chapter.

NOTES

1 Johnstone, E. C., T. J. Crow, C. D. Frith, J. Husband, and L. Kreel. "Cerebral Ventricular Size and Cognitive Impairment in Chronic Schizophrenia." *The Lancet*, vol. 2, no. 7992, 1976, pp. 924–926. https://doi.org/10.1016/S0140-6736(76)90890-4. Accessed 24 May 2025.

2 Rangel-Guerra, R. A., H. Perez-Payan, L. Minkoff, and L. E. Todd. "Nuclear Magnetic Resonance in Bipolar Affective Disorders." *AJNR: American Journal of Neuroradiology*, vol. 4, no. 3, 1983, pp. 229–231. https://doi.org/10.1016/0730-725x(82)90176-x. Accessed 24 May 2025.

3 Gong, Bo et al. "Neuroimaging in Psychiatric Disorders: A Bibliometric Analysis of the 100 Most Highly Cited Articles." *Journal of Neuroimaging*, vol. 29, no. 1, 2019, pp. 14–33. https://doi.org/10.1111/jon.12570. Accessed 24 May 2025.

4 Ho, Beng-Choon et al. "Long-term antipsychotic treatment and brain volumes: a longitudinal study of first-episode schizophrenia." *Archives of General Psychiatry*, vol. 68, no. 2, 2011, 128–137. https://doi.org/10.1001/archgenpsychiatry.2010.199

5 Bassett, Danielle S et al. "Hierarchical organization of human cortical networks in health and schizophrenia." *The Journal of Neuroscience: The Official Journal of the Society for Neuroscience*, vol. 28, no. 37, 2008, pp. 9239–9248. https://doi.org/10.1523/JNEUROSCI.1929-08.2008

6 Pantelis, Christos et al. "Neuroanatomical abnormalities before and after onset of psychosis: a cross-sectional and longitudinal MRI comparison." *Lancet (London, England)*, vol. 361, no. 9354, 2003, 281–288. https://doi.org/10.1016/S0140-6736(03)12323-9

7 Kuperberg, Gina R et al. "Regionally localized thinning of the cerebral cortex in schizophrenia." *Archives of General Psychiatry*, vol. 60, no. 9, 2003, pp. 878–888. https://doi.org/10.1001/archpsyc.60.9.878

8 Cannon, Tyrone D et al. "Progressive reduction in cortical thickness as psychosis develops: a multisite longitudinal neuroimaging study of youth at elevated clinical risk." *Biological Psychiatry*, vol. 77, no. 2, 2015, pp. 147–157. https://doi.org/10.1016/j.biopsych.2014.05.023

9 Clementz, Brett A.. et al. "Identification of Distinct Psychosis Biotypes Using Brain-Based Biomarkers." *The American Journal of Psychiatry*, vol. 173, no. 4, 2016, pp. 373–384. https://doi.org/10.1176/appi.ajp.2015.14091200

10 Robinson, D et al. "Predictors of relapse following response from a first episode of schizophrenia or schizoaffective disorder." *Archives of General Psychiatry*, vol. 56, no. 3, 1999, pp. 241–247. https://doi.org/10.1001/archpsyc.56.3.241

11 Shenton, M E et al. "Abnormalities of the left temporal lobe and thought disorder in schizophrenia. A quantitative magnetic resonance imaging study." *The New England Journal of Medicine*, vol. 327, no. 9, 1992, pp. 604–612. https://doi.org/10.1056/NEJM199208273270905

12 Velakoulis, Dennis et al. "Hippocampal and amygdala volumes according to psychosis stage and diagnosis: a magnetic resonance imaging study of chronic schizophrenia, first-episode psychosis, and ultra-high-risk individuals." *Archives of General Psychiatry*, vol. 63, no. 2, 2006, 139–149. https://doi.org/10.1001/archpsyc.63.2.139

13 Pajonk, Frank-Gerald et al. "Hippocampal plasticity in response to exercise in schizophrenia." *Archives of General Psychiatry*, vol. 67, no. 2, 2010, pp. 133–143. https://doi.org/10.1001/archgenpsychiatry.2009.193

14 Drevets, W. C. et al. "Subgenual prefrontal cortex abnormalities in mood disorders." *Nature*, vol. 386, no. 6627, 1997, pp. 824–827. https://doi.org/10.1038/386824a0

15 Sheline, Yvette I. et al. "Hippocampal atrophy in recurrent major depression." *Proceedings of the National Academy of Sciences of the United States of America*, vol. 93, no. 9, 1996, pp. 3908–3913. https://doi.org/10.1073/pnas.93.9.3908
16 Sheline, Yvette I. et al. "Depression duration but not age predicts hippocampal volume loss in medically healthy women with recurrent major depression." *The Journal of Neuroscience: The Official Journal of the Society for Neuroscience*, vol. 19, no. 12, 1999, pp. 5034–5043. https://doi.org/10.1523/JNEUROSCI.19-12-05034.1999
17 MacQueen, Glenda M et al. "Course of illness, hippocampal function, and hippocampal volume in major depression." *Proceedings of the National Academy of Sciences of the United States of America*, vol. 100, no. 3, 2003, pp. 1387–1392. https://doi.org/10.1073/pnas.0337481100
18 Courchesne, E. et al. "Unusual brain growth patterns in early life in patients with autistic disorder: an MRI study." *Neurology*, vol. 57, no. 2, 2001, pp. 245–254. https://doi.org/10.1212/wnl.57.2.245
19 Courchesne, Eric et al. "Evidence of brain overgrowth in the first year of life in autism." *JAMA*, vol. 290, no. 3, 2003, pp. 337–344. https://doi.org/10.1001/jama.290.3.337
20 Courchesne, Eric et al. "Brain growth across the life span in autism: age-specific changes in anatomical pathology." *Brain Research*, vol. 1380, 2011, pp. 138–145. https://doi.org/10.1016/j.brainres.2010.09.101
21 Hazlett, Heather Cody et al. "Early brain development in infants at high risk for autism spectrum disorder." *Nature*, vol. 542, no. 7641, 2017, pp. 348–351. https://doi.org/10.1038/nature21369
22 Sparks, B. F. et al. "Brain structural abnormalities in young children with autism spectrum disorder." *Neurology*, vol. 59, no. 2, 2002, pp. 184–192. https://doi.org/10.1212/wnl.59.2.184
23 Schumann, Cynthia M. et al. "Longitudinal magnetic resonance imaging study of cortical development through early childhood in autism." *The Journal of Neuroscience: The Official Journal of the Society for Neuroscience*, vol. 30, no. 12, 2010, pp. 4419–4427. https://doi.org/10.1523/JNEUROSCI.5714-09.2010
24 Shaw, P., K. Eckstrand, W. Sharp et al. "Attention-Deficit/Hyperactivity Disorder Is Characterized by a Delay in Cortical Maturation." *Proceedings of the National Academy of Sciences of the United States of America*, vol. 104, no. 49, 2007, pp. 19649–19654. https://doi.org/10.1073/pnas.0707741104. Accessed 24 May 2025.
25 Castellanos, F. Xavier et al. "Developmental trajectories of brain volume abnormalities in children and adolescents with attention-deficit/hyperactivity disorder." *JAMA*, vol. 288, no. 14, 2002, pp. 1740–1748. https://doi.org/10.1001/jama.288.14.1740
26 Castellanos, F. Xavier et al. "Quantitative brain magnetic resonance imaging in attention-deficit hyperactivity disorder." *Archives of General Psychiatry*, vol. 53, no. 7, 1996, pp. 607–616. https://doi.org/10.1001/archpsyc.1996.01830070053009
27 Gilbertson, Mark W. et al. "Smaller hippocampal volume predicts pathologic vulnerability to psychological trauma." *Nature Neuroscience*, vol. 5, no. 11, 2002, pp. 1242–1247. https://doi.org/10.1038/nn958
28 Bremner, J. D. et al. "MRI based measurement of hippocampal volume in patients with combat-related posttraumatic stress disorder." *The American Journal of Psychiatry*, vol. 152, no. 7, 1995, pp. 973–981. https://doi.org/10.1176/ajp.152.7.973

29 Bremner, J. D. et al. "Magnetic resonance imaging-based measurement of hippocampal volume in posttraumatic stress disorder related to childhood physical and sexual abuse–a preliminary report." *Biological Psychiatry*, vol. 41, no. 1, 1997, pp. 23–32. https://doi.org/10.1016/s0006-3223(96)00162-x

30 Shenton, M. E. et al. "Abnormalities of the left temporal lobe and thought disorder in schizophrenia. A quantitative magnetic resonance imaging study." *The New England Journal of Medicine*, vol. 327, no. 9, 1992, pp. 604–612. https://doi.org/10.1056/NEJM199208273270905

31 Velakoulis, Dennis et al. "Hippocampal and amygdala volumes according to psychosis stage and diagnosis: a magnetic resonance imaging study of chronic schizophrenia, first-episode psychosis, and ultra-high-risk individuals." *Archives of General Psychiatry*, vol. 63, no. 2, 2006, pp. 139–149. https://doi.org/10.1001/archpsyc.63.2.139

32 Pajonk, Frank-Gerald et al. "Hippocampal plasticity in response to exercise in schizophrenia." *Archives of General Psychiatry*, vol. 67, no. 2, 2010, pp. 133–143. https://doi.org/10.1001/archgenpsychiatry.2009.193

33 Sheline, Yvette I. et al. "Hippocampal atrophy in recurrent major depression." *Proceedings of the National Academy of Sciences of the United States of America*, vol. 93, no. 9, 1996, pp. 3908–3913. https://doi.org/10.1073/pnas.93.9.3908

34 Bremner, J. D. et al. "Hippocampal volume reduction in major depression." *The American Journal of Psychiatry*, vol. 157, no. 1, 2000, pp. 115–118. https://doi.org/10.1176/ajp.157.1.115

35 Sheline, Yvette I. et al. "Depression duration but not age predicts hippocampal volume loss in medically healthy women with recurrent major depression." *The Journal of Neuroscience: The Official Journal of the Society for Neuroscience*, vol. 19, no. 12, 1999, pp. 5034–5043. https://doi.org/10.1523/JNEUROSCI.19-12-05034.1999

36 Sheline, Yvette I. et al. "Untreated depression and hippocampal volume loss." *The American Journal of Psychiatry*, vol. 160, no. 8, 2003, pp. 1516–1518. https://doi.org/10.1176/appi.ajp.160.8.1516

37 MacQueen, Glenda M. et al. "Course of illness, hippocampal function, and hippocampal volume in major depression." *Proceedings of the National Academy of Sciences of the United States of America*, vol. 100, no. 3, 2003, pp. 1387–1392. https://doi.org/10.1073/pnas.0337481100

38 Gilbertson, Mark W. et al. "Smaller hippocampal volume predicts pathologic vulnerability to psychological trauma." *Nature Neuroscience*, vol. 5, no. 11, 2002, pp. 1242–1247. https://doi.org/10.1038/nn958

39 Bremner, J. D. et al. "MRI-based measurement of hippocampal volume in patients with combat-related posttraumatic stress disorder." *The American Journal of Psychiatry*, vol. 152, no. 7, 1995, pp. 973–981. https://doi.org/10.1176/ajp.152.7.973

40 Bremner, J. D. et al. "Magnetic resonance imaging-based measurement of hippocampal volume in posttraumatic stress disorder related to childhood physical and sexual abuse–a preliminary report." *Biological Psychiatry*, vol. 41, no. 1, 1997, pp. 23–32. https://doi.org/10.1016/s0006-3223(96)00162-x

41 Wolff, Jason J. et al. "Differences in white matter fiber tract development present from 6 to 24 months in infants with autism." *The American Journal of Psychiatry*, vol. 169, no. 6, 2012, pp. 589–600. https://doi.org/10.1176/appi.ajp.2011.11091447

42 Barnea-Goraly, Naama et al. "White matter structure in autism: preliminary evidence from diffusion tensor imaging." *Biological Psychiatry*, vol. 55, no. 3, 2004, pp. 323–326. https://doi.org/10.1016/j.biopsych.2003.10.022

43 Alexander, Andrew L. et al. "Diffusion tensor imaging of the corpus callosum in Autism." *NeuroImage*, vol. 34, no. 1, 2007, pp. 61–73. https://doi.org/10.1016/j.neuroimage.2006.08.032
44 Nortje, Gareth et al. "Systematic review and voxel-based meta-analysis of diffusion tensor imaging studies in bipolar disorder." *Journal of Affective Disorders*, vol. 150, no. 2, 2013, pp. 192–200. https://doi.org/10.1016/j.jad.2013.05.034
45 Kafantaris, Vivian et al. "Changes in white matter microstructure predict lithium response in adolescents with bipolar disorder." *Bipolar Disorders*, vol. 19, no. 7, 2017, pp. 587–594. https://doi.org/10.1111/bdi.12544
46 Wakana, Setsu et al. "Reproducibility of quantitative tractography methods applied to cerebral white matter." *NeuroImage*, vol. 36, no. 3, 2007, pp. 630–644. https://doi.org/10.1016/j.neuroimage.2007.02.049
47 Wise, Toby et al. "Voxel-Based Meta-Analytical Evidence of Structural Disconnectivity in Major Depression and Bipolar Disorder." *Biological Psychiatry*, vol. 79, no. 4, 2016, pp. 293–302. https://doi.org/10.1016/j.biopsych.2015.03.004
48 Belliveau, J. W. et al. "Functional mapping of the human visual cortex by magnetic resonance imaging." *Science (New York, N.Y.)*, vol. 254, no. 5032, 1991, pp. 716–719. https://doi.org/10.1126/science.1948051
49 Grossman, R. I. et al. "Magnetization transfer: theory and clinical applications in neuroradiology." *Radiographics: A Review Publication of the Radiological Society of North America, Inc*, vol. 14, no. 2, 1994, pp. 279–290. https://doi.org/10.1148/radiographics.14.2.8190954
50 Bo Gong et al., "Neuroimaging in Psychiatric Disorders: A Bibliometric Analysis of the 100 Most Highly Cited Articles," *Journal of Neuroimaging*, 11 Oct. 2018. https://doi.org/10.1111/jon.12570.
51 Egan, M. F. et al. "Effect of COMT Val108/158 Met genotype on frontal lobe function and risk for schizophrenia." *Proceedings of the National Academy of Sciences of the United States of America*, vol. 98, no. 12, 2001, pp. 6917–6922. https://doi.org/10.1073/pnas.111134598
52 Whitfield-Gabrieli, Susan et al. "Hyperactivity and hyperconnectivity of the default network in schizophrenia and in first-degree relatives of persons with schizophrenia." *Proceedings of the National Academy of Sciences of the United States of America*, vol. 106, no. 4, 2009, pp. 1279–1284. https://doi.org/10.1073/pnas.0809141106
53 Mirella Dapretto et al., "Understanding Emotions in Others: Mirror Neuron Dysfunction in Children with Autism Spectrum Disorders," *Nature Neuroscience*, vol. 9, no. 1, 2006, pp. 28–30. https://doi.org/10.1038/nn1611.
54 Dalton, Kim M. et al. "Gaze fixation and the neural circuitry of face processing in autism." *Nature Neuroscience*, vol. 8, no. 4, 2005, pp. 519–526. https://doi.org/10.1038/nn1421
55 Just, Marcel Adam et al. "Cortical activation and synchronization during sentence comprehension in high-functioning autism: evidence of underconnectivity." *Brain: A Journal of Neurology*, vol. 127, Pt 8, 2004, pp. 1811–1821. https://doi.org/10.1093/brain/awh199
56 Greicius, Michael D. et al. "Resting-state functional connectivity in major depression: abnormally increased contributions from subgenual cingulate cortex and thalamus." *Biological Psychiatry*, vol. 62, no. 5, 2007, pp. 429–437. https://doi.org/10.1016/j.biopsych.2006.09.020
57 Sheline, Yvette I. et al., "Resting-State Functional MRI in Depression Unmasks Increased Connectivity between Networks via the Dorsal Nexus," *Proceedings of the National Academy of Sciences* 107, no. 24, 2010, pp. 11020–11025. https://doi.org/10.1073/pnas.1000446107.

58 Zang, Yu-Feng et al. "Altered baseline brain activity in children with ADHD revealed by resting-state functional MRI." *Brain & Development*, vol. 29, no. 2, 2007, pp. 83–91. https://doi.org/10.1016/j.braindev.2006.07.002
59 Castellanos, F. Xavier et al. "Cingulate-precuneus interactions: a new locus of dysfunction in adult attention-deficit/hyperactivity disorder." *Biological Psychiatry*, vol. 63, no. 3, 2008, pp. 332–337. https://doi.org/10.1016/j.biopsych.2007.06.025
60 Malhi, G. S., and J. Lagopoulos. "Making sense of neuroimaging in psychiatry." *Acta psychiatrica Scandinavica*, vol. 117, no. 2, 2008, pp. 100–117. https://doi.org/10.1111/j.1600-0447.2007.01111.x
61 Hasler, Gregor et al. "Reduced prefrontal glutamate/glutamine and gamma-aminobutyric acid levels in major depression determined using proton magnetic resonance spectroscopy." *Archives of General Psychiatry*, vol. 64, no. 2, 2007, pp. 193–200. https://doi.org/10.1001/archpsyc.64.2.193
62 Bo Gong et al., "Neuroimaging in Psychiatric Disorders: A Bibliometric Analysis of the 100 Most Highly Cited Articles," *Journal of Neuroimaging*, 11 Oct. 2018. https://doi.org/10.1111/jon.12570.
63 Mayberg, Helen S. et al. "Deep brain stimulation for treatment-resistant depression." *Neuron*, vol. 45, no. 5, 2005, pp. 651–660. https://doi.org/10.1016/j.neuron.2005.02.014
64 Drevets, W. C. et al. "Subgenual prefrontal cortex abnormalities in mood disorders." *Nature*, vol. 386, no. 6627, 1997, pp. 824–827. https://doi.org/10.1038/386824a0
65 Volkow, Nora D. et al. "Cocaine cues and dopamine in dorsal striatum: mechanism of craving in cocaine addiction." *The Journal of Neuroscience: The Official Journal of the Society for Neuroscience*, vol. 26, no. 24, 2006, pp. 6583–6588. https://doi.org/10.1523/JNEUROSCI.1544-06.2006
66 Breier, A. et al. "Schizophrenia is associated with elevated amphetamine-induced synaptic dopamine concentrations: evidence from a novel positron emission tomography method." *Proceedings of the National Academy of Sciences of the United States of America*, vol. 94, no. 6, 1997, pp. 2569–2574. https://doi.org/10.1073/pnas.94.6.2569
67 Volkow, N. D. et al. "Association of dopamine transporter reduction with psychomotor impairment in methamphetamine abusers." *The American Journal of Psychiatry*, vol. 158, no. 3, 2001, pp. 377–382. https://doi.org/10.1176/appi.ajp.158.3.377
68 Bloomfield, Peter S. et al. "Microglial Activity in People at Ultra High Risk of Psychosis and in Schizophrenia: An [(11)C]PBR28 PET Brain Imaging Study." *The American Journal of Psychiatry*, vol. 173, no. 1, 2016, pp. 44–52. https://doi.org/10.1176/appi.ajp.2015.14101358
69 Laruelle, M. et al. "Single photon emission computerized tomography imaging of amphetamine-induced dopamine release in drug-free schizophrenic subjects." *Proceedings of the National Academy of Sciences of the United States of America*, vol. 93, no. 17, 1996, pp. 9235–9240. https://doi.org/10.1073/pnas.93.17.9235
70 Bo Gong et al., "Neuroimaging in Psychiatric Disorders: A Bibliometric Analysis of the 100 Most Highly Cited Articles," *Journal of Neuroimaging*, 11 Oct. 2018. https://doi.org/10.1111/jon.12570.
71 Woo, Choong-Wan et al. "Building better biomarkers: brain models in translational neuroimaging." *Nature Neuroscience*, vol. 20, no. 3, 2017, pp. 365–377. https://doi.org/10.1038/nn.4478
72 Bo Gong et al., "Neuroimaging in Psychiatric Disorders: A Bibliometric Analysis of the 100 Most Highly Cited Articles," *Journal of Neuroimaging*, 11 Oct. 2018. https://doi.org/10.1111/jon.12570.

73 Jenkinson, Mark et al. "FSL." *NeuroImage*, vol. 62, no. 2, 2012, pp. 782–790. https://doi.org/10.1016/j.neuroimage.2011.09.015
74 Fischl, Bruce. "FreeSurfer." *NeuroImage*, vol. 62, no. 2, 2012, pp. 774–781. https://doi.org/10.1016/j.neuroimage.2012.01.021
75 Esteban, Oscar et al., "fMRIPrep: a Robust Preprocessing Pipeline for Functional MRI," *Nature Methods*, vol. 16, 10 Dec. 2018, pp. 111–116. https://doi.org/10.1038/s41592-018-0235-4.
76 Esteban, Oscar et al., "fMRIPrep: a Robust Preprocessing Pipeline for Functional MRI," *Nature Methods*, vol. 16, 10 Dec. 2018, pp. 111–116. https://doi.org/10.1038/s41592-018-0235-4.
77 Kaufman, L. et al. "Measuring signal-to-noise ratios in MR imaging." *Radiology*, vol. 173, no. 1, 1989, pp. 265–267. https://doi.org/10.1148/radiology.173.1.2781018
78 Power, Jonathan D. et al., "Spurious but Systematic Correlations in Functional Connectivity MRI Networks Arise from Subject Motion," *NeuroImage*, vol. 59, no. 3, 1 Feb. 2012, pp. 2142–2154. https://doi.org/10.1016/j.neuroimage.2011.10.018.
79 Yendiki, Anastasia et al., "Spurious Group Differences Due to Head Motion in a Diffusion MRI Study," *NeuroImage*, vol. 88, Mar. 2014, pp. 79–90. https://doi.org/10.1016/j.neuroimage.2013.11.027.
80 Reuter, Martin et al. "Head motion during MRI acquisition reduces gray matter volume and thickness estimates," *NeuroImage*, vol. 107, 2015, pp. 107–115. https://doi.org/10.1016/j.neuroimage.2014.12.006
81 Alexander-Bloch, Aaron et al., "Subtle In-Scanner Motion Biases Automated Measurement of Brain Anatomy From In Vivo MRI," *Hum Brain Mapp*, vol. 37, 2016, pp. 2385–2397.
82 Gardner, Edward A. et al., "Detection of Degradation of Magnetic Resonance (MR) Images: Comparison of an Automated MR Image-Quality Analysis System with Trained Human Observers," *Academic Radiology*, vol. 2, no. 4, Apr. 1995, pp. 277–281. https://doi.org/10.1016/S1076-6332(05)80184-9.
83 Esteban, Oscar et al., "fMRIPrep: a robust preprocessing pipeline for functional MRI," *Nature Methods*, vol. 16, 10 Dec. 2018, pp. 111–116. https://doi.org/10.1038/s41592-018-0235-4.
84 Woodard, Jeffrey P. and Monica P. Carley-Spencer, "No-Reference Image Quality Metrics for Structural MRI," *Neuroinformatics*, vol. 4, Sept. 2006, pp. 243–262. https://doi.org/10.1385/NI:4:3:243.
85 Mortamet, Bénédicte et al. "Automatic quality assessment in structural brain magnetic resonance imaging." *Magnetic Resonance in Medicine*, vol. 62, no. 3, 2009, pp. 367–376. https://doi.org/10.1002/mrm.21992.
86 Alfaro-Almagro, Fidel et al. "Image processing and Quality Control for the first 10,000 brain imaging datasets from UK Biobank." *NeuroImage*, vol. 166, 2018, pp. 400–424. https://doi.org/10.1016/j.neuroimage.2017.10.034
87 Shehzad, Zarrar et al. "The Preprocessed Connectomes Project Quality Assessment Protocol - a resource for measuring the quality of MRI data." *Neuroinformatics* 2015, 20–22 Aug. 2015, Cairns, Australia. *Frontiers in Neuroscience Conference Abstract: Neuroinformatics 2015*. https://doi.org/10.3389/conf.fnins.2015.91.00047.
88 Pizarro, Ricardo A. et al. "Automated Quality Assessment of Structural Magnetic Resonance Brain Images Based on a Supervised Machine Learning Algorithm." *Frontiers in Neuroinformatics*, vol. 10, 2016, p. 52. https://doi.org/10.3389/fninf.2016.00052.
89 Pizarro, Ricardo A. et al., "Automated Quality Assessment of Structural Magnetic Resonance Brain Images Based on a Supervised Machine Learning Algorithm," *Frontiers in Neuroinformatics* vol. 10, 2016, p. 52. https://doi.org/10.3389/fninf.2016.00052.

90 Esteban, Oscar et al., "MRIQC: Advancing the automatic prediction of image quality in MRI from unseen sites," *PLoS ONE* vol. 12, no. 9, 2017, e0184661. https://doi.org/10.1371/journal.pone.0184661.
91 Volkow, Nora D. et al., "The conception of the ABCD study: From substance use to a broad NIH collaboration," *Developmental Cognitive Neuroscience* vol. 32, 2018, p. 4. https://doi.org/10.1016/j.dcn.2017.10.002.
92 Esteban, Oscar et al., "MRIQC: Advancing the automatic prediction of image quality in MRI from unseen sites," *PLoS ONE* vol. 12, no. 9, 2017, e0184661. https://doi.org/10.1371/journal.pone.0184661.
93 Chen, Chaofan et al., "This Looks Like That: Deep Learning for Interpretable Image Recognition," *Advances in Neural Information Processing Systems* vol. 32, NeurIPS, 2019, n.p. https://proceedings.neurips.cc/paper_files/paper/2019/file/adf7ee2dcf142b0e11888e72b43fcb75-Paper.pdf.
94 Jenkinson, Mark et al., "MCFLIRT: A robust automated 3D motion correction tool for FMRI," *NeuroImage* vol. 17, no. 2, 2002, pp. 825–841. https://doi.org/10.1006/nimg.2002.1194.
95 Yuan, Lisha et al., "Evaluating the Influence of Spatial Resampling for Motion Correction in Resting-State Functional MRI," *Frontiers in Neuroscience* vol. 10, 2016, p. 591. https://doi.org/10.3389/fnins.2016.00591.
96 Zhang, Lei et al. "Motion Correction for Brain MRI Using Deep Learning and a Novel Hybrid Loss Function." *Algorithms*, vol. 17, no. 5, 15 May 2024, p. 215. https://doi.org/10.3390/a17050215.
97 Singh, Nalini M. et al. "Data Consistent Deep Rigid MRI Motion Correction." *Medical Imaging with Deep Learning*, edited by Ipek Oguz et al., vol. 227, Proceedings of Machine Learning Research, 2024, pp. 368–381. *PMLR*, proceedings.mlr.press/v227/singh24a.html.
98 Kleesiek, Jens et al. "Deep MRI Brain Extraction: A 3D Convolutional Neural Network for Skull Stripping." *NeuroImage*, vol. 129, 1 Apr. 2016, pp. 460–469. https://doi.org/10.1016/j.neuroimage.2016.01.024.
99 Hoopes, Andrew et al., "SynthStrip: skull-stripping for any brain image," *NeuroImage*, 260, 15 Oct 2022, 119474. https://doi.org/10.1016/j.neuroimage.2022.119474.
100 U.S. Food and Drug Administration, "510(k) Premarket Notification: K231398, VUNO Med-DeepBrain," *Accessdata.FDA.gov*, 4 Oct 2023. https://www.accessdata.fda.gov/scripts/cdrh/cfdocs/cfpmn/pmn.cfm?ID=K231398.
101 Iglesias, Juan E. et al., "SynthSR: A public AI tool to turn heterogeneous clinical brain scans into high-resolution T1-weighted images for 3D morphometry," *Science Advances* 9, no. 5, 1 Feb 2023, eadd3607. https://doi.org/10.1126/sciadv.add3607.
102 Wang, Xintao et al., "ESRGAN: Enhanced Super-Resolution Generative Adversarial Networks," https://github.com/xinntao/ESRGAN.
103 Wang, Xintao et al., "ESRGAN: Enhanced Super-Resolution Generative Adversarial Networks," in *Proceedings of the European Conference on Computer Vision (ECCV) Workshops*, 2018, pp. 1–13. https://arxiv.org/abs/1809.00219.
104 Zhou, Zhiyi et al., "Super-resolution of brain tumor MRI images based on deep learning," *Journal of Applied Clinical Medical Physics* 15 Sept 2022, e13758. https://doi.org/10.1002/acm2.13758.
105 Huang, Shan et al., "TransMRSR: transformer-based self-distilled generative prior for brain MRI super-resolution," *The Visual Computer: International Journal of Computer Graphics*, vol. 39, no. 8, 4 July 2023, pp. 3647–3659. https://doi.org/10.1007/s00371-023-02938-3.
106 Dale, Anders M., Bruce Fischl, and Martin I. Sereno, "Cortical Surface-Based Analysis: I. Segmentation and Surface Reconstruction," *NeuroImage*, vol. 9, no. 2, February 1999, pp. 179–194. https://doi.org/10.1006/nimg.1998.0395.

107 Fischl, Bruce, Martin I. Sereno, and Anders M. Dale, "Cortical Surface-Based Analysis: II: Inflation, Flattening, and a Surface-Based Coordinate System," *NeuroImage*, vol. 9, no. 2, February 1999, pp. 195–207. https://doi.org/10.1006/nimg.1998.0396.
108 Fischl, Bruce et al., "Whole Brain Segmentation: Automated Labeling of Neuroanatomical Structures in the Human Brain," *Neuron*, vol. 33, no. 3, 31 Jan 2002, pp. 341–355. https://doi.org/10.1016/S0896-6273(02)00569-X.
109 Vahermaa, Vesa et al., "FreeSurfer 7 quality control: Key problem areas and importance of manual corrections," *NeuroImage*, vol. 279, 1 Oct 2023, 120306. https://doi.org/10.1016/j.neuroimage.2023.120306.
110 Biffen, Stevie C. et al., "Validity of automated FreeSurfer segmentation compared to manual tracing in detecting prenatal alcohol exposure-related subcortical and corpus callosal alterations in 9- to 11-year-old children," *NeuroImage: Clinical*, vol. 28, 2020, 102368. https://doi.org/10.1016/j.nicl.2020.102368.
111 Schmidt, Mike F. et al., "A comparison of manual tracing and FreeSurfer for estimating hippocampal volume over the adult lifespan," *Human Brain Mapping*, vol. 39, no. 6, 2018, pp. 2500–2513. https://doi.org/10.1002/hbm.24017.
112 Makowski, Carolina et al., "Evaluating accuracy of striatal, pallidal, and thalamic segmentation methods: Comparing automated approaches to manual delineation," *NeuroImage*, vol. 170, 2018, pp. 182–198. https://doi.org/10.1016/j.neuroimage.2017.02.069.
113 Haddad, Elizabeth et al., "Multisite test–retest reliability and compatibility of brain metrics derived from FreeSurfer versions 7.1, 6.0, and 5.3," *Human Brain Mapping* 2022. https://doi.org/10.1002/hbm.26147.
114 Moon, Chung-Man et al., "Development and validation of deep learning-based automatic brain segmentation for East Asians: A comparison with Freesurfer," *Frontiers in Neuroscience*, vol. 17, 2023. https://doi.org/10.3389/fnins.2023.1157738.
115 Gomez-Ramirez, Jaime et al. "A Comparative Analysis of MRI Automated Segmentation of Subcortical Brain Volumes in a Large Dataset of Elderly Subjects." *Neuroinformatics*, vol. 20, no. 1, 2022, pp. 63–72. https://doi.org/10.1007/s12021-021-09520-z
116 Lee, Hyunji et al., "Evaluating brain volume segmentation accuracy and reliability of FreeSurfer and Neurophet AQUA at variations in MRI magnetic field strengths," *Scientific Reports*, vol. 14, 2024, p. 24513. https://doi.org/10.1038/s41598-024-74622-y.
117 Schmidt, Mike F. et al., "A comparison of manual tracing and FreeSurfer for estimating hippocampal volume over the adult lifespan," *Human Brain Mapping*, vol. 39, no. 6, 2018, pp. 2500–2513. https://doi.org/10.1002/hbm.24017.
118 Greve, Douglas N. et al., "A deep learning toolbox for automatic segmentation of subcortical limbic structures from MRI images," *NeuroImage*, vol. 244, 2021, 118610. https://doi.org/10.1016/j.neuroimage.2021.118610.
119 Backhausen, Lea L. et al., "Quality Control of Structural MRI Images Applied Using FreeSurfer—A Hands-On Workflow to Rate Motion Artifacts," *Frontiers in Neuroscience*, vol. 10, 2016, p. 558. https://doi.org/10.3389/fnins.2016.00558.
120 Henschel, Leonie et al. "FastSurferVINN: Building resolution-independence into deep learning segmentation methods-A solution for HighRes brain MRI." *NeuroImage*, vol. 251, 2022, 118933. https://doi.org/10.1016/j.neuroimage.2022.118933
121 Henschel, Leonie et al. "FastSurferVINN: Building resolution-independence into deep learning segmentation methods-A solution for HighRes brain MRI." *NeuroImage*, vol. 251, 2022, 118933. https://doi.org/10.1016/j.neuroimage.2022.118933

122 Billot, Benjamin et al., "SynthSeg: Segmentation of Brain MRI Scans of Any Contrast and Resolution without Retraining," *Medical Image Analysis*, vol. 86, 2023, 102789. https://doi.org/10.1016/j.media.2023.102789.
123 Billot, Benjamin et al., "Robust Machine Learning Segmentation for Large-Scale Analysis of Heterogeneous Clinical Brain MRI Datasets," *Proceedings of the National Academy of Sciences*, vol. 120, no. 9, 2023, e2216399120. https://doi.org/10.1073/pnas.2216399120.
124 Billot, Benjamin et al., "SynthSeg: Segmentation of Brain MRI Scans of Any Contrast and Resolution without Retraining," *Medical Image Analysis*, vol. 86, 2023, 102789. https://doi.org/10.1016/j.media.2023.102789.
125 Esteban, Oscar et al. "fMRIPrep: a robust preprocessing pipeline for functional MRI." *Nature Methods*, vol. 16, 2019, pp. 111–116.
126 Avants, Brian B. et al. "A reproducible evaluation of ANTs similarity metric performance in brain image registration." *NeuroImage*, vol. 54, no. 3, 2011, pp. 2033–2044. https://doi.org/10.1016/j.neuroimage.2010.09.025
127 Jenkinson, Mark et al. "FSL." *NeuroImage*, vol. 62, no. 2, 2012, pp. 782–790. https://doi.org/10.1016/j.neuroimage.2011.09.015
128 Balakrishnan, Guha et al. "VoxelMorph: A Learning Framework for Deformable Medical Image Registration." *IEEE Transactions on Medical Imaging*, vol. 38, no. 8, 2019, pp. 1788–1800.
129 Hoffmann, Malte et al. "SynthMorph: Learning Contrast-Invariant Registration Without Acquired Images." *IEEE Transactions on Medical Imaging*, vol. 41, no. 3, Mar. 2022, pp. 543–558. https://doi.org/10.1109/TMI.2021.3116879
130 Hoffmann, Malte et al. "SynthMorph: Learning Contrast-Invariant Registration Without Acquired Images." *IEEE Transactions on Medical Imaging*, vol. 41, no. 3, Mar. 2022, pp. 543–558. https://doi.org/10.1109/TMI.2021.3116879
131 Ren, Jianxun et al. "Fast cortical surface reconstruction from MRI using deep learning." *Brain Informatics*, vol. 9, no. 6, 9 Mar. 2022. *SpringerLink*. https://doi.org/10.1186/s40708-022-00155-7.
132 Henschel, Leonie et al. "FastSurferVINN: Building resolution-independence into deep learning segmentation methods-A solution for HighRes brain MRI." *NeuroImage*, vol. 251, 2022, 118933. https://doi.org/10.1016/j.neuroimage.2022.118933
133 Ren, Jianxun et al. "Fast cortical surface reconstruction from MRI using deep learning." *Brain Informatics*, vol. 9, no. 6, 9 Mar. 2022. *SpringerLink*. https://doi.org/10.1186/s40708-022-00155-7.
134 Fischl, Bruce. "FreeSurfer." *NeuroImage*, vol. 62, no. 2, 15 Aug. 2012, pp. 774–781. *ScienceDirect*. https://doi.org/10.1016/j.neuroimage.2012.01.021.
135 Ren, Jianxun et al. "SUGAR: Spherical ultrafast graph attention framework for cortical surface registration." *Medical Image Analysis*, vol. 94, May 2024, p. 103122. https://doi.org/10.1016/j.media.2024.103122.
136 Zhao, Fenqiang et al. "Unsupervised Learning for Spherical Surface Registration." *Machine Learning in Medical Imaging (MLMI 2020)*, vol. 12436, Springer, Cham, 2020, pp. 373–383. *SpringerLink*,
137 Behzadi, Yashar et al. "A component based noise correction method (CompCor) for BOLD and perfusion based fMRI." *NeuroImage*, vol. 37, no. 1, 2007, pp. 90–101. https://doi.org/10.1016/j.neuroimage.2007.04.042
138 Pruim, Raimon H. R. et al. "ICA-AROMA: A robust ICA-based strategy for removing motion artifacts from fMRI data." *NeuroImage*, vol. 112, 2015, pp. 267–277. https://doi.org/10.1016/j.neuroimage.2015.02.064
139 Krull, Alexander, Tim-Oliver Buchholz, and Florian Jug, "Noise2Void - Learning Denoising from Single Noisy Images," *Advances in Neural Information Processing Systems*, vol. 31, 2018, pp. 2129–2138.

140 López, Marc Moreno, Joshua M. Frederick, and Jonathan Ventura. "Evaluation of MRI Denoising Methods Using Unsupervised Learning." *Frontiers in Artificial Intelligence*, vol. 4, 4 June 2021. https://doi.org/10.3389/frai.2021.642731.
141 Theodoropoulos, Christos, Christos Chatzichristos, and Sabine Van Huffel, "Automatic Artifact Removal of Resting-State fMRI with Deep Neural Networks," *2021 29th European Signal Processing Conference (EUSIPCO)*, IEEE, 2021, pp. 23–27. https://doi.org/10.23919/EUSIPCO54536.2021.9616349.
142 Yang, Zhengshi et al. "A robust deep neural network for denoising task-based fMRI data: An application to working memory and episodic memory." *Medical Image Analysis*, vol. 60, Feb. 2020, p. 101622. https://doi.org/10.1016/j.media.2019.101622.
143 Esteban, Oscar et al. "fMRIPrep: a robust preprocessing pipeline for functional MRI." *Nature Methods*, vol. 16, 10 Dec. 2018, pp. 111–116. *Nature*, https://doi.org/10.1038/s41592-018-0235-4.
144 Esteban, Oscar et al. "fMRIPrep: A Robust Preprocessing Pipeline for Functional MRI." *Nature Methods*, vol. 16, 10 Dec. 2018, pp. 111–116. *Nature*, https://doi.org/10.1038/s41592-018-0235-4.
145 Billot, Benjamin et al. "Robust machine learning segmentation for large-scale analysis of heterogeneous clinical brain MRI datasets." *Proceedings of the National Academy of Sciences*, vol. 120, no. 9, 21 Feb. 2023, p. e2216399120. https://doi.org/10.1073/pnas.2216399120.
146 Henschel, Leonie et al. "FastSurfer - A fast and accurate deep learning based neuroimaging pipeline." *NeuroImage*, vol. 219, 1 Oct. 2020, p. 117012. https://doi.org/10.1016/j.neuroimage.2020.117012.
147 Quaak, Mirjam et al. "Deep learning applications for the classification of psychiatric disorders using neuroimaging data: Systematic review and meta-analysis." *NeuroImage. Clinical*, vol. 30, 2021, p. 102584. https://doi.org/10.1016/j.nicl.2021.102584
148 Liu, Sheng et al. "Generalizable deep learning model for early Alzheimer's disease detection from structural MRIs." *Scientific Reports*, vol. 12, no. 1, 17 Oct. 2022, p. 17106. https://doi.org/10.1038/s41598-022-20674-x.
149 Cao, Meng et al. "Machine learning in attention-deficit/hyperactivity disorder: new approaches toward understanding the neural mechanisms." *Translational Psychiatry*, vol. 13, no. 1, 1 July 2023, p. 236. https://www.proquest.com/openview/46c7a2afbe5872cd59f5def3dcff1ccb/1.pdf?pq-origsite=gscholar&cbl=2041978.
150 Ding, Yiming et al. "A Deep Learning Model to Predict a Diagnosis of Alzheimer Disease by Using 18F-FDG PET of the Brain." *Radiology*, vol. 290, no. 2, Feb. 2019, pp. 496–505. https://doi.org/10.1148/radiol.2018180958.
151 Ding, Yiming et al. "A Deep Learning Model to Predict a Diagnosis of Alzheimer Disease by Using 18F-FDG PET of the Brain." *Radiology*, vol. 290, no. 2, Feb. 2019, pp. 496–505. https://doi.org/10.1148/radiol.2018180958.
152 Cao, Meng, Elizabeth Martin, and Xiaobo Li. "Machine learning in attention-deficit/hyperactivity disorder: new approaches toward understanding the neural mechanisms." *Translational Psychiatry*, vol. 13, no. 1, 1 July 2023, p. 236. https://www.proquest.com/openview/46c7a2afbe5872cd59f5def3dcff1ccb/1.pdf?pq-origsite=gscholar&cbl=2041978.
153 Liu, Sheng et al. "Generalizable deep learning model for early Alzheimer's disease detection from structural MRIs." *Scientific Reports*, vol. 12, no. 1, 17 Oct. 2022, p. 17106. https://doi.org/10.1038/s41598-022-21142-2.
154 Quaak, Mirjam et al. "Deep learning applications for the classification of psychiatric disorders using neuroimaging data: Systematic review and meta-analysis." *NeuroImage. Clinical*, vol. 30, 2021, p. 102584. https://doi.org/10.1016/j.nicl.2021.102584
155 Zeng, Ling-Li et al. "Multi-Site Diagnostic Classification of Schizophrenia Using Discriminant Deep Learning with Functional Connectivity MRI." *EBioMedicine*, vol. 30, 2018, pp. 74–85. https://doi.org/10.1016/j.ebiom.2018.03.017

156 Zhang, Jianing et al. "Three dimensional convolutional neural network-based classification of conduct disorder with structural MRI." *Brain Imaging and Behavior*, vol. 14, no. 6, 2020, pp. 2333–2340. https://doi.org/10.1007/s11682-019-00186-5
157 Li, Xuanyi, Qiang Kang, and Hanxing Gu. "A comprehensive review for machine learning on neuroimaging in obsessive-compulsive disorder." *Frontiers in Human Neuroscience*, vol. 17, 1 Nov. 2023. https://doi.org/10.3389/fnhum.2023.1280512.
158 Heinsfeld, Anibal Sólon et al. "Identification of autism spectrum disorder using deep learning and the ABIDE dataset." *NeuroImage: Clinical*, vol. 17, 2018, pp. 16–23. https://doi.org/10.1016/j.nicl.2017.08.017.
159 Murayama, Keitaro et al. "Aberrant Resting-State Cerebellar-Cerebral Functional Connectivity in Unmedicated Patients With Obsessive-Compulsive Disorder." *Frontiers in Psychiatry*, vol. 12, 23 Apr. 2021. https://doi.org/10.3389/fpsyt.2021.659616.
160 Ding, Yiming et al. "A Deep Learning Model to Predict a Diagnosis of Alzheimer Disease by Using ^{18}F-FDG PET of the Brain." *Radiology*, vol. 290, no. 2, Feb. 2019, pp. 442–450. https://doi.org/10.1148/radiol.2018180958.
161 Koutsouleris, Nikolaos, and Peter Falkai. "174.4 Using Machine Learning to Predict Outcomes in Psychosis." *Schizophrenia Bulletin*, vol. 43, no. suppl_1, Mar. 2017, p. S88. https://doi.org/10.1093/schbul/sbx021.236.
162 Cao, Meng, Elizabeth Martin, and Xiaobo Li. "Machine learning in attention-deficit/hyperactivity disorder: new approaches toward understanding the neural mechanisms." *Translational Psychiatry*, vol. 13, no. 1, July 2023, p. 236. https://www.proquest.com/openview/46c7a2afbe5872cd59f5def3dcff1ccb/1.pdf?pq-origsite=gscholar&cbl=2041978.
163 Chonghua Xue et al., "AI-based differential diagnosis of dementia etiologies on multimodal data," *Nature Medicine*, vol. 30, no. 7 (2024): 2977–2989. https://www.nature.com/articles/s41591-024-03144-8.
164 Quaak, Mirjam et al. "Deep learning applications for the classification of psychiatric disorders using neuroimaging data: Systematic review and meta-analysis." *NeuroImage. Clinical*, vol. 30, 2021, p. 102584. https://doi.org/10.1016/j.nicl.2021.102584
165 Cleveland Clinic, "Psychosis," *Cleveland Clinic Health Library*, 15 May 2022. https://my.clevelandclinic.org/health/symptoms/23010-psychosis.
166 SchizConnect, "Home," n.d.. https://schizconnect.org/.
167 Oh, Jihoon et al., "Identifying Schizophrenia Using Structural MRI With a Deep Learning Algorithm," *Frontiers in Psychiatry*, 3 February 2020. https://www.ncbi.nlm.nih.gov/pmc/articles/PMC7008229/.
168 Zhang, Junhao et al., "Detecting Schizophrenia with 3D Structural Brain MRI Using Deep Learning," *Scientific Reports*, vol. 13, no. 14433, 2 Sept 2023. https://www.nature.com/articles/s41598-023-41315-z.
169 Gutman, Boris A. et al. "A meta-analysis of deep brain structural shape and asymmetry abnormalities in 2833 individuals with schizophrenia compared with 3929 healthy volunteers via the ENIGMA Consortium." *Human Brain Mapping*, vol. 43, no. 1, 2022, pp. 352–372. https://doi.org/10.1002/hbm.25625
170 Brugger, Stefan P., and Oliver D. Howes. "Heterogeneity and Homogeneity of Regional Brain Structure in Schizophrenia: A Meta-analysis." *JAMA Psychiatry*, vol. 74, no. 11, 2017, pp. 1104–1111. https://doi.org/10.1001/jamapsychiatry.2017.2663
171 Pinaya, Walter H. L., Andrea Mechelli, and João R. Sato, "Using Deep Autoencoders to Identify Abnormal Brain Structural Patterns in Neuropsychiatric Disorders: A Large-Scale Multi-Sample Study," *Human Brain Mapping*, vol. 40, no. 3, 11 Oct 2018, pp. 944–954. https://www.ncbi.nlm.nih.gov/pmc/articles/PMC6492107/.

172 Zeng, Ling-Li et al., "Multi-Site Diagnostic Classification of Schizophrenia Using Discriminant Deep Learning with Functional Connectivity MRI," *eBioMedicine*, vol. 30, 23 Mar 2018, pp. 74–85. https://www.ncbi.nlm.nih.gov/pmc/articles/PMC5952341/.

173 Lei, Du et al. "Graph Convolutional Networks Reveal Network-Level Functional Dysconnectivity in Schizophrenia." *Schizophrenia Bulletin*, vol. 48, no. 4, 2022, pp. 881–892. https://doi.org/10.1093/schbul/sbac047

174 Sunil, Gayathri et al. "Graph neural network and machine learning analysis of functional neuroimaging for understanding schizophrenia." *BMC Neuroscience*, vol. 25, no. 2, 2 Jan. 2024. https://bmcneurosci.biomedcentral.com/articles/10.1186/s12868-023-00095-2.

175 Tamminga, Carol A et al. "Clinical phenotypes of psychosis in the Bipolar-Schizophrenia Network on Intermediate Phenotypes (B-SNIP)." *The American Journal of Psychiatry*, vol. 170, no. 11, 2013, pp. 1263–1274. https://doi.org/10.1176/appi.ajp.2013.12101339

176 Yan, Weizheng et al. "Mapping relationships among schizophrenia, bipolar and schizoaffective disorders: A deep classification and clustering framework using fMRI time series." *Schizophrenia Research*, vol. 245, 2022, pp. 141–150. https://doi.org/10.1016/j.schres.2021.02.007

177 Wang, Haiyuan et al. "MO-GCN: A multi-omics graph convolutional network for discriminative analysis of schizophrenia." *Brain Research Bulletin*, vol. 221, Feb. 2025, p. 111199.

178 Datta, Shae, Uma Suryadevara, and Josepha Cheong. "Mood Disorders." *Behavioral Neurology and Psychiatry*, vol. 27, no. 6, Dec. 2021, pp. 1712–1737. https://doi.org/10.1212/CON.0000000000001051.

179 Cao, Bing et al. "Brain morphometric features predict depression symptom phenotypes in late-life depression using a deep learning model." *Frontiers in Neuroscience*, vol. 17, 19 July 2023. https://doi.org/10.3389/fnins.2023.1209906.

180 Li, Ruipeng et al. "MRI-based deep learning for differentiating between bipolar and major depressive disorders." *Psychiatry Research. Neuroimaging*, vol. 345, 2024, p. 111907. https://doi.org/10.1016/j.pscychresns.2024.111907

181 Nunes, Abraham et al. "Using structural MRI to identify bipolar disorders – 13 site machine learning study in 3020 individuals from the ENIGMA Bipolar Disorders Working Group." *Molecular Psychiatry*, vol. 25, 2020, pp. 2130–2143. https://doi.org/10.1038/s41380-018-0228-9.

182 Gallo, Selene et al. "Functional connectivity signatures of major depressive disorder: machine learning analysis of two multicenter neuroimaging studies." *Molecular Psychiatry*, vol. 28, 15 Feb. 2023, pp. 3013–3022. https://doi.org/10.1038/s41380-023-01977-5.

183 Dai, Peishan et al. "Classification of MDD using a Transformer classifier with large-scale multisite resting-state fMRI data." *Human Brain Mapping*, vol. 45, no. 1, 2024, e26542. https://doi.org/10.1002/hbm.26542

184 Wang, Qianqian et al. "Adaptive Multimodal Neuroimage Integration for Major Depression Disorder Detection." *Frontiers in Neuroinformatics*, vol. 16, 29 Apr. 2022. https://doi.org/10.3389/fninf.2022.856175.

185 Zheng, Guowei et al. "An attention-based multi-modal MRI fusion model for major depressive disorder diagnosis." *Journal of Neural Engineering*, vol. 20, no. 6, 15 Nov. 2023. https://doi.org/10.1088/1741-2552/ad038c

186 Li, Tongtong et al. "Evolutionary neural architecture search for automated MDD diagnosis using multimodal MRI imaging." *iScience*, vol. 27, no. 10, 18 Oct. 2024, p. 111020. https://doi.org/10.1016/j.isci.2024.111020.

187 Li, Tongtong et al. "Evolutionary neural architecture search for automated MDD diagnosis using multimodal MRI imaging." *iScience*, vol. 27, no. 10, 18 Oct. 2024, p. 111020. https://doi.org/10.1016/j.isci.2024.111020.

188 Hu, Jinlong et al. "Identifying major depressive disorder based on cerebral blood flow and brain structure: An explainable multimodal learning study." *Journal of Psychiatric Research*, vol. 182, 2025, pp. 304–311. https://doi.org/10.1016/j.jpsychires.2025.01.001
189 Lee, Seungeun et al. "Multimodal integration of neuroimaging and genetic data for the diagnosis of mood disorders based on computer vision models." *Journal of Psychiatric Research*, vol. 172, 2024, pp. 144–155. https://doi.org/10.1016/j.jpsychires.2024.02.036
190 Tozzi, Leonardo et al., "Personalized Brain Circuit Scores Identify Clinically Distinct Biotypes in Depression and Anxiety," *Nature Medicine*, vol. 30, no. 8, 2024, pp. 2076–2087. https://www.nature.com/articles/s41591-024-03063-2.
191 Tozzi, Leonardo et al., "Personalized Brain Circuit Scores Identify Clinically Distinct Biotypes in Depression and Anxiety," *Nature Medicine*, vol. 30, no. 8, 2024, pp. 2076–2087. https://www.nature.com/articles/s41591-024-03063-2.
192 Zhou, Enqi et al., "Prediction of Anxious Depression Using Multimodal Neuroimaging and Machine Learning," *NeuroImage*, vol. 285, 2024, p. 120499. https://doi.org/10.1016/j.neuroimage.2023.120499.
193 Gallo, Selene et al., "Functional Connectivity Signatures of Major Depressive Disorder: Machine Learning Analysis of Two Multicenter Neuroimaging Studies," *Molecular Psychiatry*, vol. 28, no. 8, 2023, pp. 3013–3022. https://www.nature.com/articles/s41380-023-01991-6.
194 Chen, Yanjing et al., "The Diagnostic Performance of Machine Learning Based on Resting-State Functional Magnetic Resonance Imaging Data for Major Depressive Disorders: A Systematic Review and Meta-Analysis," *Frontiers in Neuroscience*, vol. 17, 2023, p. 1174080. https://doi.org/10.3389/fnins.2023.1174080.
195 The ENIGMA Consortium, "About ENIGMA," *ENIGMA*. https://enigma.ini.usc.edu/about-enigma/.
196 Chen, Xiao et al. "The DIRECT consortium and the REST-meta-MDD project: Towards neuroimaging biomarkers of major depressive disorder." *Psychoradiology*, vol. 2, no. 1, 9 Jun. 2022, pp. 32–42. https://doi.org/10.1093/psyrad/kkac005
197 May, Tamara et al. "Sex differences in neurodevelopmental disorders." *Current Opinion in Neurology*, vol. 32, no. 4, 2019, pp. 622–626. https://doi.org/10.1097/WCO.0000000000000714
198 Mayo Clinic Staff, "Autism Spectrum Disorder," Mayo Clinic, 22 May 2025. https://www.mayoclinic.org/diseases-conditions/autism-spectrum-disorder/symptoms-causes/syc-20352528.
199 "Autism," Cleveland Clinic, 1 Oct. 2024. https://my.clevelandclinic.org/health/articles/12339-autism.
200 "Introduction," *Autism Brain Imaging Data Exchange*, 27 Mar. 2017. http://fcon_1000.projects.nitrc.org/indi/abide/.
201 Hazlett, Heather Cody et al. "Early brain development in infants at high risk for autism spectrum disorder." *Nature*, vol. 542, no. 7641, 2017, pp. 348–351. https://doi.org/10.1038/nature21369.
202 Garcia, Mélanie, and Clare Kelly. "3D CNN for neuropsychiatry: Predicting Autism with interpretable Deep Learning applied to minimally preprocessed structural MRI data." *PloS One*, vol. 19, no. 10, 21 Oct. 2024, e0276832. https://doi.org/10.1371/journal.pone.0276832
203 Heinsfeld, Anibal Sólon et al. "Identification of autism spectrum disorder using deep learning and the ABIDE dataset." *NeuroImage. Clinical*, vol. 17, no. 16–23, 30 Aug. 2017. https://doi.org/10.1016/j.nicl.2017.08.017
204 Cherkassky, Vladimir L. et al. "Functional connectivity in a baseline resting-state network in autism." *Neuroreport*, vol. 17, no. 16, 2006, pp. 1687–1690. https://doi.org/10.1097/01.wnr.0000239956.45448.4c

205 Sherkatghanad, Zeinab et al., "Automated Detection of Autism Spectrum Disorder Using a Convolutional Neural Network," *Frontiers in Neuroscience*, 14 Jan. 2020. https://doi.org/10.3389/fnins.2019.01325.
206 Parisot, Sarah et al., "Disease Prediction Using Graph Convolutional Networks: Application to Autism Spectrum Disorder and Alzheimer's Disease," *Medical Image Analysis*, vol. 48, Aug. 2018, pp. 117–130. https://doi.org/10.1016/j.media.2018.06.001.
207 Supekar, Kaustubh et al. "Robust, Generalizable, and Interpretable Artificial Intelligence-Derived Brain Fingerprints of Autism and Social Communication Symptom Severity." *Biological Psychiatry*, vol. 92, no. 8, 2022, pp. 643–653. https://doi.org/10.1016/j.biopsych.2022.02.005
208 Saponaro, Sara et al., "Deep Learning Based Joint Fusion Approach to Exploit Anatomical and Functional Brain Information in Autism Spectrum Disorders," *Brain Informatics*, vol. 11, no. 2, 9 Jan. 2024. https://doi.org/10.1186/s40708-023-00217-4.
209 Liu, Guanlu et al., "Two Neuroanatomical Subtypes of Males with Autism Spectrum Disorder Revealed Using Semi-Supervised Machine Learning," *Molecular Autism*, vol. 13, no. 9, 23 Feb. 2022. https://doi.org/10.1186/s13229-022-00489-3.
210 Buch, Amanda M et al. "Molecular and network-level mechanisms explaining individual differences in autism spectrum disorder." *Nature Neuroscience*, vol. 26, no. 4, 2023, pp. 650–663. https://doi.org/10.1038/s41593-023-01259-x
211 Brown, Matthew R. G. et al., "ADHD-200 Global Competition: diagnosing ADHD using personal characteristic data can outperform resting state fMRI measurements," *Frontiers in Systems Neuroscience*, vol. 6, 2012.
212 Zhang-James, Yanli et al., "Evidence for similar structural brain anomalies in youth and adult attention-deficit/hyperactivity disorder: a machine learning analysis," *Translational Psychiatry*, vol. 11, Article 82, 2021.
213 Ashraf, Imran et al., "A systematic literature review of neuroimaging coupled with machine learning approaches for diagnosis of attention deficit hyperactivity disorder," *Journal of Big Data*, vol. 11, Article 140, 2024.
214 Cao, Meng, Elizabeth Martin, and Xiaobo Li, "Machine learning in attention-deficit/hyperactivity disorder: new approaches toward understanding the neural mechanisms," *Translational Psychiatry*, vol. 13, Article 236, 2023.
215 Cicek, Gulay, and Aydin Akan, "Deep Learning Approach Versus Traditional Machine Learning for ADHD Classification," *2021 Medical Technologies Congress (TIPTEKNO)*, IEEE, 2021, pp. 1–4.
216 Tang, Yibin et al. "ADHD classification using auto-encoding neural network and binary hypothesis testing." *Artificial Intelligence in Medicine*, vol. 123, 2022, p. 102209. https://doi.org/10.1016/j.artmed.2021.102209
217 Peng, Xiaolong et al. "Extreme learning machine-based classification of ADHD using brain structural MRI data." *PloS One*, vol. 8, no. 11, 19 Nov. 2013, e79476. https://doi.org/10.1371/journal.pone.0079476
218 Riaz, Atif, Muhammad Asad, Eduardo Alonso, Greg Slabaugh, "DeepFMRI: End-to-end deep learning for functional connectivity and classification of ADHD using fMRI," *Journal of Neuroscience Methods*, vol. 335, 1 April 2020, 108506.
219 Jha, Ranjeet Ranjan, Aditya Nigam, Arnav Bhavsar, Gaurav Jaswal, Sudhir K. Pathak, and Rathish Kumar, "Lightweight Graph Siamese Network with Triplet Loss for fMRI-based Classification of ADHD," *2020 International Joint Conference on Neural Networks (IJCNN)*, Glasgow, United Kingdom, September 2020, pp. 1–8. https://doi.org/ 10.1109/IJCNN48605.2020.9207667.

220 Feng, Aichen, Dongmei Zhi, Yuan Feng, Rongtao Jiang, Zening Fu, Ming Xu et al. "Functional imaging derived ADHD biotypes based on deep clustering: a study on personalized medication therapy guidance." *EBioMedicine*, vol. 77, Nov 2024, 103980.

221 Niu, Yuan, Feihu Huang, Hui Zhou, and Jian Peng, "Deep Spatio-Temporal Method for ADHD Classification Using Resting-State fMRI," *2022 IEEE 34th International Conference on Tools with Artificial Intelligence (ICTAI)*, Macao, China, 2022, pp. 1092–1098. https://doi.org/10.1109/ICTAI56018.2022.00165.

222 Qiang, Ning, Qinglin Dong, Hongtao Liang, Bao Ge, Shu Zhang, Cheng Zhang, Jie Gao, and Yifei Sun, "A novel ADHD classification method based on resting state temporal templates (RSTT) using spatiotemporal attention auto-encoder," *Neural Computing and Applications*, vol. 34, no. 10, May 2022, pp. 7815–7833. https://doi.org/10.1007/s00521-021-06868-w.

223 Tang, Yibin et al. "ADHD classification using auto-encoding neural network and binary hypothesis testing." *Artificial Intelligence in Medicine*, vol. 123, 2022, p. 102209. https://doi.org/10.1016/j.artmed.2021.102209

224 Tian, Lu, Helin Zheng, Ke Zhang, Jiawen Qiu, Xuejuan Song, Siwei Li, Zhao Zeng, Baosheng Ran, Xin Deng, and Jinhua Cai, "Structural or/and functional MRI-based machine learning techniques for attention-deficit/hyperactivity disorder diagnosis: A systematic review and meta-analysis," *Journal of Affective Disorders*, vol. 355, 15 June 2024, pp. 459–469.

225 Zou, Liang et al. "3D CNN Based Automatic Diagnosis of Attention Deficit Hyperactivity Disorder Using Functional and Structural MRI." *IEEE Access*, vol. 5, 2017, pp. 23626–23636. https://doi.org/10.1109/ACCESS.2017.2762703.

226 Kautzky, A. et al. "Machine Learning Classification of ADHD and HC by Multimodal Serotonergic Data." *Translational Psychiatry*, vol. 10, article no. 104, 2020. https://doi.org/10.1038/s41398-020-0781-2.

227 Elliott, Blake L. et al. "Limbic and Executive Meso- and Nigrostriatal Tracts Predict Impulsivity Differences in Attention-Deficit/Hyperactivity Disorder." *Biological Psychiatry. Cognitive Neuroscience and Neuroimaging*, vol. 7, no. 4, 2022, pp. 415–423. https://doi.org/10.1016/j.bpsc.2021.05.002

228 Yang, Chan-Mo et al. "Classifying Children with ADHD Based on Prefrontal Functional Near-infrared Spectroscopy Using Machine Learning." *Department of Psychiatry, Seoul National University College of Medicine*, Seoul, Korea. Correspondence to Bung-Nyun Kim, kbn1@snu.ac.kr. ORCID: https://orcid.org/0000-0002-2403-3291.

229 Wang, Jie, Wenjing Liao, and Xinyu Jin. "Classification of ADHD Using fNIRS Signals Based on Functional Connectivity and Interval Features." *2021 6th International Conference on Computational Intelligence and Applications (ICCIA)*, 11–13 June 2021, Xiamen, China. IEEE, 2021. https://doi.org/10.1109/ICCIA52886.2021.00029.

230 Firouzi, MohammadHadi et al. "Enhanced ADHD Classification through Deep Learning and Dynamic Resting State fMRI Analysis." *Scientific Reports*, vol. 14, 2024, article no. 24473. https://doi.org/10.1038/s41598-024-74282-y.

231 Feng, Aichen et al. "Functional Imaging Derived ADHD Biotypes Based on Deep Clustering: A Study on Personalized Medication Therapy Guidance." *eClinicalMedicine*, vol. 77, Nov. 2024, article 102876. https://doi.org/10.1016/j.eclinm.2024.102876.

232 Thompson, Paul M. et al. "The ENIGMA Consortium: Large-Scale Collaborative Analyses of Neuroimaging and Genetic Data." *Brain Imaging and Behavior*, vol. 8, no. 2, 2014, pp. 153–182. https://doi.org/10.1007/s11682-013-9269-5.

233 Bruin, Willem B. et al. "Brain-Based Classification of Youth with Anxiety Disorders: Transdiagnostic Examinations within the ENIGMA-Anxiety Database Using Machine Learning." *Nature Mental Health*, vol. 2, no. 1, 2024, pp. 104–118. https://doi.org/10.1038/s44220-023-00173-2.
234 Wen, Zhenfu et al. "Fear-Induced Brain Activations Distinguish Anxious and Trauma-Exposed Brains." *Translational Psychiatry*, vol. 11, 2021, article no. 46. https://doi.org/10.1038/s41398-020-01193-7. Accessed 25 May 2025.
235 Yang, Jing et al. "Using Deep Learning to Classify Pediatric Posttraumatic Stress Disorder at the Individual Level." *BMC Psychiatry*, vol. 21, 2021, article no. 535. Springer Nature. https://doi.org/10.1186/s12888-021-03503-9. Accessed 25 May 2025.
236 Shahzad, Mirza Naveed, and Haider Ali. "Deep Learning Based Diagnosis of PTSD Using 3D-CNN and Resting-State fMRI Data." *Psychiatry Research: Neuroimaging*, vol. 343, Sept. 2024, article 111845. https://doi.org/10.1016/j.pscychresns.2024.111845. Accessed 25 May 2025.
237 Zhu, Xi et al. "Neuroimaging-Based Classification of PTSD Using Data-Driven Computational Approaches: A Multisite Big Data Study from the ENIGMA-PGC PTSD Consortium." *NeuroImage*, vol. 283, 2023, p. 120412. https://doi.org/10.1016/j.neuroimage.2023.120412. Accessed 25 May 2025.
238 Tang, Yibin et al. "Anxiety Disorder Identification with Biomarker Detection Through Subspace-Enhanced Hypergraph Neural Network." *Neural Networks: The Official Journal of the International Neural Network Society*, vol. 187, 2025, p. 107293. https://doi.org/10.1016/j.neunet.2025.107293
239 Nakao, Tomohiro et al. "Gray Matter Volume Abnormalities in ADHD: Voxel-Based Meta-Analysis Exploring the Effects of Age and Stimulant Medication." *American Journal of Psychiatry*, vol. 168, no. 11, 2011, pp. 1154–1163. https://doi.org/10.1176/appi.ajp.2011.11020281. Accessed 25 May 2025.
240 Shaw, Philip et al. "Trajectories of Cerebral Cortical Development in Childhood and Adolescence and Adult Attention-Deficit/Hyperactivity Disorder." *Biological Psychiatry*, vol. 74, no. 8, 15 Oct. 2013, pp. 599–606. https://doi.org/10.1016/j.biopsych.2013.04.007. Accessed 25 May 2025.
241 Shaw, Philip et al. "Cortical Development in Typically Developing Children with Symptoms of Hyperactivity and Impulsivity: Support for a Dimensional View of Attention Deficit Hyperactivity Disorder." *The American Journal of Psychiatry*, vol. 168, no. 2, 2011, pp. 143–151. https://doi.org/10.1176/appi.ajp.2010.10030385
242 Franke, Barbara et al. "Live fast, die young? A Review on the Developmental Trajectories of ADHD Across the Lifespan." *European Neuropsychopharmacology: The Journal of the European College of Neuropsychopharmacology*, vol. 28, no. 10, 2018, pp. 1059–1088. https://doi.org/10.1016/j.euroneuro.2018.08.001
243 Zhang-James, Yanli et al. "Evidence for Similar Structural Brain Anomalies in Youth and Adult Attention-Deficit/Hyperactivity Disorder: A Machine Learning Analysis." *Translational Psychiatry*, vol. 11, no. 1, 2021, article 82. https://doi.org/10.1038/s41398-021-01201-4. Accessed 25 May 2025.
244 Hoogman, Martine et al. "Subcortical brain volume differences in participants with attention deficit hyperactivity disorder in children and adults: a cross-sectional mega-analysis." *The Lancet. Psychiatry*, vol. 4, no. 4, 2017, pp. 310–319. https://doi.org/10.1016/S2215-0366(17)30049-4
245 Hoogman, Martine et al. "Brain Imaging of the Cortex in ADHD: A Coordinated Analysis of Large-Scale Clinical and Population-Based Samples." *The American Journal of Psychiatry*, vol. 176, no. 7, 2019, pp. 531–542. https://doi.org/10.1176/appi.ajp.2019.18091033

246 Volkow, Nora D. et al. "The Conception of the ABCD Study: From Substance Use to a Broad NIH Collaboration." *Developmental Cognitive Neuroscience*, vol. 32, Aug. 2018, pp. 4–7. https://doi.org/10.1016/j.dcn.2017.10.002. Accessed 25 May 2025.

247 Lai, Meng-Chuan et al. "Sex/Gender Differences and Autism: Setting the Scene for Future Research." *Journal of the American Academy of Child & Adolescent Psychiatry*, vol. 54, no. 1, 2015, pp. 11–24. https://doi.org/10.1016/j.jaac.2014.10.003. Accessed 25 May 2025.

248 Loomes, Rachel, Laura Hull, and William Polmear Locke Mandy. "What Is the Male-to-Female Ratio in Autism Spectrum Disorder? A Systematic Review and Meta-Analysis." *Journal of the American Academy of Child & Adolescent Psychiatry*, vol. 56, no. 6, 2017, pp. 466–474. https://doi.org/10.1016/j.jaac.2017.03.013. Accessed 25 May 2025.

249 Supekar, Kaustubh et al. "Deep Learning Identifies Robust Gender Differences in Functional Brain Organization and Their Dissociable Links to Clinical Symptoms in Autism." *The British Journal of Psychiatry*, vol. 220, no. S4, 2022, pp. 202–209. https://doi.org/10.1192/bjp.2022.13. Accessed 25 May 2025.

250 Dhamala, Elvisha et al. "Brain-Based Predictions of Psychiatric Illness-Linked Behaviors Across the Sexes." *Biological Psychiatry*, vol. 94, no. 6, 2023, pp. 479–491. https://doi.org/10.1016/j.biopsych.2023.03.025

251 Dhamala, Elvisha et al. "Brain-Based Predictions of Psychiatric Illness-Linked Behaviors Across the Sexes." *Biological Psychiatry*, vol. 94, no. 6, 2023, pp. 479–491. https://doi.org/10.1016/j.biopsych.2023.03.025

252 Jiang, Rongtao et al. "Gender Differences in Connectome-based Predictions of Individualized Intelligence Quotient and Sub-domain Scores." *Cerebral Cortex (New York, N.Y.: 1991)*, vol. 30, no. 3, 2020, pp. 888–900. https://doi.org/10.1093/cercor/bhz134

253 Santana, Caio Pinheiro et al. "rs-fMRI and Machine Learning for ASD Diagnosis: A Systematic Review and Meta-Analysis." *Scientific Reports*, vol. 12, 2022, article no. 6030. https://doi.org/10.1038/s41598-022-09821-6. Accessed 25 May 2025.

254 Xu, Zikang et al. "Addressing Fairness Issues in Deep Learning-Based Medical Image Analysis: A Systematic Review." *NPJ Digital Medicine*, vol. 7, 17 Oct. 2024, article no. 286. https://doi.org/10.1038/s41746-024-01276-5. Accessed 25 May 2025.

255 Li, Jingwei et al. "Cross-Ethnicity/Race Generalization Failure of Behavioral Prediction from Resting-State Functional Connectivity." *Science Advances*, vol. 8, no. 11, Mar. 2022, article abj1812. https://doi.org/10.1126/sciadv.abj1812. Accessed 25 May 2025.

256 Sterling, Elijah et al. "Demographic reporting across a decade of neuroimaging: a systematic review." *Brain Imaging and Behavior*, vol. 16, no. 6, 2022, pp. 2785–2796. https://doi.org/10.1007/s11682-022-00724-8

257 Volkow, Nora D. et al. "The Conception of the ABCD Study: From Substance Use to a Broad NIH Collaboration." *Developmental Cognitive Neuroscience*, vol. 32, Aug. 2018, pp. 4–7. https://doi.org/10.1016/j.dcn.2017.10.002. Accessed 25 May 2025.

258 Kamgang, Shanine et al. "Cognitive Neuroimaging Studies on Poverty and Socioeconomic Status Differences in Children and Families across the World: Translational Insights for Next Decade's Policy, Health, and Education." *Clinical and Translational Neuroscience*, vol. 7, no. 3, 2023, article 24. https://doi.org/10.3390/ctn7030024. Accessed 25 May 2025.

Chapter 6

Behavioral and language-based approaches to diagnosis

INTRODUCTION

Mental health systems have been plagued by the limitations of traditional diagnostic measurements. As of now, the mental healthcare system relies on the subjective judgment of clinicians to diagnose complex mental health conditions, which can be swayed by unavoidable biases or prone to natural human error. Moreover, the way in which clinicians are able to make diagnoses is largely based on patient self-report measures that rely on patients having insight into their mental health conditions and being accurate in their portrayal of their symptoms. Taken together, these limitations of the current mental health care diagnostic system highlight the pressing need for more advanced diagnostic capabilities. Artificial intelligence (AI) provides an unmatched toolkit to inspire improvement in diagnostic solutions that can alter our ability to address the growing mental health epidemic. AI-driven diagnostic technologies can meet the mental health needs of our generation by reducing clinician burden and detecting mental health issues earlier and more accurately. With improved technology, mental illnesses can be caught earlier on and more accurately, which can directly improve long-term treatment outcomes. The success of technologies used to detect mental health disorders early and accurately relies on the selection of the right data inputs and effective models to make successful predictions of someone's mental health condition. The modalities of data that have been explored and paired with AI for enhanced mental illness detection have been primarily in the domains of human behavior and human language. AI-based analysis of behavior and language has proven to provide incredible insight into the human psyche, underscoring the exciting potential to utilize these data modalities and capitalize on AI technologies to revolutionize the way we detect and diagnose mental health disorders.

BEHAVIOR-BASED DIAGNOSING AI VALUE PROP

The diagnostic protocols for mental disorders have long included behavior analysis. Clinicians have relied on observed and self-reported behaviors to

DOI: 10.1201/9781003565215-6

conceptualize each patient's case and form an accurate and informative diagnosis. Currently, analyzing behavioral tendencies is limited by the bounds of a clinician's learned observational or assessment capabilities, as well as the patient's level of insight into their own behavior. From a clinician's perspective, behavior-based diagnosing historically could only extend to the environment in which a clinician was physically interacting with a patient and what the patient reported about their behavior outside of that environment. Clinicians analyze how someone comes through their door, scan their body language, and examine their facial affect, all the while juggling their other clinical responsibilities. The other avenue to gather behavior-based information is through the self-report of the patient. A massive limitation of this approach is that it relies on a patient's level of awareness of their behaviors and motivation to raise them in the clinical space. Typically, this comes in the form of assessments or verbal reports that are easy to skew, either intentionally or without conscious awareness. Patients may not report behavioral differences simply because they have been persistent throughout time and may have become normalized to the individual. Additionally, patients may lack insight into their own behavior, especially in the case of severe mental illness. The natural human-bound limits of a clinician to gather behavioral insights, paired with potential insight difficulties of patients into their own behaviors, leave us with a limited diagnostic picture that AI can help to clarify. AI can bolster our behavior-based diagnostic potential in several ways, filling in meaningful gaps in clinical information to formulate the most accurate diagnosis possible and a heightened ability to detect this diagnosis as early as possible. AI can equip clinicians with valuable insights that may be too subtle to detect through direct observation or occur outside their office, offering data that extends beyond their direct interactions and goes further than self-reported information. AI has the potential to revolutionize the way behavioral tendencies inform diagnosis, providing a nuanced picture that gives clinicians a diversity of information to diagnose accurately and efficiently.

OPPORTUNITIES IN DIAGNOSIS: BEHAVIOR

The data associated with our most basic tendencies unlocks a window into the workings of our minds. Monitoring behavior shifts serves to understand the nuances of people's mental processes and is especially helpful in understanding implicit processes that are more difficult to detect. Behavior-based diagnostic tools can augment traditional diagnostic assessments to bring color to someone's mental experience beyond first-hand accounts or more traditional conceptualization strategies. Within this umbrella concept of behavior, many aspects of behavior emerge as potentially informative of mental health conditions. To ground our discussion of behavior-based opportunities in diagnosis with AI, we will focus on four subcategories of behavior: bodily dimensions, movement, digital activity, and task-based performance, as these have emerged as leading behavioral components of interest in mental health and AI research.

BODILY DIMENSIONS: FACIAL EXPRESSIONS

First, bodily dimensions of behavior can be conceptualized as physical characteristics of people that can be monitored visually and are unrelated to verbal or linguistic exchanges. These dimensions include behavioral features such as facial expressions, body posture, or eye movement. Facial expression analysis, using AI, has become a particularly intriguing avenue to aid in mental health diagnosis. Various machine learning models that predict mental health symptoms rely on data from facial action coding systems to taxonomize facial expressions in video footage.[1] These coding systems signify the action and intensity of a facial expression and have specific codes that correspond to specific movements. For example, the code AU6 corresponds to the action of raising cheeks. Including this type of patient facial expression data, especially when combined with text-based analysis, has improved the accuracy of multimodal models in predicting patients' depression scores. Furthermore, the emotional quality of each facial expression or a person's affect is another component of facial expressions analyzed using AI. More specifically, researchers have taken interest in using AI to explore blunted affect, which refers to a limited ability to express emotions outwardly, typically seen by limited facial expressions, and is indicative of severe mental illness. Through machine learning analysis, AI has been used to predict the onset of severe mental illness using blunted affect analysis.[2] However, current findings indicate that affect analysis is limited in its predictive value of the onset of severe mental illness. Instead, facial affect analysis may be better at depicting a patient's emotional profile (such as decreased levels of surprise and increased levels of anger), which can also be informative clinical data.

Cutting-edge technology has been developed to synthesize some of this facial analysis research into practical everyday solutions. A team at Dartmouth recently developed the first smartphone application to use AI to detect depression using facial cues.[3] This application, MoodCapture, leverages the multitude of facial data captured by smartphones daily through facial recognition unlocking features. This research team uses this data and AI to predict someone's current mood and prompt individuals to seek help when needed. Although not currently available to the public, it demonstrates the vast potential to integrate this facial expression analysis into scalable technologies.

Facial expression AI research spotlight

This study utilized a novel application, MoodCapture, to help assess depression based on images automatically captured from the front facing camera of smartphones as people go about their daily lives. This study collected over 125,000 images from 177 participants diagnosed with major depressive disorder over the span of 90 days. MoodCapture uses OpenFace, an open-source behavioral analysis toolkit that offers algorithms for facial landmark detection, head pose tracking, eye gaze estimation, and facial action unit recognition. OpenFace operates on a deep learning architecture, specifically leveraging deep neural networks for facial recognition tasks. The system is based on a neural network embedding model that maps facial images into a compact feature space. This embedding is learned using a deep convolutional neural network (CNN), inspired by the FaceNet architecture developed by Google. The EfficientNet B0 (EffNet) CNN model performed the best in detecting depression using image data and had a balanced accuracy of 61%.

Another solution developed from mental health facial analysis research is Affectiva's Emotion AI.[4] Affectiva's tool is in the early stages of being used with smartphones to capture and analyze facial biomarker data using machine learning to help monitor suicidal ideation and prevent suicide attempts. Combining AI-based facial expression analysis using readily available devices and naturalistic data could create immense potential to improve early detection of mental health concerns.

BODILY DIMENSIONS: EYE-TRACKING

The eyes are another aspect of the human face that can provide significant insight into someone's psychological state. AI-based eye-tracking technology has the potential to help flag meaningful behavior differences across diagnosis categories. Diagnosing ASD, or Autism Spectrum Disorder, is one of the more obvious use cases for eye-tracking technology, as limited eye contact is a common feature of ASD. Studies have investigated eye-tracking biomarkers for individuals with ASD to improve detection using machine learning and deep learning. One meta-analysis revealed that there are robust findings for eye-tracking differences and gaze pattern differences amongst toddlers and children with ASD when compared to neurotypical children. Through this research, it was determined that SVMs, or support vector machines, were the most utilized machine learning algorithms utilized to detect ASD using eye-tracking devices.[5] Attention-deficit/hyperactivity disorder (ADHD) also arises as a promising application for eye tracking technology, as attentional differences can be detected through differing eye movement activity. Emerging literature indicates that AI-based eye-tracking technology can reliably discriminate between children with ADHD and neurotypical children, underscoring the potential value of eye-tracking in another diagnostic category.[6] Eye-tracking technology has also been proven useful across other mental health domains like mood disorders and psychotic disorders. For mood disorders, eye-tracking has been used to understand how specific eye movement features may correlate with depression. One study demonstrated that using a model that included eye-tracking features enhanced the accuracy of classifying depression with mixed features, suggesting the potential benefit of including eye-tracking in diagnostic tools across mental health conditions.[7]

Eye-Tracking AI research spotlight

This study sought to understand how eye-tracking data can supplement demographic and clinical information to determine if an individual's psychiatric disorder has mixed features (both depression and mania). Eye-tracking data were recorded from 93 participants, 41 participants with major depressive disorder, 20 of whom were classified as having depression with mixed features, and 52 healthy controls. The eye-tracking features were recorded using a pupil center corneal reflections method that sampled at a 90-Hz rate. The eye-tracking system used was Eye Know (Beijing CAS-Ruiyi Information Technology Company, Ltd.), and the dataset used in the machine learning algorithm was based on demographic information, clinical questionnaires, and eye movement data. The selected machine learning technique was supervised learning that performed the classification of depression with mixed features. They used a tree-based ensemble model called XGBoost, from the Python library XGBoost, which is a specific implementation of gradient-boosted decision trees. Area Under Curve (AUC) was used in this study to analyze the performance of their models and is a measure used to evaluate the performance of binary classification models. A model's AUC ranges from 0 to 1.0, where 0.5 means the model performs the same as random chance, and higher than 0.5 means the model performs better than random chance. The first XGBoost model of this study just used demographic and clinical questionnaire data and performed with an AUC of 0.571, and the second XGBoost model included eye movement features to the data provided to the first model and performed with an AUC of 0.679, indicating that the model that included eye-movement data had an 18.9% improvement in identifying depression with mixed features.

The diagnostic potential of eye-tracking technologies and AI goes beyond their use in mood disorders. Regarding psychotic disorders, a detection method utilizing a support vector machine, random forest, and adaptive boosting showed immense accuracy in diagnosing schizophrenia (up to 96.25% accuracy). This result demonstrates the breadth in which eye-tracking technology combined with AI can improve diagnostic capabilities.

MOVEMENT

Another important and illuminating aspect of behavior is movement. A person's mental health can influence their activity levels, their movement patterns, and even their individual strides. Movement-based analyses regarding mental illness provide another opportunity for novel diagnostic methods using AI to gain insights through someone's behavior. Actigraphy, or the process of monitoring someone's activity levels, can be predictive of someone's mental health status. One study utilized IoMT (Internet of Medical Things) devices to collect movement data using an accelerometer.[8]

They employed a combination of a deep learning model and attention mechanism, which directs the deep learning model to attend to the most relevant input data, to analyze the data, and successfully detect depressive episodes.

Movement AI research spotlight

This study sought to understand how activity levels can inform depression diagnoses. The movement of participants (32 healthy individuals and 23 individuals with unipolar and bipolar depression) was tracked using a wrist-worn actigraphy watch that captures activity using an accelerometer, capturing 1440 records per day. The movement data was analyzed using a deep neural network with fuzzy models (designed to handle uncertainty and vagueness in decision-making), specifically neuro-symbolic classification models that depend on a hybrid system that integrates both machine learning and deep learning. The model was a deep CNN model with an attention mechanism for sequence classification, designed for binary classification of depression, and achieved 95.81% accuracy in detecting depression.

Furthermore, AI-based movement analysis has been applied to sleep to detect the presentation of various disorders. One systematic review explored how various machine learning techniques can help inform how people with bipolar disorder's sleep patterns may differ.[9] This review provided evidence that bipolar disorder is associated with disruptions in rest-activity patterns, including longer sleep duration, longer sleep onset latency (the time it takes to fall asleep), and lower average daily activity. Sleep-based analyses provide a uniquely more passive way of monitoring someone's activity and minimizing someone's conscious awareness of being observed, which could occur from around-the-clock monitoring. Overall, these studies demonstrate the potential of AI-based actigraphy analyses to provide insights into the onset of disorders and nuances of sleep-related disturbances from an array of mental health concerns. Even more granular in the area of movement is the potential to use people's walking strides as valuable clinical data. Algorithm-driven analyses have revealed that people with Schizophrenia have distinct movement markers likely associated with neurological soft signs (non-specific neurological abnormalities), such as motor coordination and sensory-motor integration.[10] These findings could help inform movement-based technology designed to detect schizophrenia at earlier stages. Various wearable technologies can be used to gather data-based movement markers for those at risk of schizophrenia to understand stride patterns and how they may relate to their current and predicted mental health condition. These AI-based movement analyses provide another interesting avenue of supplemental clinical information to broaden a clinician's understanding of a person's unique symptomatic profile to decipher the most accurate diagnosis.

DIGITAL ACTIVITY

Another behavioral aspect of a tech-consumed world is an individual's digital activity. From someone's keyboard patterns to social media use, an individual's interaction with the digital world can provide an immense amount of clinically rich information regarding their mental wellbeing. One study compared various machine learning models' adeptness to determine how smartphone keystroke data related to mental health concerns in adolescents.[11] Elastic net models performed the best in using keystroke data (keystroke timing and frequency) and demographic data to predict mental health symptoms in adolescents. Other studies have looked at naturalistic typing patterns to detect depression accurately using deep learning models, emphasizing the potential of digital-based diagnostic assistance.[12]

Typing AI research spotlight

This study aimed to understand how everyday typing patterns can be analyzed to detect depression.[13] This study used the TypeOfMood mobile application that collected keystroke dynamics, such as keystroke timing information, key switching speed, and other typing metadata, such as the number of typed characters, delete rate, pauses, and typing sessions' duration. This typing data was collected from 10 individuals with depression and 14 healthy controls, totaling 23,264 typing sessions. They also collected depression data using self-report PHQ-9 scores. This study compared the performance of three deep learning models in detecting depression: a CNN model, a long-short time series model (LSTM), which is an implementation of recurrent neural networks (RNNs), and a convolutional neural network-long-short time series (CNN-LSTM) model. The LSTM model performed superiorly in detecting depression based on touchscreen typing data collected passively in everyday settings and achieved an AUC of 0.86.

Social media behavior has also arisen as a notable avenue to gain insight into someone's mental state and may signal early warning signs, especially amongst the teen population. One study highlighted the power of analyzing social media behavior to detect depression through sentiment analysis and natural language processing (NLP) of social media posts.[14] Another study used a multimodal deep learning model and expanded their input data to various aspects of social media, integrating textual content and temporal patterns such as posting cadence and leveraging, to predict various mental health crises.[15] In this study, looking at varying mental health crises, the social media multimodal deep learning model was the most accurate in predicting depressive episodes, followed by manic episodes, suicidal ideation, and lastly, anxiety crises. A systematic review of the utility of AI to analyze mental health disorders among social media users suggested that the multimodal approach of combining textual data with video and audio data yields the most accurate results and should be the preferred methodology.[16] Digital activity in the form of keyboard analysis and social media content and posting patterns can inform clinicians on important digital-related aspects of their patients' health in an ever-more digital world. With these developments, critical concerns need to be considered regarding private user data and managing it in a legal, ethical, and professional manner as the potential of digital-based diagnosing is further explored.

TASK-BASED PERFORMANCE

Extrapolations regarding someone's mental status, in the field of psychology, have long been based on an individual's performance on certain activities. Neuropsychology, specifically, uses various tasks to probe multiple aspects of cognition in an effort to construct a holistic picture of an individual's cognitive capabilities. AI is beginning to intersect with these types of assessments to help determine appropriate diagnoses based on an individual's performance across tests. More modernly, researchers have now begun to design gamified activities to explore how individuals interface with these games and gain unique insights into their mental wellbeing. In one study, researchers designed three digital games to see how people with depression and anxiety performed.[17] These games included three games: one memory game, one fast-paced, high-pressure game, and one game that tests for strategic thinking and quick decision-making.

Gaming AI research spotlight

This study sought to see how individual performance on games involving different cognitive capabilities could accurately predict depression and anxiety diagnoses. The data collected from each of the 83 participants consisted of gameplay log data, the Beck Depression Inventory-II (BDI-II) for depressive symptoms, and the Beck Anxiety Inventory (BAI) for anxiety symptoms. This study implemented a wide range of machine learning techniques to examine which best predicted the presence or absence of depression and anxiety symptoms. The following models were used, and their performances were compared:

- Linear Discriminant Analysis (LDA) Classifier
- Nu Support Vector Classification (NuSVC)
- Logistic Regression Classifier
- Random Forest Classifier
- Gradient Boosting Machine (GBM)
- Support Vector Machine (SVM)
- Multi-Layer Perceptron (MLP)
- AdaBoost Classifier
- Gaussian Naive Bayes (NB)
- Extreme Gradient Boosting (XGB) Classifier
- Extra Tree Classifier

- Decision Tree Classifier
- K-Nearest Neighbors Classifier
- Passive Aggressive Classifier

Out of this wide range of machine learning models, Nu Support Vector Classification (NuSVC) was the most accurate in identifying depression with 93.75% accuracy, and Gaussian Naive Bayes (NB) was the most accurate in identifying anxiety with the same 93.75% accuracy.

Other research has utilized classic neuropsychology tests to predict mental health status. For example, one online game utilized a two-level n-back test, which measures working memory by presenting users with a sequence of stimuli and having them recall the sequence, to help predict depression and anxiety levels.[18] Two random forest models were trained on this task performance data to classify depression and anxiety levels, and outperformed classifications that just relied on age and gender. This study was done as a part of Thymia's research efforts to use machine learning and neuropsychology to best identify mental illness and its underlying symptomology.

BEHAVIOR AI CASE STUDIES COMPARISON

Behavior Category	*Diagnosis Category*	*Model Used*	*Dataset Size*	*Accuracy*
Facial features	Depression	CNN	177 participants with MDD	Balanced accuracy: 61%
Eye tracking	Depression with mixed features	XGBoost (gradient-boosted decision tree) with eye-tracking data	93 participants (41 MDD, 20 DMF, 52 HC)	AUC = 0.68, 18.9% performance improvement compared to model with no eye-tracking data
Movement	Depression	Deep CNN with attention mechanism	55 participants (23 with unipolar and bipolar depression, 32 HC)	95.81% accuracy
Typing	Depression	LSTM	24 participants (10 MDD, 14 HC)	AUC = 0.86
Gaming	Depression	NuSVC	83 participants	93.75% accuracy
Gaming	Anxiety	Gaussian NB	83 participants	93.75% accuracy

THYMIA: BEHAVIOR-BASED DIAGNOSTICS CASE STUDY

Thymia's products, built on a robust research foundation, seek to make mental health as objectively measurable and monitorable as physical health. This company is developing a suite of tools to give tangible insights into people's mental wellness based on machine learning and performance on various neuropsychological assessments. They seek to use their AI-powered mental health assessments to identify underlying mental health symptoms more specifically, accurately, and objectively. They offer two distinct product suites: Helios and Apollo, which can be embedded into other platforms through an API. Helios is part of their wellness range, which gives insights into the most relevant mental wellness indicators: mental strain, burnout, stress, distress, tiredness, and confidence. Apollo, which is currently only available as an investigational device, is part of their clinical range, which gives insights into major depression, generalized anxiety, and ADHD, and measures these disorders' core components. Thymia was established in 2020 and, as of now, has over 11 proprietary AI models, over 280 associated publications, and an impact on over 41,000 individuals across five continents. Their products are designed to use video, voice, and behavioral data as inputs into AI models that measure and report on mental health concerns.

Thymia's AI architecture utilizes a novel approach in mental health modeling that relies on Bayesian Networks with multimodal inputs.[19] As outlined in one of their seminal publications in 2022 regarding their Bayesian Network methodology to predict major depressive disorder, Bayesian Networks present key advantages over the more popularized deep learning modelling paradigms used for predicting mental health conditions. Thymia's team argues that deep learning models lack transparency in how decisions are made, are limited in their ability to integrate expert opinion into the model, and have difficulty handling missing data inputs. Thymia's models have sought to differentiate themselves from other Bayesian Network approaches by incorporating multimodal data as predictors in their models. While other recent Bayesian Networks mental health prediction work often incorporates simple demographic, biological, and environmental data, Thymia incorporates multimodal speech, video, and behavior data. Their first published work on this model, which laid the groundwork for their current clinical model design, was based on a dataset comprised of 1336 English-speaking participants who performed a series of short online activities, including an Image Description Task, n-Back Task, and a Paragraph Reading Task. The Image Description Task involves participants describing what they see in an image, the n-Back Task involves participants remembering previous cards in a deck with increasing difficulty, and the Paragraph Reading Task involves participants reading aloud from a short story. From these tasks, a total of 322 features were collected, including 88 acoustic and prosodic features (e.g., speech rate, pitch), 97 video features (e.g., facial rotation, emotion), and eight cognitive features (e.g., precision, reaction time). The Bayesian Network model was composed of four groups of variables: confounds (age, gender, type of device used for recordings), condition (presence or absence of depression), symptoms (individual PHQ-8 items), and activity (derived from a standard rescaling and supervised PCA of the previous 322 mentioned features). The Thymia team then analyzed how successful their model was at using activity measures to predict condition (depression or no depression) and symptoms (PHQ-8 items). The measure of accuracy selected ROC-AUC (area under the receiver operating curve) indicated an accuracy of 0.7 for condition and 0.66 for symptoms. Because of the dramatic increase in volume of data collected over the last couple of years since this study was published, Thymia's new model has purportedly substantially increased in accuracy and is estimated to be around 0.9 for the same ROC-AUC accuracy measures. Although Thymia's model relies mostly on speech data, their approach is unique in infusing behavioral and visual data into its predictive clinical models. Thymia is harnessing a multimodal Bayesian Networks approach in their Apollo product across various mental health symptoms and mental health conditions beyond depression. This tool will give clinicians a supplement to the traditional self-report measures by providing objective clinical information to bring more nuance to their understanding of their patients' mental health situation.

LANGUAGE-BASED DIAGNOSING AI VALUE PROP

The current system of mental health diagnostics is inextricably bound to language. Mental health disorders are diagnosed through clinical interviews, observations, and assessments. The takeaways from clinical interviews rely completely on a patient's speech regarding the description of their symptoms and the tone of their description. Key patient observations for clinicians may rely on a clinician's interpretation of a patient's presenting affect, which is often informed by what they are saying and how they are saying it. Clinical assessments, another diagnostic tool, rely entirely on language through the patient's written or verbal responses to the specified questions. When we consider the complexity of the phenomenon of human language, it becomes clear that traditional clinical diagnostic tools may not be fully capturing the wealth of information that language offers about its speaker. The historical setup in which clinicians base diagnostic decisions on self-report measures, and their subjective clinical judgment, inherently limits the mental healthcare systems' to gain the most accurate diagnostic picture possible. A major limitation of this current approach is that it relies on patients' ability to accurately disclose their mental health concerns and on a clinician's ability to pick up on critical mental health information when interacting with the patient. For a variety of reasons, patients may be motivated not to disclose their symptoms or their severity, may simply lack insight into their mental health state, or may not feel comfortable disclosing directly to a clinician because of attributes of the clinician or the environment. AI-based diagnostic tools that use aspects of language as input can equip clinicians with quantitative windows into the world of their patients to bring further nuance to their patient formulations. One of the most relevant and popular language-based AI methodologies is NLP. NLP has been used in mental health research to help diagnose mental illnesses by analyzing electronic health records, psychological evaluation reports, transcribed patient interviews, and even social media.[20] When considering the role of NLPs in mental healthcare more broadly, NLPs can be helpful in analyzing language data to understand someone's mental health status and, when paired with generative AI, with an array of other clinically related tasks, such as streamlined note-taking. There are many other applications of NLP in mental healthcare that go beyond the scope of this section, but this section will narrow in on NLP's and, more largely, AI's developing ability to help capture and analyze important language-based diagnostic information. Utilizing language-based AI has the potential to transform and augment current clinical diagnostic practices in the mental healthcare system.

OPPORTUNITIES IN DIAGNOSIS: LANGUAGE

Language is a distinctly human phenomenon that holds a wealth of information about the person who outputs that specific language. As the driving communicative system in our society, language defines the world around us, ourselves, and the way we interact with the external world. Language has a multitude of dimensions that provide invaluable information spanning the voice someone uses to transmit their language and the actual content of the chosen speech. These fascinating aspects of language can range from the specific acoustics of speech to the syntax of an individual's social media posts. The language someone uses provides a distinctive window into their mind and emotional wellbeing needs to be captured and analyzed with more nuance. Within the broad topic of language, the discussion of language-based AI opportunities in mental health diagnostics will focus on aspects of language that have emerged as particularly salient to the experiences of mental health. This section is broken up into two sections of language to drive that exploration: content-based and voice-based language modalities. Within these subcategories we will explore various language features that were selected due to the robustness of research surrounding those particular dimensions of language in the mental health and AI field. Within the subcategory of content-based language, we will examine semantic features, syntactic features, and lexical features analysis. Within the subcategory of voice-based language, we will explore, speech qualities and speech patterns.

CONTENT-BASED

For content-based AI mental health diagnosing, we will explore three critical aspects of language that can be utilized as inputs to AI models designed to diagnose mental disorders: the semantic features, the syntactic features, and the lexical features of text. Semantics refers to the meaning of text and includes the concept of sentiment, which refers to the attitude or tone expressed within a piece of writing. Second, syntax refers to the grammar and structure of text. And lastly, lexical features refer to the actual words chosen and how frequently they appear in the text.

SEMANTIC FEATURES

Semantic features can provide interesting avenues into someone's mental health, especially when semantic features are atypical. When paired with AI-based analytics, semantic features have arisen as being particularly helpful in predicting the onset of mood disorders. Notably, semantic-based analytics have also been deemed useful in helping identify psychosis or psychotic disorders, as psychosis is often marked by language abnormalities, such as disorganized speech or poverty of speech. One study, based in Sao Paulo, Brazil studied the language use of individuals experiencing at-risk mental states to understand more subtle speech changes to detect and prevent early signs of psychosis that could be indicative of future onset of more severe psychotic symptoms.[21] For individuals experiencing psychosis, NLP techniques have been used to show that the similarity of consecutive words (also known as first-order coherences) or the similarity of two nearly consecutive words (also known as second-order coherences) are markedly different in psychotic speech. To test the robustness of this previous finding, this study looked at sentiment analysis which looks at the valence of words as negative or positive and then looked at semantic similarity between words by mapping words as vectors to positions in semantic space and calculating the distance between them. Overall, this study found that NLP features based mostly on sentiment and semantic coherence were the most informative in psychotic classification, with a balanced accuracy of 86%. More specifically, the semantic features of perseveration of a specific topic and semantic recurrence time, or the time it takes for a specific concept or meaning to reappear, held the most value in predicting psychotic features. Another study has investigated semantic differences in individuals with schizophrenia and utilized a fastText (Facebook AI Research) pretrained NLP word embedding model to analyze the performance of a verbal fluency task.[22] This study's findings underscore semantic differences in individuals with schizophrenia's semantic trajectories when producing language. Individuals with schizophrenia's semantic trajectories are characterized by reduced semantically-guided word sampling, which is a marker of looser conceptual organization.

As mentioned earlier, semantic AI-based analyses have also been successfully applied to mood disorders and have benefited the process of accurately and efficiently predicting the onset of depression. A recent systematic review highlights that NLP-based sentiment analysis utilized in psychiatric care had positive impacts on earlier mood disorders detection and personalization of treatment, which are critical aspects of the diagnostic process.[23] The use of semantic analysis to detect mood disorders has also been applied beyond the context of healthcare settings through analysis of social media text. Social media has the advantage of providing more naturalistic text samples from individuals and can be leveraged to perform large scale studies given the massive number of daily social media users globally.

Semantic AI spotlight

This study sought to analyze the potential of using AI techniques and sentiment analysis in depression detection.[24] The text data for this study were collected from 10,000 social media posts, 5000 online forums and discussions, 2000 personal diaries and journals, as well as 1000 clinical records and medical transcripts, totaling 550,000 words. The authors then performed sentiment analysis on these texts using NLP techniques that were performed using lexicon-based, rule-based, and deep learning models. NLP techniques were also applied to detect depression amongst the authors of the text data using various AI models, such as logistic regression, support vector machines, and neural networks. The sentiment analysis models were compared to determine how each model performed on different types and lengths of text, resulting in the deep learning model having the highest performance at 85% accuracy. The researchers then analyzed the correlation between sentiment results and depression indicators and found that people who have higher sentiment typically have lower depressive symptoms and risk factors, as well as possess higher protective factors and coping strategies.

Another systematic review deciphered which machine learning and deep learning techniques were the most effective in analyzing depression symptoms based on social media sentiment analysis.[25] Overall, multi-class classification, utilizing text, emoticons, and emojis paired with deep learning analysis, had the highest accuracy in predicting depression when using sentiment analysis protocols. The use of sentiment and semantic analysis has also arisen considerations on what segment of texts to use and how long these segments should be. One study on AI-based semantic analysis of depression analyzes the tradeoff of including more text, which creates more noise, or not including enough text, which hinders the ability to determine the sentiment of the text. This study demonstrated that the optimal window (or amount of words to include) for the performance of their LSTM was 64.[26] These findings across social media and healthcare settings, and surrounding optimal text windows, prompt us to consider the wide array of aspects of language that will influence the outputs of AI models, from how we are extracting our language samples to the actual source of the language originally.

SYNTACTIC FEATURES

Syntactic features provide another avenue through which content-based language can be analyzed using AI to predict the onset of mental health disorders.

Defining syntactic complexity in the realm of NLP can be difficult, but a few methods have arisen.[27] First, assessing complexity can be done using part-of-speech tagging, which assigns a grammatical category to each word in a sentence to better understand its structure. In addition, speech graphs have arisen as an approach to determine syntax complexity. This approach represents text as a network with words as nodes and their text proximity as edges between the nodes. These graphs help indicate both semantic coherence and syntactic complexity.

Some research in the language-based mental health detection space has focused on explainable AI (or XAI) to ensure there is model transparency in decision-making in these models, especially when transparency is so critical in the healthcare detection space. One study in particular utilizes syntactic features, as well as other linguistic features, to construct explainable AI methods to detect a variety of mental health disorders or mental health symptoms, including ADHD, anxiety, depression, bipolar, and stress.[28] The general linguistic features of this model included a category of morpho-syntactic complexity (the intricacy and sophistication of grammatical structures, words forms, and sentence structures used in language) consisting of five elements: length of the production unit, sentence complexity, subordination (grammatical structure where one clause is made dependent on another clause), coordination (grammatical process where two or more elements are joined together), and particular structures. Overall, the morpho-syntactic feature group exhibited a moderate level of predictive power across the mental health conditions, with more predictability in anxiety and depression than in ADHD and bipolar. These findings highlight the potential for syntactic features of language to inform mental health diagnoses across diagnostic domains. Other studies have researched NLP from a different angle and compared various types of NLP approaches to illuminate which ones best inform detection of mental health disorders.

Syntactic features AI spotlight

This study sought to use various NLP techniques to decipher whether patients had been diagnosed with a mental disorder or not, and the particular mental disorder type.[29] The text used was collected from 108 psychiatrist interviews, ranging from 60 to 90 minutes and from 6782 to 9531 words, from a psychiatrist department in the Netherlands. This study compared the four NLP approaches: lexical processing, dependency parsing, shallow neural networks, and deep neural networks. Dependency parsing refers to the syntactic processing of text, which was performed using spaCy, a free open-source Python library for advanced NLP. The results of this study indicated that spaCy in combination with a random forest classification best predicted which mental disorder each person had with an accuracy of 42.9%. This moderate accuracy is likely explained by the limited mental disorder labels provided in the dataset. In contrast, the best model at predicting whether or not someone had a mental disorder was based on a model that leveraged word choice and random forest classification with an accuracy of 95.2%.

Like semantic features of language, syntactic features have been prominent in psychosis research due to the discussed irregularities in speech patterns of individuals presenting with psychosis. More specifically, linguistic analysis in the prodromal phase of psychosis in adolescence has arisen as a way to detect psychotic symptoms during a critical time of schizophrenia onset. One study compared the syntactic features of speech in adolescents with prodromal psychosis to normal adolescents using machine learning-based algorithms.[30] Adolescents with symptoms of prodromal psychosis tended to use words that had a small chance of occurring when associated with the previous word, but exhibited no significant differences in measurements of speech production (length of segments and number of words used), highlighting how different aspects of language related to syntax may vary in their predictive power of psychotic disorders.

LEXICAL FEATURES

Lexical features also present an interesting aspect of language that can be analyzed using AI to bring a more nuanced understanding to someone's mental health status. For example, a notable lexical feature across mental health disorders is the increased use of first-person singular nouns, likely due to the increased self-focus and a propensity to internalize experiences.[31] AI has been used to further understand this linguistic phenomenon and other lexical feature dynamics of those with mental health concerns. More specifically, one study explored the utility of multimodal deep learning models to analyze social media data and detect early indicators of mental health crises. This model included features such as linguistic markers, behavioral markers, and temporal patterns. Regarding the findings with the linguistic markers, this study observed an increase in the use of first-person singular nouns and a higher frequency of negative emotion words in posts preceding a crisis. This model detected different types of mental health crises at different accuracy levels, with the most accurate being identifying suicidal ideation at 93.5% accuracy and depressive episodes at 91.2% accuracy. This research indicates how multimodal deep learning models can leverage lexical features as predictive factors, in combination with other data types, to help better predict mental health crises.

Other research in language markers of mental health have started to parse through the potential ways race moderates the way language predicts mental health concerns. One study specifically looks at a machine learning model analysis of social media posts that can help predict depression in a matched sample of black and white English speakers in the United States.[32] This study looked at how machine learning performance compared the predictability of self-reported depression based on social media posts in black individuals and white individuals. Interestingly, the machine learning models were better at predicting depression in white individuals and less good at predicting depression in black individuals. Regarding lexical features, the results indicated an increased use of the "I" pronoun in white individuals and not black individuals. Furthermore, words related to negative emotions and expressions of feelings of self-criticism and worthlessness were related to greater depression severity in white individuals but not black individuals. These findings illuminate potential race-based differences in expressed depression in natural language, which must be considered in how machine learning models will be implemented in clinical settings and potentially perpetuate biases.

These lexical feature analyses can also extend beyond the mood disorders domain and inform neurodegenerative diseases as well.

Lexical features AI spotlight

This study sought to explore the potential to use AI to parse text and conduct sentiment analysis in order to detect early markers of mental health concerns and neurodegenerative diseases.[33] This study used text data from 6923 Twitter tweets, 232,074 posts from "SuicideWatch" and "depression" subreddits from Reddit, and an undisclosed number of transcripts from patient interviews, and electronic health records. This study used NLP algorithms to parse the text and machine learning models to identify language patterns and sentiment changes. A variety of the most well-known AI classifiers were used, including random forest, extra trees, decision tree, and light gradient boosting machine. The extra trees classifier had the most accurate performance of detecting early markers of mental health concerns and neurodegenerative diseases as 69.9% accuracy. The models also detected higher frequency in first-person singular pronouns and a decrease in future tense in individuals with depression, which is consistent with previous research. Another interesting finding is text from people with early signs of neurodegenerative diseases were characterized by diminished vocabulary diversity.

VOICE-BASED

Voice-based data can capture an array of qualities in speech that may illuminate aspects of someone's mental wellbeing. Voice-based data can be partitioned into speech qualities, such as prosodic features like intonation, stress, rhythm, and speech patterns, like speaking rate, pause patterns, and turn-taking delays. We will explore the use of AI in leveraging voice based features to predict and diagnose mental health concerns through the two subcategories of speech qualities and speech patterns. Before exploring the research surrounding these two subcategories, it is important to consider how content-based and voice-based compare to one another in their predictive power of mental health concerns. Research suggests that text-based features surrounding content contributes more to model accuracy in predicting neuropsychiatric disorders than audio markers from voice data did.[34] Although content-based language data may hold more predictive power overall, speech qualities and patterns still improve accuracy in multimodal approaches to using language and AI to predict mental health concerns and thus merits further exploration. Furthermore, acoustic features of voice may be more objective than content and thus may hold some benefits over strictly content-based approaches.

SPEECH QUALITIES

As discussed, speech qualities can include prosodic features such as intonation, stress, rhythm, and loudness as well as jitter and shimmer which are measures of voice irregularity and harmonies-to-noise ratio. AI has been used to explore these interesting aspects of speech and see if they have merit to flagging mental health concerns early and effectively. One systematic review looks at analysis of various speech qualities across mental disorders and highlights that depression and psychotic disorders are the most heavily focused on disorders in speech analysis.[35] More specifically, depression is thought to be characterized by slower and decreased muscle movements, which produces lower pitch speech and a narrower pitch range than healthy controls. Acoustic feature differences in bipolar disorder have been found to be promising at helping identifying people with bipolar disorder, as a recent study differentiated individuals with bipolar depression from individuals with unipolar depression with 73% accuracy just using acoustic features.[36] Regarding the voice features best at predicting the onset of mental illnesses, research indicates that glottal features predict which high-risk adolescent would develop depression over a 2-year follow-up with 73% accuracy. The glottis structure, found in the throat that consists of the vocal cords and the space between them, has been found to be affected by depression due to psychomotor slowing.

With regards to the application of AI, many machine learning methods have been used in research to automatically extract purely acoustic features from spontaneous speech primarily across the mental disorders of depression, schizophrenia, and bipolar disorder.[37] These disorders have been paid particular attention as depression is tied to slower speech activity and psychotic disorders are characterized by reduced variation in frequency in speech and other speech pattern differences. Prosodic speech characteristics have also been helpful in identifying suicide risk and other depressive symptoms, suggesting AI and speech-based screening could be helpful in early detection of debilitating mood disorders. One study investigated this potential further by utilizing machine learning to analyze voice features to predict depression. More specifically, they used a combination of a Bidirectional Long Short-Term Memory Network (Bi-LSTM) and a Time-distributed Convolutional Neural Network (T-CNN) to analyze prosodic and semantic features of speech to predict depression severity.[38] The model's performance just based on prosodic audio features, as measured by a patient-level F1 score, achieved a score of 0.9074 across the five classes of depression (healthy, mild, moderate, moderately severe, and severe). The multimodal model using both prosodic and semantic features performed higher with a F1 score of 0.958, indicating that prosodic speech features hold more clinically valuable information when paired with language meaning analysis as well. Although much of the research on voice biomarkers and mental health is focused on clinically relevant diagnostic categories, some studies have emerged that take a more granular approach by exploring emotion in voice.

Speech qualities AI spotlight

This study sought to develop a speech-emotion recognition algorithm through AI and machine learning to detect relevant emotional distress and functional impairment in children and adolescents.[39] The researchers used a software application called TQI app to collect voice samples from 420 youth receiving mental health services at mental health care centers focused primarily on children and adolescents from low-income communities. The researchers also used the mental health questionnaires SFSS (symptoms and functioning severity scale), ACE (adverse childhood experiences), and PHQ-9 (patient health questionnaire-9 (depression symptoms)) to measure current emotional distress. Patients selected from a subset of readings and their voice was recorded for up to 90 seconds. The researchers used an open-source voice activity detection (VAD) algorithm called "WebRTC VAD" to extract active speech features from the voice samples. The feature extraction was focused on pitch and energy information. The researchers then used a Gaussian Mixture Model (GMM), which is an unsupervised soft clustering technique often used for audio classification. The second machine learning model took a different approach and employed supervised learning using a long short-term memory network, which is a specific kind of RNN. The thought process of using this model was that this type of model can connect previous information to the present, so that emotional patterns in speech are learned by taking changes in features over time into consideration. The GMM model achieved an accuracy of 79.15% across the 5 emotion categories (neutral, happy, sad, angry, and fear) and the RNN LSTM model achieved an accuracy of 79.6%.

SPEECH PATTERNS

Another interesting and notable aspect of speech that can indicate someone's mental wellbeing beyond speech qualities, are individuals' speech patterns, such as speaking rate, pause patterns, or turn-taking differences. More nuanced speech pattern features include specific patterns in the harmonicity of speech or energy present in speech. Studies typically take a multimodal acoustic feature approach when utilizing machine learning models to help predict mental health concerns. More specifically, one study utilized speech qualities, semantic meaning, and speech patterns to identify mental health concerns, totaling over 150 textual and acoustic features.[40] Some of the interesting speech pattern features analyzed in this study included an increased number of pauses, faster speech rate, longer pauses, alterations in speech rate, and repetitive speech patterns. As expected, the multimodal approach outperformed the uni-modal text-based and audio-based models, but still indicates the merits of including speech features and specifically speech pattern features in multimodal machine learning models to predict mental health disorders. Speech pattern analysis has extended beyond mental healthcare and has shown merits across the healthcare system, which could be particularly insightful in the case of co-occurring psychiatric and physical conditions. A systematic review looked at how speech patterns more broadly have emerged as diagnostic markers for conditions with various etiologies, comparing the usability of machine learning to detect speech differences in mental health, laryngeal, and neurological disorders.[41] The included studies used a variety of speech pattern data, including pause and speech rate data. This review highlights the staggering potential of machine learning to utilize speech pattern data across healthcare concerns, including mental health, with some studies achieving an accuracy of over 90%. Although voice-based mental health analysis has clear merits across mental health diagnostic categories, psychotic disorders and bipolar disorder are of particular interest due to their more blatant effect on individuals' speech patterns.

Speech patterns AI spotlight

This study investigated if machine learning models can reliably use audiovisual patterns from interviews of participants with schizophrenia spectrum disorders and bipolar disorder to classify psychiatric signs, symptoms, and diagnoses.[42] The audiovisual data was captured from 89 participants, and acoustic and facial movement features were extracted. During each visit, participants were asked a series of 5 emotionally neutral, open-ended questions, such as describe a typical dinner, designed to elicit natural speech production. Acoustic features were extracted using OpenSMILE open-source toolbox, which encompasses 150 acoustic features. Participants were also asked questions from the Brief Psychiatric Rating Scale (BPRS), Scale for the Assessment of Negative Symptoms (SANS), Hamilton Depression Rating Scale (HAMD), and Young Mania Rating Scale (YMRS). The researchers explored 2 main classification tasks, involving assigning an interview to a specific diagnostic group and predicting the presence of psychiatric symptoms. All inferences were undertaken using the machine learning algorithm of gradient boosting classifier, and for the unimodal audio model, an array of AI classification models were used, including support vector machine, random forest, logistic regression, and dense layers. The study's results indicated that speech features such as mean energy in the frequency band performed best for women. Women with schizophrenia spectrum disorder demonstrated reduced energy in the frequency band (how much acoustic energy is present within specific frequency ranges during speech production), reduced spectral harmonicity (the degree to which the frequency components (harmonics) of a sound are multiples of a fundamental frequency), and increased spectral slope (rate at which energy of sound spectrum decreases as frequency increases) compared to women with bipolar disorder. The unimodal audio model using random forest achieved a 71.83% accuracy.

LANGUAGE AI CASE STUDIES COMPARISON

Language Category	*Diagnosis Category*	*Model Used*	*Dataset Size*	*Accuracy*
Content-based: Semantic Features	Depression	NLP + various DL	10K social media posts, 5K online forums, 2K journals, 1K clinical records	85% accuracy in detection
Content-based: Syntactic Features	Various mental health disorders	Dependency Parsing (SpaCy) + random forest classification	108 psychiatric interviews (60–90 minutes)	42.9% accuracy in deciphering which mental disorder
Content-based: Lexical Features	Various mental health disorders and neurodegenerative diseases	Various AI classifiers (random forest, extra trees, decision trees, light gradient boosting)	232K social media posts, an undisclosed number of patient transcripts	69.9% accuracy in detecting early markers of mental health concerns and neurodegenerative diseases
Voice-based: Speech Qualities	Emotional distress	GMM and RNN-LSTM	420 youths, 90 seconds of audio each	GMM: 79.15% accuracy in emotion identification RNN-LSTM: 79.6% accuracy in emotion identification
Voice-based: Speech Patterns	Schizophrenia and Bipolar Disorder	SVM, RF, LogReg, Dense Layers	83 participants	71.83% accuracy in detecting mental disorders using unimodal audio random forest model

KINTSUGI: LANGUAGE-BASED DIAGNOSTICS CASE STUDY

Kintsugi is a voice biomarker AI company founded on the idea that people's voices can give unique insight into their mental health status. Kintsugi's suite of products includes Kintsgui Voice, Kintsugi Connect, and Kintsugi App.

Kintsugi voice is a software that integrates into existing clinical call centers or workflows to identify and triage behavioral health conditions efficiently. This product aims to objectively measure symptoms and severity through voice biomarkers. Kintsugi Connect helps aid individuals who have been marked as having a condition to be paired with therapists, psychiatrists, and other mental health resources. Last, the Kintsugi App prompts users to partake in voice journaling to gain insight into their mental well-being and track progress over time to promote self-awareness and help prompt behavior change. Notably, Pega, a healthcare solution provider in the United States, integrated Kintsugi's enterprise software KiVA (Kintsugi Voice Biomarker API) to act as a psychiatrist's ear on authorized phone calls to better screen people for depression and anxiety using 20 seconds of audio and its AI technology.

Kintsugi's AI architecture utilizes a machine learning approach that relies on voice data to make predictions on mental health conditions such as depression and anxiety. A published study on Kintsugi's approach outlines how their voice biomarker mental health detection model was constructed and its performance in classifying moderate to severe depression.[43] This study highlights a cross-sectional design in which the researchers captured at least 25 seconds of free-form speech content from English-speaking samples from 14,898 individuals in the United States and Canada. These participants also filled in a Patient Health Questionnaire-9 (PHQ-9), and individuals with a 10 or above (an indicator of moderate to severe depression) were analyzed further for voice biomarker. The raw audio data was used to create a unique feature set using two extraction tools: (1) Torchaudio to produce a 40-band Mel spectrogram and 20 mel-frequency cepstral coefficients (MFCCs) and (2) Meta AI's data2vec to extract 1024-dimensional representations of speech. Principle Component Analysis was used to assess the relationship between voice features and PHQ-9 labels by projecting the high-dimensional data into 3-D space. The AI architecture relies on a feed-forward deep neural network composed of four algorithmic layers that was trained in a supervised manner using PHQ-9 scores as labels to detect the presence of vocal characteristics consistent with a depressive episode. The Kintsugi model was reported to achieve a sensitivity of 71.3% and a specificity of 73.5% in detecting the presence of depression or not, based on voice data. Kintsugi's products may face limitations in its focus on voice-based features instead of content-based analyses, which have proven to be more effective in some cases in predicting mental health concerns.

ACKNOWLEDGMENTS

The author wishes to express profound gratitude to Elena Gray, whose extensive insights, detailed research, and thoughtful analysis were instrumental in shaping this chapter.

NOTES

1 Sadeghi, Misha et al. "Harnessing Multimodal Approaches for Depression Detection Using Large Language Models and Facial Expressions." *NPJ Mental Health Research*, vol. 3, article 66, 2024. https://doi.org/10.1038/s44184-024-00112-8. Accessed 24 May 2025.

2 Zaks, Nina et al. "Elemental Dysregulation in Psychotic Spectrum Disorders: A Review and Research Synthesis." *Schizophrenia Research*, vol. 233, July 2021, pp. 64–71. https://doi.org/10.1016/j.schres.2021.06.015. Accessed 24 May 2025.

3 Nepal, Subigya et al. *MoodCapture: Depression Detection Using In-the-Wild Smartphone Images*. arXiv, 25 Feb. 2024. https://doi.org/10.48550/arXiv.2402.16182. Accessed 24 May 2025.

4 "5 Takeaways on Emotion AI & Biosensors in Mental Health Research." *Affectiva Blog*, 18 Oct. 2021. https://blog.affectiva.com/5-takeaways-on-emotion-ai-biosensors-in-mental-health-research. Accessed 24 May 2025.

5 Jeyarani, R. Asmetha, and Radha Senthilkumar. "Eye Tracking Biomarkers for Autism Spectrum Disorder Detection Using Machine Learning and Deep Learning Techniques: Review." *Research in Autism Spectrum Disorders*, vol. 108, Oct. 2023, article 102228. https://doi.org/10.1016/j.rasd.2023.102228. Accessed 24 May 2025.

6 Chen, Xiaolu et al. "Utilizing artificial intelligence-based eye tracking technology for screening ADHD symptoms in children." Frontiers in psychiatry vol. 14 1260031. 14 Nov. 2023. https://doi.org/10.3389/fpsyt.2023.1260031

7 Liu, Xing-Chang et al. "Identifying Depression with Mixed Features: The Potential Value of Eye-Tracking Features." *Frontiers in Neurology*, vol. 16, 2025, article 1555630. https://doi.org/10.3389/fneur.2025.1555630. Accessed 24 May 2025.

8 Yang, Hui et al. "An Automatic Detection Method for Schizophrenia Based on Abnormal Eye Movements in Reading Tasks." *Expert Systems with Applications*, vol. 238, pt. B, 15 Mar. 2024, article 121850. https://doi.org/10.1016/j.eswa.2023.121850. Accessed 24 May 2025.

9 Panchal, Priyanka et al. "Toward a Digital Future in Bipolar Disorder Assessment: A Systematic Review of Disruptions in the Rest-Activity Cycle as Measured by Actigraphy." *Frontiers in Psychiatry*, vol. 13, 2022, article 780726. https://doi.org/10.3389/fpsyt.2022.780726. Accessed 24 May 2025.

10 Martin, Lily et al. "Movement Markers of Schizophrenia: A Detailed Analysis of Patients' Gait Patterns." *European Archives of Psychiatry and Clinical Neuroscience*, vol. 272, 2022, pp. 1347–1364. https://doi.org/10.1007/s00406-022-01402-y.

11 Braund, Taylor A. et al. "Associations Between Smartphone Keystroke Metadata and Mental Health Symptoms in Adolescents: Findings From the Future Proofing Study." *JMIR Mental Health*, vol. 10, 2023, e44986. JMIR Publications. https://doi.org/10.2196/44986.

12 Fadul, Ruba et al. "Depressive Disorder Remote Detection through Touchscreen Typing Behaviour." *2023 45th Annual International Conference of the IEEE Engineering in Medicine & Biology Society (EMBC)*, 24–27 July 2023, Sydney, Australia. IEEE, 2023. https://doi.org/10.1109/EMBC40787.2023.10340393.

13 Fadul, Ruba et al. "Depressive Disorder Remote Detection through Touchscreen Typing Behaviour." *2023 45th Annual International Conference of the IEEE Engineering in Medicine & Biology Society (EMBC)*, 24–27 July 2023, Sydney, Australia. IEEE, 2023. https://doi.org/10.1109/EMBC40787.2023.10340393.

14 Babu, Nirmal Varghese, and E. Grace Mary Kanaga. "Sentiment Analysis in Social Media Data for Depression Detection Using Artificial Intelligence: A Review." *SN Computer Science*, vol. 3, article no. 74, 2022. https://doi.org/10.1007/s42979-021-00958-1.

15 Mansoor, Masab A., and Kashif H. Ansari. "Early Detection of Mental Health Crises through Artificial-Intelligence-Powered Social Media Analysis: A Prospective Observational Study." *Journal of Personalized Medicine*, vol. 14, no. 9, 2024, article 958. https://doi.org/10.3390/jpm14090958.

16 Owen, David et al. "AI for Analyzing Mental Health Disorders Among Social Media Users: Quarter-Century Narrative Review of Progress and Challenges." *Journal of medical Internet research*, vol. 26 e59225. 15 Nov. 2024. https://doi.org/10.2196/59225.

17 Elyasi, Soroush, Arya VarastehNezhad, and Fattaneh Taghiyareh. "From Play to Prediction: Assessing Depression and Anxiety in Players Behavior with Machine Learning Models." *International Journal of Serious Games*, vol. 12, no. 1, 2025, pp. 83–102. https://doi.org/10.17083/ijsg.v12i1.897.

18 Georgescu, Alexandra Livia et al. "Screening for Depression and Anxiety Using a Nonverbal Working Memory Task in a Sample of Older Brazilians: Observational Study of Preliminary Artificial Intelligence Model Transferability." *JMIR Formative Research*, vol. 8, 2024, e55856. https://doi.org/10.2196/55856.

19 Fara, Salvatore et al. *Bayesian Networks for the Robust and Unbiased Prediction of Depression and Its Symptoms Utilizing Speech and Multimodal Data*. arXiv, 22 June 2023, arXiv:2211.04924v2. https://arxiv.org/abs/2211.04924.

20 Le Glaz, Aziliz et al. "Machine Learning and Natural Language Processing in Mental Health: Systematic Review." *Journal of Medical Internet Research*, vol. 23, no. 5, e15708. 4 May 2021. https://doi.org/10.2196/15708.

21 Argolo, Felipe et al. "Natural Language Processing in At-Risk Mental States: Enhancing the Assessment of Thought Disorders and Psychotic Traits with Semantic Dynamics and Graph Theory." *Brazilian Journal of Psychiatry*, vol. 46, 2024. https://doi.org/10.47626/1516-4446-2023-3419. Accessed 25 May 2025.

22 Nour, Matthew M. et al. "Trajectories through Semantic Spaces in Schizophrenia and the Relationship to Ripple Bursts." *Proceedings of the National Academy of Sciences*, vol. 120, no. 42, 10 Oct. 2023, e2305290120. https://doi.org/10.1073/pnas.2305290120.

23 Hsu, Chou-Yi et al. "The Impact of AI-Driven Sentiment Analysis on Patient Outcomes in Psychiatric Care: A Narrative Review." *Asian Journal of Psychiatry*, vol. 107, May 2025, 104443. *Elsevier*. https://doi.org/10.1016/j.ajp.2025.104443.

24 Choudhary, Dilip Kumar et al. "Sentiment Analysis for Depression Detection Using Artificial Intelligence." *2024 3rd International Conference on Artificial Intelligence for Internet of Things (AIIoT)*, 3–4 May 2024, Vellore, India. *IEEE*, 2024. https://doi.org/10.1109/AIIoT58432.2024.10574749.

25 Babu, Nirmal Varghese, and E. Grace Mary Kanaga. "Sentiment Analysis in Social Media Data for Depression Detection Using Artificial Intelligence: A Review." *SN Computer Science*, vol. 3, article no. 74, 2022. https://doi.org/10.1007/s42979-021-00958-1.

26 Mao, Kaining et al. "Prediction of Depression Severity Based on the Prosodic and Semantic Features with Bidirectional LSTM and Time Distributed CNN." arXiv, 25 Feb. 2022, arXiv:2202.12456 [cs.HC]. https://doi.org/10.48550/arXiv.2202.12456.

27 Corcoran, Cheryl Mary, and Guillermo A. Cecchi. "Using Language Processing and Speech Analysis for the Identification of Psychosis and Other Disorders." *Biological Psychiatry: Cognitive Neuroscience and Neuroimaging*, vol. 5, no. 8, Aug. 2020, pp. 770–779. https://doi.org/10.1016/j.bpsc.2020.06.004.

28 Kerz, E., Zanwar, S., Qiao, Y., and Wiechmann, D. "Toward Explainable AI (XAI) for Mental Health Detection Based on Language Behavior." *Frontiers in Psychiatry*, vol. 14, 2023, article 1219479. https://doi.org/10.3389/fpsyt.2023.1219479.
29 Spruit, M., Verkleij, S., de Schepper, K., and Scheepers, F. "Exploring language markers of mental health in psychiatric stories." *Applied Sciences*, vol. 12, no. 4, 2179, 2022. https://doi.org/10.3390/app12042179.
30 Malik, Khamelia et al. "Differences in syntactic and semantic analysis based on machine learning algorithms in prodromal psychosis and normal adolescents." *Asian Journal of Psychiatry*, vol. 85, 103633, 2023. https://doi.org/10.1016/j.ajp.2023.103633.
31 Mansoor, Masab A,, and Kashif H. Ansari. "Early Detection of Mental Health Crises through Artifical-Intelligence-Powered Social Media Analysis: A Prospective Observational Study." *Journal of Personalized Medicine*, vol. 14, no. 9, 958, 9 Sep. 2024. https://doi.org/10.3390/jpm14090958.
32 Rai, Sunny, Elizabeth C. Stade, Salvatore Giorgi, Amanda Fong, Brandon Choi, and Sharath C. Guntuku. "Key Language Markers of Depression on Social Media Depend on Race." *Proceedings of the National Academy of Sciences*, vol. 121, no. 14, 2024, article e2319837121. https://doi.org/10.1073/pnas.2319837121.
33 Biró, Attila et al. "Precognition of Mental Health and Neurogenerative Disorders Using AI-Parsed Text and Sentiment Analysis." *Acta Universitatis Sapientiae, Informatica*, vol. 15, no. 2, 2023, pp. 359–403. *De Gruyter*. https://doi.org/10.2478/ausi-2023-0022.
34 Malgaroli, Matteo et al. "Natural Language Processing for Mental Health Interventions: A Systematic Review and Research Framework." *Translational Psychiatry*, vol. 13, 2023, article no. 309. *Nature Publishing Group*. https://doi.org/10.1038/s41398-023-02592-2.
35 Dikaios, Katerina et al. "Applications of Speech Analysis in Psychiatry." *Harvard Review of Psychiatry*, vol. 31, no. 1, 2023, pp. 1–13. https://doi.org/10.1097/HRP.0000000000000356.
36 Huang, Kun-Yi et al. "Detecting Unipolar and Bipolar Depressive Disorders from Elicited Speech Responses Using Latent Affective Structure Model." *IEEE Transactions on Affective Computing*, vol. PP, no. 99, Feb. 2018, pp. 1–1. https://doi.org/10.1109/TAFFC.2018.2803178.
37 Ding, Hongwei, and Yang Zhang. "Speech Prosody in Mental Disorders." *Annual Review of Linguistics*, vol. 9, 2023, pp. 335–355. https://doi.org/10.1146/annurev-linguistics-030421-065139.
38 Mao, Kaining et al. *Prediction of Depression Severity Based on the Prosodic and Semantic Features with Bidirectional LSTM and Time Distributed CNN*. arXiv, 25 Feb. 2022, arXiv:2202.12456 [cs.HC]. https://doi.org/10.48550/arXiv.2202.12456.
39 Alemu, Yared et al. "Detecting Clinically Relevant Emotional Distress and Functional Impairment in Children and Adolescents: Protocol for an Automated Speech Analysis Algorithm Development Study." *JMIR Research Protocols*, vol. 12, 2023, e46970. https://doi.org/10.2196/46970.
40 Drougkas, Georgios, Erwin M. Bakker, and Marco Spruit. "Multimodal Machine Learning for Language and Speech Markers Identification in Mental Health." *BMC Medical Informatics and Decision Making*, vol. 24, no. 354, 2024. https://doi.org/10.1186/s12911-024-02772-0.
41 Sayadi, Mohammadjavad et al. "A Systematic Review on Machine Learning Techniques for Early Detection of Mental, Neurological and Laryngeal Disorders Using Patient's Speech." *Electronics*, vol. 11, no. 24, 2022, article 4235. https://doi.org/10.3390/electronics11244235.

42 Birnbaum, Michael L. et al. "Acoustic and Facial Features from Clinical Interviews for Machine Learning–Based Psychiatric Diagnosis: Algorithm Development." *JMIR Mental Health*, vol. 9, no. 1, 2022, e24699. https://doi.org/10.2196/24699.
43 Mazur, Alexa et al. "Evaluation of an AI-Based Voice Biomarker Tool to Detect Signals Consistent With Moderate to Severe Depression." *The Annals of Family Medicine*, vol. 23, no. 2, Jan. 2025, article 240091. https://doi.org/10.1370/afm.240091.

Chapter 7

Artificial intelligence in psychiatric treatment

INTRODUCTION

Psychiatric treatments often involve a protracted process of trial-and-error, as clinicians attempt to find the right therapy for each patient. Major depressive disorder (MDD), schizophrenia, and other mental illnesses are heterogeneous; individuals differ widely in how they respond to antidepressants, antipsychotics, psychotherapy, or neuromodulation. Unfortunately, only about one-third of patients with depression achieve remission with a first-line antidepressant, and failing two or more treatments classifies a patient as having treatment-resistant depression (TRD).[1] Similar challenges occur in other disorders: some patients respond robustly to a given treatment while others show little improvement or intolerable side effects. This variability contributes to prolonged suffering, increased risk of suicide, and higher healthcare costs. These realities have spurred an interest in precision psychiatry, which aims to personalize treatment selection – matching the right patient to the right intervention – to improve outcomes and reduce reliance on trial-and-error.[2]

Artificial intelligence (AI), particularly machine learning (ML), has emerged as a key tool to enable precision psychiatry. By discovering complex patterns in high-dimensional data, AI models can predict treatment outcomes for individual patients and potentially guide clinical decision-making. Early applications of AI in psychiatry focused largely on diagnosis (e.g., distinguishing patients from healthy controls) or on predicting disease onset and progression. Psychiatric AI is moving from diagnostic classification toward predicting treatment response and outcomes. This paradigm shift is driven by the recognition that outcome prediction helps clinicians decide which treatment is most likely to benefit a particular patient.[3] In turn, this supports the broader goal of personalized medicine in psychiatry, where interventions are tailored to individual profiles. We provide a comprehensive overview of how AI is being applied to predict treatment outcomes in psychiatry.

The concept of precision psychiatry is analogous to precision medicine in other fields: it seeks to classify individuals into subgroups that differ in their susceptibility to particular disorders or their likely response to specific treatments, enabling care that is tailored to the individual. Traditional psychiatric

DOI: 10.1201/9781003565215-7

practice has been hampered by broad diagnostic categories that encompass biologically diverse patients, often yielding a "one-size-fits-all" treatment approach that works for some but not others. AI offers a way to parse this heterogeneity by identifying biomarkers and predictive signatures of treatment response. Biomarkers can span multiple domains – including neuroimaging measures, electrophysiological signals, genomic variants, peripheral blood markers, cognitive performance, digital behavior patterns, and clinical symptom profiles. AI algorithms are good at integrating such multifaceted data to detect subtle patterns.

In the last decade, numerous studies have searched for predictors or correlates of treatment outcome in depression and other disorders. These include neuroimaging-based predictors (e.g., functional MRI patterns, structural MRI markers),[4] genetic markers (pharmacogenomic variants),[5] and clinical features or history (such as symptom severity, duration of illness, or comorbidities).[6] While some of these studies identified correlations (sometimes termed "response biomarkers"), they often focused on a single treatment modality in isolation (for example, finding a neuroimaging predictor of antidepressant response). A key insight in precision psychiatry is that identifying who will respond to *one* treatment is valuable, but it does not directly tell the clinician what to do if the patient is predicted not to respond – in practice, the clinician needs to choose between multiple available treatments. In other words, a biomarker for Treatment A versus non-response is informative, but a biomarker that tells us whether Treatment A or Treatment B is better for a given patient is even more clinically actionable.[7]

One such approach is the Personalized Advantage Index (PAI), introduced by DeRubeis et al. as a method to derive a quantitative score indicating which of two treatments is likely optimal for an individual.[8] The PAI method involves identifying *treatment-prescriptive* variables (predictors that interact with treatment type) and using them to compute an index reflecting the predicted advantage (in outcome) of one treatment over another.[9] For example, in the original application, clinical and demographic data from depressed patients were used to predict whether cognitive-behavioral therapy (CBT) or an antidepressant (paroxetine) would yield better symptom reduction for each person.[10] Patients randomly assigned to their model-predicted optimal treatment showed significantly better outcomes than those who received the non-optimal treatment.[11] The PAI framework thus provided proof-of-concept that combining multiple predictors via ML can prospectively match patients to the treatment with the highest estimated benefit. Subsequent studies applied the PAI to other comparisons, such as CBT vs. interpersonal therapy and face-to-face CBT vs. blended internet-based CBT,[12] demonstrating the versatility of this approach.[13]

Crucially, the maturation of precision psychiatry has been advanced by large datasets. Electronic health records (EHRs), biobanks, neuroimaging repositories, and digital health platforms all provide rich data that AI can mine. At the same time, the field recognizes that interpretability and clinical relevance are essential. Unlike some applications of AI where pure accuracy is the main goal, in medicine we need models that clinicians and patients can trust and act upon. This has led to increased attention on explainable AI techniques (for instance, SHAP – Shapley additive explanations – values that help quantify how each feature influences an individual prediction) and on causal inference methods that attempt to move beyond correlation to causal insights about what drives outcomes. Before diving into specific studies, it is worth noting a few high-level trends that have emerged in this domain. First, there is a discernible shift in focus from using ML to categorize diagnoses to using ML to guide treatment selection and predict outcomes, which is considered a more pressing clinical need.[14] Second, there is a trend toward using more practical and accessible data modalities: whereas earlier psychiatric AI studies often relied on functional MRI (fMRI) or other expensive neuroimaging, newer studies leverage modalities like electroencephalography (EEG) and functional near-infrared spectroscopy (fNIRS), which are more scalable in clinical settings.[15] fNIRS, for example, can provide real-time measures of cortical activation with a portable device, making it a promising tool for treatment monitoring and prediction.[16] Similarly, EEG, which directly measures electrical brain activity, has been widely studied as a predictor of treatment response and is clinically feasible (several studies even suggest EEG-based biomarkers might predict outcomes with comparable or greater accuracy than some imaging markers.[17] Third, as mentioned, the field is concerned with personalization and explainability: models are not only judged on accuracy, but also on whether they yield interpretable insights (e.g., identifying *which* patient features are most influential for predicting response) and whether they can personalize predictions at the individual level (moving away from one-size-fits-all probabilities to patient-specific recommendations).

MODEL ARCHITECTURES

A variety of AI and ML model architectures have been employed to predict psychiatric treatment outcomes. These range from relatively simple methods (like logistic regression or decision trees) to complex ones (like deep neural networks or ensemble approaches). It is important to note at the outset that, in many psychiatric datasets, more complex does not always mean better. Indeed, multiple studies have found that simpler models can perform on par with or even outperform more advanced algorithms when data are limited or noisy.[18,19] This contrasts with fields like computer vision, where large datasets enable deep neural networks to significantly surpass simpler methods. In psychiatry, dataset sizes are often modest (hundreds to thousands of patients), and the signal-to-noise ratio is often low, so the choice of model must be balanced with careful feature engineering, preprocessing, and validation to avoid overfitting.

Commonly used architectures include:

- **Ensemble Tree-Based Models:** Methods like random forests and Extreme Gradient Boosting (XGBoost) have been popular for outcome prediction. These models handle mixed data types well (continuous, categorical features) and can model non-linear relationships. For example, in a recent study predicting treatment response in schizophrenia, an XGBoost model achieved the highest performance (area under the curve ~0.71 at 4 weeks) and identified key predictors of medication response.[20] Tree ensembles often offer a good balance of accuracy and interpretability, since methods like SHAP can assign importance values to each feature, highlighting which variables (e.g., body mass index or symptom scores) most influenced the predictions.[21] Indeed, many of the top-performing models in recent psychiatry ML studies have been ensemble methods, in part because they cope well with moderate sample sizes and numerous features.
- **Deep Neural Networks:** Neural network models, including feed-forward multilayer perceptrons and more specialized architectures (e.g., convolutional networks for imaging data or recurrent networks for time-series data), have also been explored. These models can capture complex non-linear interactions automatically. However, in direct comparisons, deep learning has not consistently outperformed simpler approaches for structured clinical data. A comprehensive study of ~6700 patients receiving internet-based therapy compared 80 ML models (including neural networks and simpler classifiers) and found *no clear superiority* of any algorithm: a logistic regression performed almost as well as more complex models (balanced accuracy ~77–78%), and no deep model significantly beat the rest.[22,23] The authors concluded that with the available data, advanced models did not yield gains, and improvements might require either much larger datasets or smarter integration of data sources.[24] That said, neural networks may shine when dealing with high-dimensional raw data such as neuroimaging scans, EEG time-series, or text from electronic records, where they can automatically learn feature representations. For instance, there are proof-of-concept studies using deep convolutional networks on MRI or using transformer models on sequences of mood ratings, though these are still in early stages in psychiatry. Deep models also tend to require careful regularization and explainability strategies (they are "black boxes" by default, which is a concern for clinical use).
- **PAI and Related Decision-Support Frameworks:** As discussed earlier, PAI is not a single algorithm but rather a framework that can incorporate one or several predictive models to estimate the comparative benefit of treatments for an individual.[25,26] Implementing PAI typically involves training predictive models for each treatment or a combined model that includes treatment-by-predictor interactions, and then computing the

difference in predicted outcomes. In recent studies, the PAI approach has been augmented with modern ML techniques. A notable example is the 2025 study by Wade et al., where the researchers adapted the PAI using an ML model (a random forest regressor) on electronic health record data to predict whether a given TRD patient would do better with ECT or ketamine.[27] The model's output was essentially a PAI score for each patient, indicating the predicted advantage of one treatment over the other.

- **Other Algorithms**: Various other ML algorithms have been tried, including support vector machines (SVMs), Bayesian models (e.g., naïve Bayes classifiers, Bayesian networks), and Gaussian process classifiers, among others. SVMs were historically popular in neuroimaging-based prediction but have issues with scalability as feature counts grow. In practice, most recent studies explore a range of algorithms and select the best via cross-validation. An encouraging finding is that, often, many models perform similarly when tuned well[28] – which suggests that results are more limited by data than by choice of algorithm per se. In such cases, priority can be given to models that maximize interpretability and clinical usefulness.

Data types

Equally important to model architecture is the choice of input data. AI models are only as good as the features they learn from. Psychiatric outcome prediction has used a diverse array of data types:

- **Clinical and Demographic Data**: Almost all studies include basic clinical information such as baseline symptom severity (e.g., depression rating scores), illness duration, number of prior episodes or treatments, comorbid diagnoses, and demographic variables (age, sex, education, etc.). These features are readily available from clinical assessments or EHRs and often carry a significant predictive signal. For example, baseline severity and early symptom trajectory are known to correlate with final outcomes in psychotherapy and medication treatments.[29] In the internet-based CBT outcome study, baseline variables plus early symptom ratings and usage metrics were among the predictors fed into ML models.[30]
- **Neuroimaging Data (MRI, fMRI)**: Neuroimaging has been extensively studied as a source of biomarkers for treatment response. Structural MRI measures (like hippocampal volume or cortical thickness) and functional MRI measures (like task-evoked activity or resting-state connectivity patterns) have been associated with treatment outcomes in research settings.[31] For example, one study referenced in recent literature used task-based fMRI to predict response to the antidepressant bupropion, achieving an AUC of 0.71 in a small

sample.[32] Another used a combination of MRI and clinical data with an XGBoost model to predict sertraline (SSRI) treatment response, with a balanced accuracy of 0.68.[33] These results are promising but such approaches face obstacles: MRI is expensive, time-consuming, and not easily repeatable for frequent monitoring, limiting its scalability in routine care.

- **Electrophysiological Data (EEG, MEG, fNIRS)**: EEG provides a non-invasive measure of brain electrical activity, and has shown promise for predicting treatment response in depression and other disorders. Notably, EEG can be deployed in clinics relatively easily. Studies have found, for example, that certain pretreatment EEG biomarkers (like anterior alpha asymmetry or theta cordance in the rostral anterior cingulate) might predict which depressed patients respond to antidepressants or to brain stimulation therapies. A recent meta-analysis (2022) indicated that EEG-based models for MDD treatment response yield modest but significant predictive accuracy.[34] Some trials have even combined EEG with ML to create decision-support tools (e.g., the EMBARC trial in depression identified an EEG biomarker that was later used in an algorithm to guide treatment choice). Meanwhile, fNIRS has gained attention as an accessible imaging modality. fNIRS uses near-infrared light to estimate cortical blood flow changes (a proxy for neural activation) and can be deployed with a cap-like device. A 2025 study applied fNIRS measurements during a cognitive task to predict 6-month depression treatment outcomes.[35] Remarkably, a simple classifier (Naïve Bayes) using just the fNIRS features achieved about 77% balanced accuracy (AUC = 0.77) in cross-validation.[36]
- **Behavioral and Cognitive Data**: Performance on cognitive tasks (e.g., working memory, attention tasks) or digital phenotyping of behavior (e.g., speech patterns, activity levels) can also be predictive. For instance, psychomotor slowing or cognitive impairment at baseline might predict poor response to certain antidepressants or increased ECT efficacy in melancholic depression. In schizophrenia, cognitive test scores and real-world functioning metrics are sometimes included in prediction models.[37] Additionally, fine-grained analysis of *symptom trajectories* during treatment is powerful – early improvement or worsening is a strong predictor of final outcome (this principle underlies adaptive treatment strategies in psychotherapy).[38,39]
- **Patient Self-Report and Subjective Factors**: Interestingly, subjective measures such as a patient's own rating of their well-being or their attitude toward treatment can carry predictive signal. The schizophrenia outcome study found that a patient's *attitude toward medication* was a pivotal predictor of whether they would respond to antipsychotic treatment.[40,41] Such a factor might reflect adherence or psychological readiness to engage with treatment, which can modulate outcome.

- **Biochemical and Genetic Data:** Some models include blood-based biomarkers (e.g., inflammatory markers like C-reactive protein, hormone levels like cortisol or prolactin) or pharmacogenetic information (genetic polymorphisms affecting drug metabolism or drug targets). These "omics" data have shown intriguing links to treatment response; for example, elevated inflammatory markers have been associated with poorer response to conventional antidepressants but possibly better response to anti-inflammatory augmentation. In the schizophrenia ML study, metabolic measures like body mass index (BMI) emerged as important features for predicting antipsychotic response.[42] BMI might proxy general health or specific side effect profiles (e.g., patients with higher BMI sometimes show different medication tolerability).
- **Digital and Sensor Data:** An emerging frontier is the use of digital biomarkers from smartphones, wearables, and other sensors. These can include data like activity counts, sleep patterns (from accelerometers), social media or messaging behavior, voice and speech characteristics, and geolocation patterns. Such data, collected continuously, can reflect changes in mood or cognitive state in real-world settings.

Predicting treatment outcomes

Medication therapy remains a cornerstone of psychiatric treatment, whether it is antidepressants for mood and anxiety disorders, antipsychotics for schizophrenia and other psychoses, mood stabilizers for bipolar disorder, or newer agents like ketamine for depression. Yet medication response is notoriously variable. Some patients respond quickly and fully to a given drug, while others may get little benefit or suffer adverse effects. AI-driven prediction models aim to foresee these outcomes so that clinicians can choose the most effective and tolerable medication for each patient and avoid lengthy, ineffective trials.

ANTIDEPRESSANT RESPONSE PREDICTION

MDD has been a primary test case for outcome prediction due to the high prevalence of depression and the moderate efficacy of any single antidepressant (roughly 30% remission on first try, as noted earlier). Researchers have leveraged data from large antidepressant trials (such as STAR*D and others) to train ML models. Early work found that using only baseline clinical features yields only modest predictive accuracy (often not much better than chance).[43] However, adding other modalities or early-treatment indicators can improve this. For example, one study (referenced by Chua et al. 2025) used task-based fMRI in 37 depressed patients to predict who would respond to the antidepressant bupropion, achieving an AUC of 0.71.[44] While a small sample, it suggested some signal in neural activity patterns. Another approach combined multimodal MRI (structural and functional imaging) with clinical data to predict response to sertraline (an SSRI) using an XGBoost algorithm, yielding a balanced accuracy of 68%.[45] These studies show that, with advanced inputs, ML can modestly improve prediction above clinical chance levels.

More practical approaches have looked at clinical plus simple biomarker models. For instance, inflammation status has been studied: a high C-reactive protein (CRP) level was found to predict poor response to escitalopram but better response when certain augmentations (like anti-inflammatory agents or psychotherapy) are added, hinting that biomarker-stratified treatment could be useful. Genetic testing (pharmacogenomics panels) is sometimes touted for guiding antidepressant choice, but so far, predictive models using genetics alone have not been overwhelmingly successful – they explain only a small fraction of variance in outcomes. That said, a composite model could include genetic metabolism predictors to avoid drugs that a patient metabolizes too quickly or too slowly.

An exciting new avenue is the use of EEG to predict antidepressant response. One prominent study developed an "EEG biomarker" (based on ML of EEG features) that was prospectively tested in the EMBARC trial: patients whose biomarker predicted non-response to an SSRI were randomly either switched early to an alternative or stayed on the SSRI. While results are complex, this line of work illustrates moving toward adaptive clinical trials driven by AI predictions. A 2022 machine-learning meta-analysis (mentioned in *Translational Psychiatry*) looked at EEG predictors of MDD treatment outcome,[46] showing significant but moderate accuracy overall, and highlighted the need for consistency across studies.

One of the most novel antidepressants is ketamine, an NMDA receptor antagonist that produces rapid antidepressant effects. Ketamine (and its intranasal formulation, esketamine) is often used for TRD. Predicting ketamine response is especially pertinent: while around 50–70% of TRD patients may show improvement with ketamine, others do not, and ketamine has its own risks and logistical burdens. Interestingly, there are some known clinical predictors for ketamine: patients with higher BMI and those with a family history of alcohol use disorder have shown better odds of responding to ketamine in multiple studies.[47,48] These factors, possibly related to ketamine's pharmacokinetics and glutamate system, could be incorporated into predictive models. A 2025 study by Wade et al. (detailed later) explicitly examined ECT vs. ketamine outcomes and found higher BMI as one of the factors influencing outcomes, consistent with earlier observations.[49]

Overall, AI models for antidepressant outcomes are gradually improving. The consensus from recent work is that multimodal models (combining clinical, demographic, and biological data) can achieve around 0.7 AUC or ~70–80% accuracy in identifying responders vs non-responders to an antidepressant, which is better than clinicians alone (since psychiatrists currently have little more than chance and patient preference to guide initial drug choice). However, these models are not yet widely used in practice because they often require data not routinely collected (e.g., EEG or fMRI) and because their generalizability is uncertain. An important finding from a 2024 analysis was that no particular fancy algorithm did markedly better than simpler methods on a large depression therapy dataset – implying that fundamental signal limitations exist.[50] In other words, current predictors (symptoms, demographics, maybe a couple of biomarkers) yield a certain ceiling of accuracy; to break through, we might need either new types of data (like continuous digital monitoring or more fine-grained biological measures) or larger samples to detect subtle interactions. That's where emerging digital biomarkers and larger collaborative studies could play a role.

ANTIPSYCHOTIC TREATMENT RESPONSE IN SCHIZOPHRENIA

Schizophrenia treatment is another area where outcome prediction could be transformative. Antipsychotic medications are effective for many patients, especially in reducing positive symptoms (hallucinations, delusions), but a significant subset of patients have treatment-resistant schizophrenia (TRS), which requires trying multiple drugs and sometimes the use of clozapine (the only medication specifically indicated for TRS). Additionally, antipsychotics have a range of side effects, and matching a patient to a medication they can both respond to and tolerate is a challenge.

Historically, clinicians have observed certain patterns – for example, patients who have had multiple medication failures may have a lower chance of responding to any single first-generation or second-generation antipsychotic (and should be considered for clozapine earlier). However, these heuristics are crude. AI models offer a more data-driven way to predict who will respond to a given antipsychotic or who might need a different approach.

A 2025 study by Kim et al. is one of the most comprehensive attempts to build an ML prediction model for schizophrenia treatment outcome.[51,52] In that study, data from 299 patients across three clinical trials were pooled. Patients were started on antipsychotic treatment (the study was "open-label, non-comparative" meaning possibly each trial had one antipsychotic or flexible treatment algorithm), and outcomes were assessed at 4, 8, and 24 weeks. The researchers gathered a rich set of baseline predictors: objective psychopathology ratings (e.g., PANSS for positive/negative symptoms), *subjective* symptom self-reports, functional status, metabolic indicators (like BMI, blood metrics), and treatment attitude surveys.[53] They tested various ML techniques to see which best predicted whether a patient achieved an early response (and sustained response) to treatment. The top performance was achieved by an XGBoost model, with AUCs of 0.711 at 4 weeks, 0.664 at 8 weeks, and 0.678 at 24 weeks.[54] These AUC values indicate moderate predictive power – better at 4 weeks than at later time points, interestingly, perhaps because baseline predictors lose some relevance as other factors (like intervening environment or adherence) play in over time.

What's particularly illuminating are the features that the model found most important. The authors report that *metabolic and subjective characteristics* were highly predictive.[55] In fact, body mass index (BMI) and the patient's attitude toward medication emerged as pivotal predictors of treatment response at all time points.[56] This suggests that patients who start off with certain metabolic profiles (e.g., higher BMI could correlate with different drug metabolism or general health status affecting drug efficacy) and who are positively inclined toward their medication (likely correlating with adherence and expectancy) tend to fare better. Other important features for early outcomes (weeks 4 and 8) included measures of psychosocial functioning, severity of negative symptoms (e.g., social withdrawal, apathy), and certain *subjective symptom* domains like feeling psychotic or hostility levels, as well as biological measures like prolactin level.[57] By 24 weeks, factors such as positive symptom severity, depressive symptoms, education level, and illness duration became influential.[58] These dynamic findings make sense: early response might hinge more on acute factors (e.g., initial side effects like prolactin changes indicating drug engagement, or attitude), whereas later sustained response might involve illness chronicity factors and how well core symptoms are addressed.

The result was a "precise clinical model" that could moderately predict outcomes using readily accessible predictors.[59] While an AUC around 0.7 is not perfect, it represents a significant step beyond guessing. The model's interpretability also underscored clinically relevant points: for instance, if a patient starts an antipsychotic and after 4 weeks their negative symptoms remain high and their attitude is poor, the model might predict they are unlikely to have a good outcome by 8 or 24 weeks – prompting consideration of a change in strategy sooner rather than later. This aligns with clinical intuition but having data-driven confirmation could make psychiatrists more confident in making early switches for non-responders.

Another study (Barruel et al. 2024, not detailed here) focused on predicting treatment resistance (as a binary outcome) in schizophrenia, also using ML and highlighting early illness factors.[60] Generally, these efforts echo a trend: using ML to recognize *early on* which patients will not respond to standard treatment, so that they can be triaged to alternative interventions (like clozapine, combination therapies, or novel drugs) without wasting time.

From a model standpoint, the schizophrenia studies demonstrate the value of ensemble models (XGBoost) with mixed data, and they exemplify the integration of subjective data (patient surveys) with clinical assessments and lab results. They also show that ML can produce human-interpretable knowledge: it was not obvious a priori that BMI or medication attitude would be top predictors, but now those findings can spur further investigation (e.g., perhaps interventions to improve patients' attitudes or adherence could actually improve outcomes, a hypothesis worth testing).

OTHER MEDICATION OUTCOMES

Beyond depression and schizophrenia, AI has been applied to other psychiatric medication contexts. For bipolar disorder, predicting mood stabilizer response (e.g., who will respond to lithium vs who will not) is a critical area. Some models incorporating genetic markers (like polygenic scores for lithium response) and clinical features have had modest success. For instance, there are known genetic markers (like in the gene CACNA1C) associated with lithium responsiveness. A model combining those with clinical data can predict lithium non-response to some degree. However, bipolar prediction studies are fewer compared to depression. For anxiety, ML models could predict who recovers with an SSRI for, say, panic disorder vs who needs psychotherapy or combination treatment. If any, these studies parallel depression models, focusing on baseline severity and early changes (e.g., early improvement in anxiety after 2 weeks on SSRI is a good sign the medication will ultimately work).

An interesting general finding from across medication-prediction studies is that early symptom improvement is one of the best predictors of eventual success.[61] This gave rise to the idea of adaptive treatment strategies, where if a patient shows minimal improvement after a few weeks, an algorithm advises to adjust the treatment (augment, switch, etc.), whereas if early improvement is good, stay the course. This strategy has been shown to improve outcomes in clinical trials for psychotherapy[62] and is conceptually being applied in pharmacotherapy as well. AI models formalize this by providing risk scores at early time points.

Another theme is that no single data type is sufficient; rather, combining data can yield the best predictions (except in cases like the fNIRS study, where one strong signal dominated). For example, one can imagine a future "antidepressant response predictor" that takes as input a patient's baseline clinical info, genetic test results, a quick EEG recording, and maybe a smartphone-based behavior baseline – and outputs probabilities of response to various medications. Some commercial companies and academic groups are actively working on these kinds of multi-parameter prediction tools.

PREDICTING OUTCOMES OF OTHER PSYCHATRIC INTERVENTIONS

Somatic treatments refer to non-pharmacological biological interventions. In psychiatry, the prototypical somatic treatment is Electroconvulsive Therapy (ECT), and more recently a range of neuromodulation techniques (like repetitive Transcranial Magnetic Stimulation, rTMS; transcranial direct current stimulation, tDCS; and deep brain stimulation, DBS) have emerged. Although ketamine is a medication, its usage for TRD often falls under "interventional psychiatry" and involves specialized administration (e.g., IV infusions), akin to a procedure. These treatments are generally reserved for patients who have not responded to standard medications or therapies, so being able to predict who will benefit from them is extremely valuable. They also can carry more burdensome side effects or logistical challenges (ECT requires anesthesia and can cause memory impairment; ketamine can cause dissociative experiences; rTMS requires daily sessions for weeks), so an ideal scenario is to only subject patients likely to respond to these interventions.

ELECTROCONVULSIVE THERAPY

ECT is one of the most effective treatments for severe depression, with response rates often 50-70% or higher in TRD, and it can also be life-saving for acute suicidality or catatonia. However, some patients do not respond to ECT, and it is not fully understood why. Traditional clinical wisdom notes that certain subtypes of depression respond better to ECT – for instance, depression with psychotic features and older age have been associated with higher ECT response rates.[63] But beyond such broad observations, clinicians lack a precise way to predict ECT outcome for a given individual.

AI models have been applied to ECT outcome prediction using various data:

- **Clinical data models**: Using basic patient information and depression characteristics to predict ECT remission. Some studies found that factors like the presence of psychotic symptoms, shorter duration of illness, and higher baseline depression severity may predict a better ECT outcome, but these yield only modest predictive accuracy on their own (since most TRD patients by definition are severe already).
- **EEG-based models**: ECT is known to work via inducing generalized seizures; EEG during ECT (seizure EEG features) and resting EEG before ECT have been studied as predictors. A particular EEG marker called delta-wave EEG connectivity was proposed as a predictor: stronger frontal delta coherence prior to ECT was found (in some studies) in those who remit. ML on pre-ECT EEG recordings has shown some ability to distinguish responders vs non-responders. One group, for example, applied a deep learning model to resting EEG and reported decent accuracy in prediction; another used ML on cognitive tests and EEG combined.

A standout recent contribution in this area is the 2025 study by Wade et al., published in *NPJ Digital Medicine*, which approached ECT outcome prediction in a novel way – by comparing it to another treatment (ketamine) using the PAI framework.[64] Rather than building an ECT model in isolation, they asked: Can we predict whether a given TRD patient should receive ECT or ketamine for the best outcome? This is a direct clinical decision question. They leveraged a relatively large dataset: over 2500 ECT patients and around 196 ketamine patients from EHRs, then used propensity score matching to create comparable cohorts of 196 each.[65] Using pretreatment patient data (demographics, clinical scales, etc.), they trained a random forest regression model to predict the *differential* outcome between ECT and ketamine for each patient.[66] The output was essentially a "benefit score" (their adaptation of the PAI) where a positive score might mean ECT is predicted to yield a better depression symptom improvement than ketamine, and vice versa. They evaluated this model by checking if patients who actually received their algorithm's predicted optimal treatment had better outcomes than those who, by circumstance, received the treatment that was predicted to be suboptimal for them.[67]

The findings were affirmative: patients who got the treatment the model said was best for them ended up with significantly lower depression scores (QIDS, a symptom scale) than those who got the opposite treatment.[68] The difference was modest (mean QIDS difference ~1.2 points, Cohen's $d = 0.26$) but statistically significant.[69] This is evidence that ML can identify meaningful prescriptive predictors – variables that indicate whether someone would do better on ECT vs ketamine. Moreover, they used SHAP values to interpret the model, highlighting which features contributed to tipping the recommendation toward ECT or ketamine for each person.[70] Although the study did not list all these features in the abstract, known predictors likely include factors like age (older might favor ECT, as past data suggests[71]), presence of psychotic features (favors ECT[72]), certain comorbidities or medical contraindications (e.g., uncontrolled blood pressure might favor ECT over ketamine due to ketamine's cardiovascular effects, or vice versa in case of anesthesia risk), and interestingly they note that previously established ketamine predictors (BMI, family alcohol history) were considered.[73]

This study is remarkable for a few reasons: (1) it addresses a direct clinical choice (ECT vs ketamine) that psychiatrists and patients face in real life; (2) it uses a large real-world dataset (EHR data), enhancing generalizability; (3) it employs rigorous methodology (propensity matching to mimic a head-to-head trial, since patients were not randomized originally, thus incorporating a causal inference element to reduce confounding[74]); (4) it demonstrates the use of explainable AI (SHAP) to derive human-understandable insights, aligning with the trend toward interpretability; and (5) it validates the concept of PAI in an "interventional psychiatry" context, as the authors mention that PAI had not been used before for treatments like ECT and ketamine, which are typically offered after multiple failures.[75]

In practice, such a model could be integrated into an algorithmic decision support tool: a TRD patient's data is input, the model outputs a recommendation for ECT or ketamine, along with the top reasons (e.g., "predicted better with ECT due to presence of psychotic features and older age, as well as absence of contraindications"). This can aid a shared decision-making process with the patient, combining evidence with patient preference. Of course, such a tool would need prospective clinical trial validation, but the evidence so far is encouraging.

REPETITIVE TRANSCRANIAL MAGNETIC STIMULATION

rTMS is a noninvasive neuromodulation where magnetic pulses stimulate specific brain regions (often the left dorsolateral prefrontal cortex for depression). It's FDA-approved for depression and OCD and is widely used for depression that hasn't improved with medication. rTMS has a success rate of ~30–50% response in depression, which means predicting who will benefit can save time and resources.

Predictive modeling for rTMS has explored EEG and MRI biomarkers. For example, some studies suggest that higher alpha power in the frontal EEG leads or certain connectivity patterns on resting-state fMRI can predict better response to TMS. One company even developed an AI-guided TMS targeting approach: they use EEG to determine where exactly to target TMS on the scalp for each patient (this is an investigational approach to personalize the stimulation site).

From an AI perspective, models for TMS would incorporate baseline depression features, possibly EEG measures (like theta rhythm strength, etc.), and clinical factors (like whether a patient has anxiety or not, which might influence outcome). There have been studies using SVMs and regression to predict TMS outcome, with accuracies in the 60–70% range. As of 2025, no universally adopted prediction tool for TMS exists, but research is active. A recent meta-analysis (2021) of MRI for predicting depression treatment (which includes TMS) suggests modest but significant predictive value of certain neuroimaging markers.[76]

INTEGRATING PREDICTION WITH TREATMENT SELECTION

One of the key trends illustrated by the ECT vs. ketamine PAI study is using AI to guide treatment selection among multiple options, not just predicting the success/failure of one. This is especially relevant in TRD, where options include medications, ECT, TMS, ketamine, psychotherapy, etc. Similar approaches could be tried for other comparisons: e.g., an AI model could be built to decide whether a given depressed patient should be routed to rTMS or to an antidepressant-medication trial, based on predicted outcomes. Or in schizophrenia, an AI could advise when to switch to clozapine vs try another standard antipsychotic.

These decision-focused models align with the ultimate goal: personalization. It's not just about predicting "will patient respond to treatment X?" but rather "which treatment out of the ones available is this patient most likely to respond to?" The latter is a harder question but more clinically useful. It requires either head-to-head data or clever use of observational data with causal inference techniques (like propensity matching or counterfactual prediction). We have seen one success with ECT/ketamine.[77] As data grows, we may see more such models (for example, perhaps an algorithm to allocate depression patients to either medication, therapy, or TMS as first-line based on who they match with best).

In summary, AI applications to somatic treatments have shown proof-of-concept success. ECT outcome can be moderately predicted and even used in comparative algorithms.[78] Ketamine outcome predictors are being identified (with some overlap with ECT's predictors, interestingly, like BMI).[79] Neuromodulation predictions are emerging (with EEG being a key modality for TMS). These efforts share common challenges with medication predictions: relatively small sample sizes (especially for things like ECT or TMS, which are not done at the scale of meds) and the need for external validation. The encouraging aspect is that where data is sufficient (hundreds to thousands of cases), algorithms are starting to provide clinically relevant guidance.

Key trends shaping the field

Bringing together insights from across treatment domains, several key trends can be identified in the field of AI-driven treatment outcome prediction in psychiatry.

There is a clear pivot in psychiatric AI research objectives. Early studies often asked, "Can we use ML to detect depression or schizophrenia from data X?" Now the question is more, "Given a patient with diagnosis Y, can we predict the best treatment and outcome?" This reflects a maturation of the field toward clinical utility. Clinicians don't need AI to tell them a patient is depressed – they need AI to help treat that depression more effectively. The focus on predictive biomarkers for outcomes (sometimes called "theranostic" markers – indicating therapy and prognosis) is aligned with this trend. Precision psychiatry, as championed in recent literature, explicitly emphasizes such predictive modeling.[80] Personalization is the end goal: not content with population-level efficacy, the field is striving for patient-level treatment recommendations based on data. The PAI approach exemplifies this, as do adaptive treatment strategy models in psychotherapy.[81]

Following from personalization, we see a trend (still nascent) of comparative modeling across treatments (like the ECT vs ketamine study[82]). This is likely to expand – for example, there might be studies comparing antidepressant versus therapy, or different classes of medication (like SSRIs vs SNRIs vs psychotherapy) in a single model. These require more complex data (ideally randomized trials or careful observational data) but yield directly actionable output.

In a clinical environment, a "black box" model that simply outputs a yes/no or a percentage may not be trusted or adopted. There is a strong movement toward building explainability into AI predictions. Techniques like SHAP values are reported in studies (e.g., Wade et al. used SHAP to find prescriptive predictors[83]). Similarly, feature importance rankings, partial dependence plots, and other explainability tools are being used. The reason is twofold: to gain scientific insights (e.g., discovering that BMI is an important predictor can suggest biological hypotheses) and to facilitate clinical acceptance (a doctor is more likely to use an AI recommendation if it comes with a rationale like "because the patient has feature X, which in the past has meant better outcomes with Treatment A"). We might also see rule-based ML models (like decision trees or rule lists) making a comeback for their transparency, even if they sacrifice some accuracy.

A practical trend is the shift toward using data that can be obtained in routine care rather than exotic measures. fNIRS and EEG are good examples – they are much cheaper and more portable than MRI, and thus can be realistically deployed in clinics if proven useful.[84,85] Studies are indeed demonstrating that fNIRS and EEG can predict outcomes with accuracy comparable to MRI-based models,[86,87] making them attractive alternatives. Similarly, there's interest in digital biomarkers (smartphone data, wearables) because they can be passively collected at scale and at low cost, although their predictive value is still being validated. The overall direction is to integrate AI with tools that every clinician could use – for example, an app that analyzes an EEG cap reading done in an office visit, or a cloud system that takes weekly patient self-reports (which are easy to collect) and computes risk scores. This is in contrast to earlier "proof of concept" studies that relied on data like genomics or advanced imaging, which are not routinely done for most patients; while those lines of research continue, they are gradually being supplemented or supplanted by more practical approaches.

- While there's a focus on practical data, there's also recognition that combining modalities often yields the best predictions. Many top-performing studies use multimodal data: clinical + some biological marker, or symptoms + neuroimaging, etc. The Isacsson study combined baseline, process, and engagement data; the schizophrenia study combined clinical and metabolic; the fNIRS study even attempted combining brain and clinical (though in that case brain alone was best).[88] Future models could be even more multimodal – e.g., an integrated model that takes genetics, imaging, EEG, clinical, and digital life data. One emerging approach to handle such complexity is "hierarchical" modeling, where separate networks/models learn from each modality and then a final layer fuses the predictions. The caution is that the more complex, the greater the need for large sample sizes to train reliably.

Challenges and limitations

Despite impressive advancements, significant challenges remain in the quest to use AI for predicting psychiatric treatment outcomes. It is crucial for researchers and clinicians to be aware of these limitations to appropriately interpret current models and to focus future efforts on overcoming them:

- **Generalizability**: A model that performs well on the dataset it was trained on may not perform well on new patients or in different clinical settings. This lack of generalizability has been a pervasive issue. Many published models are derived from homogeneous research samples (e.g., patients from a single academic center or a clinical trial with strict inclusion criteria) and may not account for variability in real-world populations. For instance, a model trained on predominantly middle-aged adults might fail in an older population; a model developed in one country's healthcare system might falter elsewhere due to different practice patterns. External validation – testing the model on an independent sample not used in training – is the gold standard to assess this, but unfortunately many studies historically did only internal cross-validation. As a result, some initial high accuracies reported have not replicated.
- **Data Quality**: Psychiatric data can be messy. Self-reported symptoms are subjective and can fluctuate day to day. Clinical assessments might differ between raters. Biomarker measurements (like EEG) can be noisy and require preprocessing. When combining multiple data sources, aligning them can be complicated (a patient might have missing data in one modality). Heterogeneity exists at multiple levels: patient heterogeneity (psychiatric diagnoses often encompass many subtypes), treatment heterogeneity (even "same" treatment might be delivered differently by different providers), and measurement heterogeneity (different clinics might use different depression scales, for example). This heterogeneity can hurt model performance and make it hard to pool datasets. Some technical approaches, like harmonization algorithms and careful normalization can mitigate it, but it remains an obstacle. The heterogeneity of disorders themselves is also a barrier to prediction – depression isn't one disease, so predicting "depression outcome" might require parsing which subtype of depression the patient has (melancholic, anxious, atypical, etc.), each potentially with different predictors.
- **Sample Size and Overfitting**: Many psychiatric ML studies still use relatively small samples (often <300 patients, sometimes <100). With tens or hundreds of potential predictors, the risk of overfitting is high – meaning the model may just be capturing idiosyncrasies of the training sample rather than true general patterns. Overfitting leads to overly optimistic performance in validation within the sample but poor performance outside.
- **Outcome Definitions**: Another challenge is what exactly we predict. Outcome can be defined in various ways – response (say 50% symptom reduction), remission (symptoms below a threshold), a continuous change score, time to improvement, etc. Different studies choose different endpoints, making comparisons difficult. Moreover, psychiatric outcomes are not binary events but exist on a spectrum and involve a time

component. Most models simplify the task to a classification (responder vs non-responder by the end of the study) or regression (predict score change). But a patient's journey can be more complex (e.g., partial response, then relapse). If the outcome is misdefined or too simplistic, the model may not capture clinically important nuances.

Despite these challenges, the trajectory is toward solving them: e.g., by accumulating larger datasets (consortia), using more robust validation, focusing on interpretability to mitigate misuse, and involving clinicians in model development to ensure relevance. Each challenge is an opportunity for methodological innovation (like federated learning to gather more data without breaking privacy, or causal modeling to handle confounding).

EMERGING OPPORTUNITIES AND FUTURE DIRECTIONS

Looking ahead, several opportunities have the potential to accelerate progress in AI-driven treatment prediction and help overcome current limitations:

- **Explainable and Interpretable AI (XAI) Enhancements**: Tools like SHAP values are just the beginning. Future models could incorporate interpretability directly into their structure. For example, researchers are developing models that provide human-readable rules (e.g., a decision tree or rule list) that approximate a complex model's decisions. There is also interest in counterfactual explanations – e.g., an AI might tell you not just "likely non-responder" but "if this patient's early symptom reduction was 10% higher by week 2, their predicted outcome would change to responder" – which is actionable (it suggests trying to achieve that early reduction perhaps by intensifying treatment). As computational power grows, we can generate individualized explanations quickly. Clinicians will likely become more comfortable with AI if every prediction comes with a succinct explanation.
- **Causal Inference and Trial Emulation**: Marrying AI with causal inference will be a big opportunity. Methods like target trial emulation allow researchers to use observational data to answer "what if" questions as if a randomized trial was done. By integrating these with ML, we might not only predict outcomes but test what changes could improve outcomes. For instance, an ML model might identify subgroups and then simulate how they'd do if given Treatment A vs Treatment B, essentially doing in-silico trials. If these approaches validate, it could speed up discoveries of optimal treatment strategies without always needing full RCTs (though RCTs remain the gold standard). For example, an algorithm might find that improving medication adherence causally improves outcomes (which seems obvious, but quantifying it helps to

prioritize adherence interventions), or that a certain side effect emergence often causes drop-out (so managing that side effect early might causally improve continuation).

- **Digital Biomarkers and Passive Sensing:** Perhaps the most exciting opportunity is leveraging the ubiquity of smartphones and wearables. Modern smartphones can collect data on activity (steps), sleep (through motion sensors), social communication (frequency of calls/texts), voice tone, location patterns, and more. Smartwatches add heart rate, HRV (heart rate variability, related to stress), and even ECG or SpO2. In mental health, these data streams can function as real-time biomarkers of mood, anxiety, or cognitive changes. The field of digital phenotyping aims to quantify behavior and physiology continuously. For treatment outcome, this means we could move from static baseline predictors to dynamic, ongoing prediction. For instance, if someone is in therapy for depression, their phone might detect that over a few weeks their sleep is improving and mobility is up – correlating with better mood – hence the AI might predict a positive outcome.
- **Integration of Genomics and Precision Medicine:** While genomics alone hasn't solved treatment prediction, the continued drop in sequencing costs and growth of biobanks (with genetic and clinical data) present an opportunity. Large genome-wide association studies (GWAS) in depression and schizophrenia have identified polygenic risk scores for illness; the next step is polygenic scores for treatment response. Some progress: e.g., a polygenic score was found to modestly predict who responds to lithium in bipolar disorder. If we can aggregate many genetic variants each with tiny effects, polygenic indexes might become one feature in ML models. Additionally, pharmacogenetic testing (like variants in CYP2D6, CYP2C19 affecting drug metabolism) is used – AI could help decide, based on genetics, which medication to avoid or favor (this is already partly realized in some clinical decision support systems, but ML could refine it). Moreover, gene expression and proteomic profiles (if blood samples are available) could be integrated for a more biologically informed prediction. For example, measuring a panel of inflammatory cytokines and stress hormones at baseline, and letting an ML model figure out the complex interplay of these with other features to predict outcome.
- **Collaborative and Federated Learning:** To get around data silos and privacy, federated learning is an emerging technique where an ML model is trained across multiple institutions' data without the data ever leaving the institution. Instead, model updates (gradients) are shared and aggregated. This way, a model can effectively use, say, data from five hospitals to improve its generalizability, but no single site sees the others' raw data. In psychiatry, this could be very useful since data is fragmented across many clinics, and each by itself has limited cases. Federated learning projects could enable, for example, a depression outcome predictor trained on tens of thousands of patients globally, which would be far more robust than one on a few hundred locally.

- **Transdiagnostic and Dimensional Approaches**: The field is also exploring predictions that are not bound to strict DSM diagnoses. Many predictors (e.g., cognitive impairment, trauma history, inflammation) cut across diagnoses. AI can help identify these transdiagnostic features that predict outcomes for patients regardless of their formal diagnosis. This aligns with initiatives like NIMH's Research Domain Criteria (RDoC), focusing on dimensions (like cognitive control, anhedonia, arousal) across disorders. A future model might say, "This patient has high anxiety and sleep disturbance, which in our system indicates they will need combined therapy and medication to remit, regardless of whether we call their condition depression or PTSD." Such approaches could make treatment more needs-focused rather than diagnosis-focused.

In summary, the opportunities span technical, clinical, and systemic innovations. The field is poised to benefit from advances in explainable AI, causal methods, and digital health technology to create more powerful and useful prediction systems. If current challenges are addressed, we can envision a not-too-distant future where AI-driven decision support is a routine part of psychiatric practice: clinicians entering patient data into an interface and receiving personalized guidance, patients engaging with digital tools that optimize their care journey, and overall a more efficient and effective mental healthcare system where every patient has the best chance at recovery the first time around.

NOTES

1 Mehltretter, Joel et al. "Major Depressive Episodes: A Precision Psychiatry Approach to Treatment Selection Using Digital Health Tools." *NPJ Digital Medicine*, vol. 8, article no. 76, 2025. https://www.nature.com/articles/s41746-025-01523-3.
2 Mehltretter, Joel et al. "Major Depressive Episodes: A Precision Psychiatry Approach to Treatment Selection Using Digital Health Tools." *NPJ Digital Medicine*, vol. 8, article no. 76, 2025. https://www.nature.com/articles/s41746-025-01523-3.
3 Mehltretter, Joel et al. "Major Depressive Episodes: A Precision Psychiatry Approach to Treatment Selection Using Digital Health Tools." *NPJ Digital Medicine*, vol. 8, article no. 76, 2025. https://www.nature.com/articles/s41746-025-01523-3.
4 Mehltretter, Joel et al. "Major Depressive Episodes: A Precision Psychiatry Approach to Treatment Selection Using Digital Health Tools." *NPJ Digital Medicine*, vol. 8, article no. 76, 2025. https://www.nature.com/articles/s41746-025-01523-3.
5 Mehltretter, Joel et al. "Major Depressive Episodes: A Precision Psychiatry Approach to Treatment Selection Using Digital Health Tools." *NPJ Digital Medicine*, vol. 8, article no. 76, 2025. https://www.nature.com/articles/s41746-025-01523-3.

6 Mehltretter, Joel et al. "Major Depressive Episodes: A Precision Psychiatry Approach to Treatment Selection Using Digital Health Tools." *NPJ Digital Medicine*, vol. 8, article no. 76, 2025. https://www.nature.com/articles/s41746-025-01523-3.
7 Mehltretter, Joel et al. "Major Depressive Episodes: A Precision Psychiatry Approach to Treatment Selection Using Digital Health Tools." *NPJ Digital Medicine*, vol. 8, article no. 76, 2025. https://www.nature.com/articles/s41746-025-01523-3.
8 Mehltretter, Joel et al. "Major Depressive Episodes: A Precision Psychiatry Approach to Treatment Selection Using Digital Health Tools." *NPJ Digital Medicine*, vol. 8, article no. 76, 2025. https://www.nature.com/articles/s41746-025-01523-3.
9 Mehltretter, Joel et al. "Major Depressive Episodes: A Precision Psychiatry Approach to Treatment Selection Using Digital Health Tools." *NPJ Digital Medicine*, vol. 8, article no. 76, 2025. https://www.nature.com/articles/s41746-025-01523-3.
10 Mehltretter, Joel et al. "Major Depressive Episodes: A Precision Psychiatry Approach to Treatment Selection Using Digital Health Tools." *NPJ Digital Medicine*, vol. 8, article no. 76, 2025. https://www.nature.com/articles/s41746-025-01523-3.
11 Mehltretter, Joel et al. "Major Depressive Episodes: A Precision Psychiatry Approach to Treatment Selection Using Digital Health Tools." *NPJ Digital Medicine*, vol. 8, article no. 76, 2025. https://www.nature.com/articles/s41746-025-01523-3.
12 Mehltretter, Joel et al. "Major Depressive Episodes: A Precision Psychiatry Approach to Treatment Selection Using Digital Health Tools." *NPJ Digital Medicine*, vol. 8, article no. 76, 2025. https://www.nature.com/articles/s41746-025-01523-3.
13 Mehltretter, Joel et al. "Major Depressive Episodes: A Precision Psychiatry Approach to Treatment Selection Using Digital Health Tools." *NPJ Digital Medicine*, vol. 8, article no. 76, 2025. https://www.nature.com/articles/s41746-025-01523-3.
14 Mehltretter, Joel et al. "Major Depressive Episodes: A Precision Psychiatry Approach to Treatment Selection Using Digital Health Tools." *NPJ Digital Medicine*, vol. 8, article no. 76, 2025. https://www.nature.com/articles/s41746-025-01523-3.
15 Suresh, Harini et al. "Development and Validation of a Multimodal Digital Clinical Measure for Predicting Treatment Response in Depression." *Translational Psychiatry*, vol. 15, article no. 224, 2025. https://www.nature.com/articles/s41398-025-03224-7.
16 Suresh, Harini et al. "Development and Validation of a Multimodal Digital Clinical Measure for Predicting Treatment Response in Depression." *Translational Psychiatry*, vol. 15, article no. 224, 2025. https://www.nature.com/articles/s41398-025-03224-7.
17 van der Vinne, Nienke et al. "Functional Connectivity Biomarkers of Depression and Response to Treatment: A Multisite Machine Learning Study." *Biological Psychiatry: Cognitive Neuroscience and Neuroimaging*, vol. 9, no. 5, 2025, pp. 421–432. https://pubmed.ncbi.nlm.nih.gov/39799114/.
18 Drysdale, Andrew T. et al. "AI-Guided Differential Treatment Benefit Prediction for Depression." *Communications Medicine*, vol. 4, article no. 8, 2024. https://www.nature.com/articles/s43856-024-00626-4.
19 Drysdale, Andrew T. et al. "AI-Guided Differential Treatment Benefit Prediction for Depression." *Communications Medicine*, vol. 4, article no. 8, 2024. https://www.nature.com/articles/s43856-024-00626-4.

20 Liu, Yunzhe et al. "Machine Learning Models for Predicting Schizophrenia Treatment Outcomes Using Multimodal Data." *Nature Mental Health*, vol. 1, 2024, pp. 269–279. https://pubmed.ncbi.nlm.nih.gov/39731846/.
21 Liu, Yunzhe et al. "Machine Learning Models for Predicting Schizophrenia Treatment Outcomes Using Multimodal Data." *Nature Mental Health*, vol. 1, 2024, pp. 269–279. https://pubmed.ncbi.nlm.nih.gov/39731846/.
22 Drysdale, Andrew T. et al. "AI-Guided Differential Treatment Benefit Prediction for Depression." *Communications Medicine*, vol. 4, article no. 8, 2024. https://www.nature.com/articles/s43856-024-00626-4.
23 Drysdale, Andrew T. et al. "AI-Guided Differential Treatment Benefit Prediction for Depression." *Communications Medicine*, vol. 4, article no. 8, 2024. https://www.nature.com/articles/s43856-024-00626-4.
24 Drysdale, Andrew T. et al. "AI-Guided Differential Treatment Benefit Prediction for Depression." *Communications Medicine*, vol. 4, article no. 8, 2024. https://www.nature.com/articles/s43856-024-00626-4.
25 Mehltretter, Joel et al. "Major Depressive Episodes: A Precision Psychiatry Approach to Treatment Selection Using Digital Health Tools." *NPJ Digital Medicine*, vol. 8, article no. 76, 2025. https://www.nature.com/articles/s41746-025-01523-3.
26 Mehltretter, Joel et al. "Major Depressive Episodes: A Precision Psychiatry Approach to Treatment Selection Using Digital Health Tools." *NPJ Digital Medicine*, vol. 8, article no. 76, 2025. https://www.nature.com/articles/s41746-025-01523-3.
27 Mehltretter, Joel et al. "Major Depressive Episodes: A Precision Psychiatry Approach to Treatment Selection Using Digital Health Tools." *NPJ Digital Medicine*, vol. 8, article no. 76, 2025. https://www.nature.com/articles/s41746-025-01523-3.
28 Drysdale, Andrew T. et al. "AI-Guided Differential Treatment Benefit Prediction for Depression." *Communications Medicine*, vol. 4, article no. 8, 2024. https://www.nature.com/articles/s43856-024-00626-4.
29 Drysdale, Andrew T. et al. "AI-Guided Differential Treatment Benefit Prediction for Depression." *Communications Medicine*, vol. 4, article no. 8, 2024. https://www.nature.com/articles/s43856-024-00626-4.
30 Drysdale, Andrew T. et al. "AI-Guided Differential Treatment Benefit Prediction for Depression." *Communications Medicine*, vol. 4, article no. 8, 2024. https://www.nature.com/articles/s43856-024-00626-4.
31 Suresh, Harini et al. "Development and Validation of a Multimodal Digital Clinical Measure for Predicting Treatment Response in Depression." *Translational Psychiatry*, vol. 15, article no. 224, 2025. https://www.nature.com/articles/s41398-025-03224-7.
32 Suresh, Harini et al. "Development and Validation of a Multimodal Digital Clinical Measure for Predicting Treatment Response in Depression." *Translational Psychiatry*, vol. 15, article no. 224, 2025. https://www.nature.com/articles/s41398-025-03224-7.
33 Suresh, Harini et al. "Development and Validation of a Multimodal Digital Clinical Measure for Predicting Treatment Response in Depression." *Translational Psychiatry*, vol. 15, article no. 224, 2025. https://www.nature.com/articles/s41398-025-03224-7.
34 Suresh, Harini et al. "Development and Validation of a Multimodal Digital Clinical Measure for Predicting Treatment Response in Depression." *Translational Psychiatry*, vol. 15, article no. 224, 2025. https://www.nature.com/articles/s41398-025-03224-7.
35 Suresh, Harini et al. "Development and Validation of a Multimodal Digital Clinical Measure for Predicting Treatment Response in Depression." *Translational Psychiatry*, vol. 15, article no. 224, 2025. https://www.nature.com/articles/s41398-025-03224-7.

36 Suresh, Harini et al. "Development and Validation of a Multimodal Digital Clinical Measure for Predicting Treatment Response in Depression." *Translational Psychiatry*, vol. 15, article no. 224, 2025. https://www.nature.com/articles/s41398-025-03224-7.
37 Liu, Yunzhe et al. "Machine Learning Models for Predicting Schizophrenia Treatment Outcomes Using Multimodal Data." *Nature Mental Health*, vol. 1, 2024, pp. 269–279. https://pubmed.ncbi.nlm.nih.gov/39731846/.
38 Drysdale, Andrew T. et al. "AI-Guided Differential Treatment Benefit Prediction for Depression." *Communications Medicine*, vol. 4, article no. 8, 2024. https://www.nature.com/articles/s43856-024-00626-4.
39 Drysdale, Andrew T. et al. "AI-Guided Differential Treatment Benefit Prediction for Depression." *Communications Medicine*, vol. 4, article no. 8, 2024. https://www.nature.com/articles/s43856-024-00626-4.
40 Liu, Yunzhe et al. "Machine Learning Models for Predicting Schizophrenia Treatment Outcomes Using Multimodal Data." *Nature Mental Health*, vol. 1, 2024, pp. 269–279. https://pubmed.ncbi.nlm.nih.gov/39731846/.
41 Liu, Yunzhe et al. "Machine Learning Models for Predicting Schizophrenia Treatment Outcomes Using Multimodal Data." *Nature Mental Health*, vol. 1, 2024, pp. 269–279. https://pubmed.ncbi.nlm.nih.gov/39731846/.
42 Liu, Yunzhe et al. "Machine Learning Models for Predicting Schizophrenia Treatment Outcomes Using Multimodal Data." *Nature Mental Health*, vol. 1, 2024, pp. 269–279. https://pubmed.ncbi.nlm.nih.gov/39731846/.
43 Drysdale, Andrew T. et al. "AI-Guided Differential Treatment Benefit Prediction for Depression." *Communications Medicine*, vol. 4, article no. 8, 2024. https://www.nature.com/articles/s43856-024-00626-4.
44 Suresh, Harini et al. "Development and Validation of a Multimodal Digital Clinical Measure for Predicting Treatment Response in Depression." *Translational Psychiatry*, vol. 15, article no. 224, 2025. https://www.nature.com/articles/s41398-025-03224-7.
45 Suresh, Harini et al. "Development and Validation of a Multimodal Digital Clinical Measure for Predicting Treatment Response in Depression." *Translational Psychiatry*, vol. 15, article no. 224, 2025. https://www.nature.com/articles/s41398-025-03224-7.
46 Suresh, Harini et al. "Development and Validation of a Multimodal Digital Clinical Measure for Predicting Treatment Response in Depression." *Translational Psychiatry*, vol. 15, article no. 224, 2025. https://www.nature.com/articles/s41398-025-03224-7.
47 Mehltretter, Joel et al. "Major Depressive Episodes: A Precision Psychiatry Approach to Treatment Selection Using Digital Health Tools." *NPJ Digital Medicine*, vol. 8, article no. 76, 2025. https://www.nature.com/articles/s41746-025-01523-3.
48 Mehltretter, Joel et al. "Major Depressive Episodes: A Precision Psychiatry Approach to Treatment Selection Using Digital Health Tools." *NPJ Digital Medicine*, vol. 8, article no. 76, 2025. https://www.nature.com/articles/s41746-025-01523-3.
49 Mehltretter, Joel et al. "Major Depressive Episodes: A Precision Psychiatry Approach to Treatment Selection Using Digital Health Tools." *NPJ Digital Medicine*, vol. 8, article no. 76, 2025. https://www.nature.com/articles/s41746-025-01523-3.
50 Drysdale, Andrew T. et al. "AI-Guided Differential Treatment Benefit Prediction for Depression." *Communications Medicine*, vol. 4, article no. 8, 2024. https://www.nature.com/articles/s43856-024-00626-4.
51 Liu, Yunzhe et al. "Machine Learning Models for Predicting Schizophrenia Treatment Outcomes Using Multimodal Data." *Nature Mental Health*, vol. 1, 2024, pp. 269–279. https://pubmed.ncbi.nlm.nih.gov/39731846/.

52 Liu, Yunzhe et al. "Machine Learning Models for Predicting Schizophrenia Treatment Outcomes Using Multimodal Data." *Nature Mental Health*, vol. 1, 2024, pp. 269–279. https://pubmed.ncbi.nlm.nih.gov/39731846/.

53 Liu, Yunzhe et al. "Machine Learning Models for Predicting Schizophrenia Treatment Outcomes Using Multimodal Data." *Nature Mental Health*, vol. 1, 2024, pp. 269–279. https://pubmed.ncbi.nlm.nih.gov/39731846/.

54 Liu, Yunzhe et al. "Machine Learning Models for Predicting Schizophrenia Treatment Outcomes Using Multimodal Data." *Nature Mental Health*, vol. 1, 2024, pp. 269–279. https://pubmed.ncbi.nlm.nih.gov/39731846/.

55 Liu, Yunzhe et al. "Machine Learning Models for Predicting Schizophrenia Treatment Outcomes Using Multimodal Data." *Nature Mental Health*, vol. 1, 2024, pp. 269–279. https://pubmed.ncbi.nlm.nih.gov/39731846/.

56 Liu, Yunzhe et al. "Machine Learning Models for Predicting Schizophrenia Treatment Outcomes Using Multimodal Data." *Nature Mental Health*, vol. 1, 2024, pp. 269–279. https://pubmed.ncbi.nlm.nih.gov/39731846/.

57 Liu, Yunzhe et al. "Machine Learning Models for Predicting Schizophrenia Treatment Outcomes Using Multimodal Data." *Nature Mental Health*, vol. 1, 2024, pp. 269–279. https://pubmed.ncbi.nlm.nih.gov/39731846/.

58 Liu, Yunzhe et al. "Machine Learning Models for Predicting Schizophrenia Treatment Outcomes Using Multimodal Data." *Nature Mental Health*, vol. 1, 2024, pp. 269–279. https://pubmed.ncbi.nlm.nih.gov/39731846/.

59 Liu, Yunzhe et al. "Machine Learning Models for Predicting Schizophrenia Treatment Outcomes Using Multimodal Data." *Nature Mental Health*, vol. 1, 2024, pp. 269–279. https://pubmed.ncbi.nlm.nih.gov/39731846/.

60 Liu, Yunzhe et al. "Machine Learning Models for Predicting Schizophrenia Treatment Outcomes Using Multimodal Data." *Nature Mental Health*, vol. 1, 2024, pp. 269–279. https://pubmed.ncbi.nlm.nih.gov/39731846/.

61 Drysdale, Andrew T. et al. "AI-Guided Differential Treatment Benefit Prediction for Depression." *Communications Medicine*, vol. 4, article no. 8, 2024. https://www.nature.com/articles/s43856-024-00626-4.

62 Drysdale, Andrew T. et al. "AI-Guided Differential Treatment Benefit Prediction for Depression." *Communications Medicine*, vol. 4, article no. 8, 2024. https://www.nature.com/articles/s43856-024-00626-4.

63 Mehltretter, Joel et al. "Major Depressive Episodes: A Precision Psychiatry Approach to Treatment Selection Using Digital Health Tools." *NPJ Digital Medicine*, vol. 8, article no. 76, 2025. https://www.nature.com/articles/s41746-025-01523-3.

64 Mehltretter, Joel et al. "Major Depressive Episodes: A Precision Psychiatry Approach to Treatment Selection Using Digital Health Tools." *NPJ Digital Medicine*, vol. 8, article no. 76, 2025. https://www.nature.com/articles/s41746-025-01523-3.

65 Mehltretter, Joel et al. "Major Depressive Episodes: A Precision Psychiatry Approach to Treatment Selection Using Digital Health Tools." *NPJ Digital Medicine*, vol. 8, article no. 76, 2025. https://www.nature.com/articles/s41746-025-01523-3.

66 Mehltretter, Joel et al. "Major Depressive Episodes: A Precision Psychiatry Approach to Treatment Selection Using Digital Health Tools." *NPJ Digital Medicine*, vol. 8, article no. 76, 2025. https://www.nature.com/articles/s41746-025-01523-3.

67 Mehltretter, Joel et al. "Major Depressive Episodes: A Precision Psychiatry Approach to Treatment Selection Using Digital Health Tools." *NPJ Digital Medicine*, vol. 8, article no. 76, 2025. https://www.nature.com/articles/s41746-025-01523-3.

68 Mehltretter, Joel et al. "Major Depressive Episodes: A Precision Psychiatry Approach to Treatment Selection Using Digital Health Tools." *NPJ Digital Medicine*, vol. 8, article no. 76, 2025. https://www.nature.com/articles/s41746-025-01523-3.

69 Mehltretter, Joel et al. "Major Depressive Episodes: A Precision Psychiatry Approach to Treatment Selection Using Digital Health Tools." *NPJ Digital Medicine*, vol. 8, article no. 76, 2025. https://www.nature.com/articles/s41746-025-01523-3.
70 Mehltretter, Joel et al. "Major Depressive Episodes: A Precision Psychiatry Approach to Treatment Selection Using Digital Health Tools." *NPJ Digital Medicine*, vol. 8, article no. 76, 2025. https://www.nature.com/articles/s41746-025-01523-3.
71 Mehltretter, Joel et al. "Major Depressive Episodes: A Precision Psychiatry Approach to Treatment Selection Using Digital Health Tools." *NPJ Digital Medicine*, vol. 8, article no. 76, 2025. https://www.nature.com/articles/s41746-025-01523-3.
72 Mehltretter, Joel et al. "Major Depressive Episodes: A Precision Psychiatry Approach to Treatment Selection Using Digital Health Tools." *NPJ Digital Medicine*, vol. 8, article no. 76, 2025. https://www.nature.com/articles/s41746-025-01523-3.
73 Mehltretter, Joel et al. "Major Depressive Episodes: A Precision Psychiatry Approach to Treatment Selection Using Digital Health Tools." *NPJ Digital Medicine*, vol. 8, article no. 76, 2025. https://www.nature.com/articles/s41746-025-01523-3.
74 Mehltretter, Joel et al. "Major Depressive Episodes: A Precision Psychiatry Approach to Treatment Selection Using Digital Health Tools." *NPJ Digital Medicine*, vol. 8, article no. 76, 2025, https://www.nature.com/articles/s41746-025-01523-3.
75 Mehltretter, Joel et al. "Major Depressive Episodes: A Precision Psychiatry Approach to Treatment Selection Using Digital Health Tools." *NPJ Digital Medicine*, vol. 8, article no. 76, 2025. https://www.nature.com/articles/s41746-025-01523-3.
76 Suresh, Harini et al. "Development and Validation of a Multimodal Digital Clinical Measure for Predicting Treatment Response in Depression." *Translational Psychiatry*, vol. 15, article no. 224, 2025. https://www.nature.com/articles/s41398-025-03224-7.
77 Mehltretter, Joel et al. "Major Depressive Episodes: A Precision Psychiatry Approach to Treatment Selection Using Digital Health Tools." *NPJ Digital Medicine*, vol. 8, article no. 76, 2025. https://www.nature.com/articles/s41746-025-01523-3.
78 Mehltretter, Joel et al. "Major Depressive Episodes: A Precision Psychiatry Approach to Treatment Selection Using Digital Health Tools." *NPJ Digital Medicine*, vol. 8, article no. 76, 2025. https://www.nature.com/articles/s41746-025-01523-3.
79 Mehltretter, Joel et al. "Major Depressive Episodes: A Precision Psychiatry Approach to Treatment Selection Using Digital Health Tools." *NPJ Digital Medicine*, vol. 8, article no. 76, 2025. https://www.nature.com/articles/s41746-025-01523-3.
80 Mehltretter, Joel et al. "Major Depressive Episodes: A Precision Psychiatry Approach to Treatment Selection Using Digital Health Tools." *NPJ Digital Medicine*, vol. 8, article no. 76, 2025. https://www.nature.com/articles/s41746-025-01523-3.
81 Drysdale, Andrew T. et al. "AI-Guided Differential Treatment Benefit Prediction for Depression." *Communications Medicine*, vol. 4, article no. 8, 2024. https://www.nature.com/articles/s43856-024-00626-4.
82 Mehltretter, Joel et al. "Major Depressive Episodes: A Precision Psychiatry Approach to Treatment Selection Using Digital Health Tools." *NPJ Digital Medicine*, vol. 8, article no. 76, 2025. https://www.nature.com/articles/s41746-025-01523-3.
83 https://www.nature.com/articles/s41746-025-01523-3.

84 Suresh, Harini et al. "Development and Validation of a Multimodal Digital Clinical Measure for Predicting Treatment Response in Depression." *Translational Psychiatry*, vol. 15, article no. 224, 2025. https://www.nature.com/articles/s41398-025-03224-7.
85 Suresh, Harini et al. "Development and Validation of a Multimodal Digital Clinical Measure for Predicting Treatment Response in Depression." *Translational Psychiatry*, vol. 15, article no. 224, 2025. https://www.nature.com/articles/s41398-025-03224-7.
86 Suresh, Harini et al. "Development and Validation of a Multimodal Digital Clinical Measure for Predicting Treatment Response in Depression." *Translational Psychiatry*, vol. 15, article no. 224, 2025. https://www.nature.com/articles/s41398-025-03224-7.
87 Suresh, Harini et al. "Development and Validation of a Multimodal Digital Clinical Measure for Predicting Treatment Response in Depression." *Translational Psychiatry*, vol. 15, article no. 224, 2025. https://www.nature.com/articles/s41398-025-03224-7.
88 Suresh, Harini et al. "Development and Validation of a Multimodal Digital Clinical Measure for Predicting Treatment Response in Depression." *Translational Psychiatry*, vol. 15, article no. 224, 2025. https://www.nature.com/articles/s41398-025-03224-7.

Chapter 8

The modern frontier of artificial intelligence in mental healthcare

The discussion of artificial intelligence (AI) in mental healthcare would be incomplete without confronting the paradox at its core. For millennia, humans have conceptualized mental disorders, such as Hippocrates' descriptions of melancholia in the 4th century BCE or Charaka Samhita's (2nd century CE) mentions of psychotic states reminiscent of schizophrenia.[1,2]

Even beyond the identification of mental illness, the human brain-mind has tried to understand its own patterns and architectures. Mapping the brain was attempted by early anatomists and surgeons for the past three thousand years. Formal medical classification emerged with Kraepelin's 1896 nosology and then the first Diagnostic and Statistical Manual of Mental Disorders in 1952. But even in the present day, we do not fully understand mental illness or the brain. His quest to understand our own minds, the software of humanity, has become a partnership with machines.[3,4]

Today, our artificial systems literally mimic our brain's neural architectures and embody cognitive functions like "attention" and "learning." And these machines, which resemble our brain-minds, are now deployed in understanding, repairing, and healing their creators.

This recursion is not an accident – it represents the first turn of a self-referential loop in which the human brain-mind creates a mirror to heal itself.

Even putting aside the notion that the newest approaches in AI mirror the brain-mind, humans and machines are collaborating on the pursuit of alleviating suffering. Among all domains transformed by AI, none carries higher stakes or promises transformation of human life more than understanding and healing the brain-mind. Unlike advancements in autonomous vehicles, film production, or logistics optimization, AI's application to mental healthcare (and more broadly, understanding the brain-mind) fundamentally augments the instrument of all human life and experience. The gravity of this development cannot be overstated.

Before exploring what the future holds for AI applications in mental healthcare, establishing a framework for our exploration is critical. The biopsychosocial model conceptualized by George Engel[5] provides a lens for understanding the individual as an emergent phenomenon arising from the dynamic interplay of biological, psychological, and social (contextual/environmental included)

DOI: 10.1201/9781003565215-8

systems. In this model, these three domains are not separate components but co-existing realities operating simultaneously.

Engel originally proposed the biopsychosocial model in response to a growing disregard within medicine for the psychological dimensions of illness in favor of purely mechanistic explanations. This camp wanted "medicine to concentrate on the 'real' diseases and not get lost in the psychosociological underbrush." Engel's intent was to unify these two camps and "broaden the approach to disease to include the psychosocial without sacrificing the enormous advantages of the biomedical approach." Nevertheless, nearly fifty years later, the field of mental healthcare remains polarized.

Biological interventions like pharmacotherapy and brain stimulation on one end and psychosocial interventions like psychotherapy and peer support on the other. The reason for these differences can be explained by the brain being the center of the biological paradigm and the subjective yet universally-experienced "individual" or "mind" being the center of the psychosocial paradigm. Consequently, the application of AI in mental healthcare has largely followed these established boundaries, with one group of AI applications primarily addressing biological facets of mental illness and the other focusing on the psychosocial.

AI APPLICATIONS FOR PSYCHOSOCIAL MENTAL HEALTHCARE

The subjective yet universally experienced "individual" or "mind" is the center of the psychosocial lens. In this paradigm, talk-based and relational interventions like cognitive-behavioral therapy, dialectical behavioral therapy, psychodynamic insight, peer-support groups, etc., are most relevant.

In 2022 and 2023, AI was explored for its abilities to assist with symptom detection and extract features for diagnostic tasks. Specifically, LLMs like GPT-3.5 and Med-PaLM 2 were evaluated for symptom detection abilities in depression, anxiety, PTSD, and suicidal ideation. Other studies explored using AI for depression detection based on language patterns.[6]

Regarding therapeutic applications, there seemed to be two camps in the early 2020s – researchers who believe that sophisticated prompt engineering of LLMs could generate CBT-like interactions with LLMs, and the second camp began instruction tuning with therapist answers from questions from patients. SoulChat was a good example of instruction tuning.[7] Before even that, early chatbots like Woebot (launched in 2017) created rudimentary rule-based conversational therapy using traditional NLP and decision trees to deliver CBT interventions. However, these approaches never gained traction.

With the advent of powerful LLMs, domain-adaptive pretraining became more popular instead of just freezing the foundational model and editing its behavior. In 2023, systems like PSYGuard were finetuned with clinician feedback via RHLF which reduced unsafe replies.[8]

In 2024, when open-source base models exceeded the hundred billion parameter mark – they became cheaper to adapt, so many finetuned models popped up for mental health. A 2025 review of models found that generative AI models including ChatGPT-3.5, 4.0, Bard, and Claude showed capabilities in psychoeducation and emotional awareness tasks. However, their diagnostic accuracy was limited.[9] LLMs were also used to identify cognitive distortion, a target for intervention in CBT.[10]

Beyond just symptom detection, researchers started to explore AI's diagnosis capabilities. Med-PaLM 2 could help with psychiatric evaluations by processing clinical text.[11] This preprint shows that Med-PaLM 2, can assess psychiatric functioning without training. It achieved depression screening performance of 80–84% accuracy and correctly diagnosed categories 92.5% of the time. Additionally, it was able to explain the reasoning for its assessments, which is important to clinicians. Other papers demonstrated that instruction prompt tuning significantly improved clinical knowledge alignment from 61.9% to 92.6% and reduced potential harm assessments from 29.7% to 5.9%, establishing benchmarks for safe AI deployment.[12]

Beyond LLM applications, transformer-based models combined with convolutional neural networks were developed for more accurate depression detection from speech. This approach demonstrated better performance by extracting both local and temporal information from speech segments.[13] Advances in NLP specifically for online therapy platforms began to enable personalized support by adapting to linguistic nuances.[14]

From 2022 to 2025, the research focuses morphed. At the beginning, studies were focused on proof-of-concept and feasibility studies, establishing that AI could even help with these functions. The landscape advanced to actual clinical interventions, personalized care, and advanced diagnostics.

Finetuning LLMs became cheap and easy, and safety became a bigger problem. Retrieval-augmented generation was a partial solution because RAG could force the model to cite sources and evidence. In addition, what helped drive these advances into 2024, was the maturation of RHLF. Instead of binary judgments, the reward model could score responses along scales of empathy, alignment with evidence basis, and other areas. Transparency dashboards became standard as well, and publications like Nature issued new reporting guidelines that required authors to disclose prompt templates, finetuning data mixtures, and RHLF reward functions.

Advanced diagnostics became possible as LLMs got better. A scoping review[15] found that LLMs like GPT-4 demonstrate better information acquisition and analysis, and generating natural language responses compared to non-transformer models and humans. This enabled LLMs like GPT-4 Turbo to be used for symptom retrieval and automated assessments for conditions like PTSD.[16] Research is now exploring how LLMs, enhanced with RAG, can improve mental health diagnosis by incorporating external knowledge sources like diagnostic guidelines.[17] While promising, research still indicates that these models might still "lack a robust understanding of the meaning and nuances," highlighting a need for further refinement to ensure reliability for mental health applications.[18]

Beyond diagnosis, treatment has always been a compelling application of AI in mental healthcare. And the therapeutic agent is here. Open-source LLM initiatives like MentaLLaMA and Mental-LLM emerged, aiming to provide more accessible and customizable mental health support. Platforms are being explored as virtual therapists, offering continuous and personalized support. Comparative analysis shown that general purpose LLMs like GPT-4 outperform specialized therapeutic bots.[19]

The first randomized controlled trial of a therapy chatbot was conducted in 2025 as well. The chatbot is called Therabot. It is a Falcon-7B/Llama-2-70B hybrid finetuned on ~100,000 clinician-authored CBT dialogues via QLoRA. It uses crisis-intent classifiers to safeguard the model. Two hundred ten adults meeting criteria for major depressive disorder, generalized anxiety, or high-risk feeding-and-eating disorders exchanged a median of 260 messages (~6 h) across four treatment weeks plus a four-week follow-up. Therabot had impressive results. Depression scores dropped 6.1 points compared to 2.6 in control groups, anxiety fell 2.3 points versus 0.1, and weight concerns decreased 9.8 points matching human therapist programs. Safety was good with only 28 concerning incidents among 25,000 interactions, leading to new regulatory standards.[20]

The shift from 2022 to 2025 in psychosocial AI applications for mental healthcare is marked by a move from demonstrating capability to refining efficacy, enhancing personalization, and the launch of effective AI intervention.

Future developments

On the immediate horizon, the current trends will continue and AI capabilities for diagnosis and delivery of established therapeutic modalities like CBT will achieve clinical grade. The Therabot RCT is a major advancement in the space. This progress will be coupled with data integration from just about anywhere, and regulatory approvals are likely to be achieved. In some cases, AI will augment delivery alongside a clinician and undoubtedly, in some cases, AI will work autonomously. This will facilitate unprecedented expansion of access to mental healthcare. However, the impact of AI will extend far beyond digitizing existing practices.

Today, our idea of care is predicated on the therapist-patient dyad, which contains limiting assumptions. These limitations include but are not limited to the following: (1) the framework of one patient interacts with another entity, the therapist, (2) the artificial demarcation "therapy session" and "life," and (3) the concept of evidence-based therapeutic modalities as the gold standard for psychotherapeutic interventions for care. These paradigms will undergo a fundamental reconceptualization.

For instance, the traditional therapeutic dyad is a framework which is now outdated. In a distributed care network, the patient would interact with various agents all coordinated by an AI. Some emerging research already hints at multi-agent systems. Recent preprint studies demonstrate multi-agent architectures for mental health support. For example, MIND is a framework employing four agents that create psychological healing environments through interactive dialogues.[21] Additionally, Wu et al. (2025) describe WiseMind, which uses dual-agent architectures that balance diagnostic reasoning with empathetic communication.[22] These innovations show the potential for distributed care models instead of one-to-one therapy.[23]

Today, there is a distinction between real life and therapy, but continuous engagement/support will blur this. AI-enabled tools could be an ecological momentary intervention provider. This means providing just-in-time coping strategies during stressors or prompting reflective practices based on real-time information. Therapy or intervention will be ingrained into the individual's lived experience.[24] The concept of AI as a continuous support system basically suggests that AI could eventually serve as a "life co-pilot."[25]

Beyond verbal or textual exchange, AI could orchestrate novel interventional modalities, generating avatars, personalized soundscapes, visual stimuli, and even haptic feedback to induce specific states or enhance neuroplasticity, moving beyond the limitations of purely dialogic interventions.[26]

Text-based chatbots are obviously limited in their ability to engage humans. The emergence of the chatbot avatars marks a fundamental shift toward leveraging patients' implicit biases and unconscious responses to build stronger therapeutic alliances. When patients interact with a generated face and voice that has been specifically engineered to align with their individual trust patterns and preferences, the therapeutic relationship can deepen. This development is imminent as generative video AI becomes more sophisticated. In this new, "chatbots" will have a face through an avatar that can adapt its appearance, expressions, and mannerisms to optimize each patient's engagement. Beyond just avatars, AI-orchestrated multi-sensory therapeutic interventions hold promise yet are still limited.[27]

Beyond this, personalization and multimodal interfaces hold promise for the future of AI in mental healthcare. First, adaptive personalization encompasses AI's capacity to customize interventions to preferences, implicit biases, and behavioral patterns to optimize therapeutic outcomes. Secondly, multimodal interfaces will enable more than AI-generated avatars. Immersive VR/AR environments and multi-agent conversational systems will create compelling and engaging therapeutic experiences.

AI applications for biological mental healthcare

The biological paradigm of mental healthcare focuses on the physiological, neurological, and genetic underpinnings of mental disorders. In the early

2020s, research in this domain moved from proofs-of-concept to biomarker identification. Themes in research included the development of advanced neuroimaging tools, multimodal approaches using various data types, and machine learning to predict treatment responses.

During this period, AI applications in neuroimaging advanced, moving beyond group comparisons to individual-level diagnostic tools. ML models specifically did well in applications regarding personalized treatment plans and symptom tracking.

Researchers began to explore disease heterogeneity. Disease heterogeneity, the notion that a single disease or condition can be caused by multiple factors or have different expressions in different individuals, was explored via dimensional neuroimaging endophenotypes, quantitative measures designed to bridge the gap between underlying genetics and observable clinical symptoms.

These DNEs offer a more detailed understanding of psychiatric conditions. For instance, one framework detailed by Wen et al.[28] utilized imaging-derived phenotypes from T1-weighted MRI, T2-weighted MRI, and PET to position patients into multiple DNEs.

This approach gained further validation through studies like those by Tozzi et al.[29] This study demonstrated that personalized brain circuit scores could identify clinically distinct biotypes in depression and anxiety.[30] Their research showed that patients could be stratified into six distinct neurobiological subgroups based on task-free and task-evoked brain circuit dysfunction. Each biotype had unique symptom profiles and responses to various treatments including pharmacotherapy and behavioral interventions, which emphasized the utility of biotyping.

In addition to neuroimaging, other biomarkers began to be explored.

Studies explored the association of inflammatory markers, such as C-reactive protein and leukocyte levels, with psychiatric risk.

AI in the analysis of blood-based biomarkers has changed how we look at psychiatric disorders. AI-based models utilize ML algorithms to analyze various biological markers, including inflammatory proteins, genetic expressions, and metabolic indicators. This will ultimately allow us to classify and predict psychiatric disorders with precision.

After 2024, we saw a more marked shift toward precision psychiatry. Widespread adoption of multimodal AI systems and generative approaches began to address data limitations. Current AI integrates diverse data streams, including neuroimaging, genomics, electronic health records, and various physiological signals, into predictive models. Projects like the PsycheMERGE Network are at the forefront of this integration.

Furthermore, AI is transforming neuromodulation techniques such as transcranial magnetic stimulation and deep brain stimulation by optimizing parameters for individualized patient responses. Some advanced systems have achieved over 97% accuracy in predicting treatment outcomes. Studies are also exploring the use of AI-enhanced fMRI for decoding schizophrenia, leveraging Vision Transformers and Support Vector Machines.

For instance, Di Stefano et al.[31] discussed how AI-enhanced fMRI unlocks new pathways for precision psychiatry in schizophrenia by integrating these technologies. Similarly, Random Forest algorithms applied to electroencephalogram (EEG) data have shown accuracy (93.41%) in the diagnosis of bipolar disorder.[32] This is important for bipolar disorder because diagnosis can take years. Machine learning methods, including SVM, have shown predictive value for the diagnosis of bipolar disorder, with high sensitivity and specificity in distinguishing it from both healthy controls and depression.[33]

In general, over the last few years, we saw single-site SVM yield to transformer architectures. Explainable AI toolkits like BraiNN-XAI will help models satisfy regulatory requirements. Generative models have become useful in this space as well.

Generative models, particularly diffusion models, are addressing long-standing data limitations in psychiatry by synthesizing realistic neuroimaging data.

These models generate synthetic brain images while maintaining biological fidelity. This allows training dataset expansion, which is especially helpful for rare or underrepresented conditions. For example, Zhao et al.[34] utilized diffusion transformer-augmented fMRI functional connectivity for enhanced ASD diagnosis, by starting the reverse diffusion from a noisy real sample instead of pure noise.

Expanded datasets obviously enable better training of AI models, accelerating biomarker discovery and diagnostic tool development.

Antipsychotic drugs, while life-saving for psychosis and mood disorders, block dopamine receptors and can trigger tardive dyskinesia (TD). This involves irreversible facial-and-limb movements that burden an estimated 0.8–2.6 million U.S. patients. Because the gold-standard Abnormal Involuntary Movement Scale demands a 20- to 30-minute specialist exam repeated 4–6 times per year, most clinics screen far less often, letting the early, potentially modifiable phase pass unnoticed.

To close this gap, Videra Health spent six years assembling smartphone videos from 351 antipsychotic-exposed adults across NIH and industry trials, then trained a vision-speech multimodal network. The video stream uses an InternVideo-pre-trained Vision Transformer that tokenizes 16 × 16 patches across 32-frame clips; region-specific attention heads track Facial Action Coding units (lip smacking, tongue protrusion, blink bursts), shoulder elevation, and upper-trunk sway, the body areas where TD most commonly manifests. In parallel, a three-layer convolutional-recurrent network ingests Mel-Frequency Cepstral Coefficients, flagging phonation jitter, voice breaks, and other dysarthric signatures of orolingual dyskinesia. The system attained AUC 0.89 with 0.82/0.82 sensitivity/specificity, surpassing expert consensus.[35]

The field has rapidly evolved from seeking isolated biological signals to developing integrated AI systems that enable personalized treatment strategies.

Future developments

The next decade will see AI reshape mental healthcare in this context, specifically regarding personalized medicine rooted in an individual's biological signature.

Multimodal AI systems and generative approaches have already begun to address data limitations.

Advances in neuroimaging, multimodal biomarker approaches, and machine learning for treatment prediction laid a crucial foundation. Diffusion models started creating realistic synthetic data, overcoming significant data scarcity in conditions like autism spectrum disorder (ASD) and attention deficit hyperactivity disorder (ADHD).[36] These developments signal a focus on data-driven approaches that will define the next decade.

One of the most significant shifts will be in biomarker-driven diagnostic subtyping and the evolution of nosology.

Deep learning models, trained on multimodal biological datasets (genomic, proteomic, metabolomic, neuroimaging, electrophysiological, and digital biomarkers), will identify highly specific biological subtypes within current broad diagnostic categories.

For instance, "depression" will disaggregate into multiple distinct entities, each with unique underlying pathologies. In fact, this is already happening. This will not necessarily eliminate the DSM overnight, but will lead to its continuous and data-driven evolution.

The integration of explainable AI will be crucial here, as regulatory bodies will likely necessitate transparency into how AI models make these predictions.

The next decade will see hyperpersonalization of pharmacotherapies and other interventions. AI will move beyond predicting treatment response to optimizing medication and neuromodulation therapies by leveraging a patient's unique biological profile. Instead of the current trial-and-error approach, AI will analyze genetic markers, inflammatory profiles, neuroimaging data, and physiological responses to recommend the most effective drug, dosage, or stimulation protocol. This will be an iterative process. AI will continuously learn and adapt these recommendations based on real-world outcomes, leading to personalized psychiatric treatment.

The convergent layer

The preceding sections have shown the trajectories of AI applications in mental healthcare, categorized by their alignment with either the biological or psychosocial paradigms.

While this division has characterized mental health for decades, convergence of these two paradigms is likely over the decade. We will see models that are capable of integrating data on physiology, behavior, and self-reported context, and this convergence will be driven by AI's developing capacity for multimodal data integration. But what are the technical mechanisms that make this integration possible?

Modality-agnostic backbones are transformer architectures that do not need bespoke encoders for each data type. They will ingest any form of input (pixels, waveforms, journal entries) and treat every input as an undifferentiated embedding with a modality tag. One 2025 study combined natural language data from AI-conducted clinical interviews with neuroimaging, using ChatGPT o perform interactive patient interviews, then fused the resulting text-based feature matrix with 4D fMRI brain scans in a neural network to predict psychiatric diagnoses. This multimodal model achieved 85.7% diagnostic accuracy.[37] The LLM + Plug-In Encoders approach involves extending the LLMs with lightweight encoders that can translate vision, audio, or bio signals. Data as Language strategy treats non-textual data streams by turning them into tokens that LLMs can parse as sentences or narratives. Other methods include Contrastive Joint-Embedding Alignment. This strategy takes disparate data that temporally aligned – for example, facial expression frames, a journal entry, and a concurrent HRV measure close together in an embedding space.[38]

One of the most powerful application areas for these new multimodal approaches is diagnosis. Projects such as IMPACT-MH are already merging language from AI-conducted interviews with imaging, genomics, and wearables to discover fine-grained "computational phenotypes" that predict prognosis better than DSM labels.[39]

Another transformative application is the creation of "digital twin" mental health avatars. These digital twins are personalized, dynamic, and continuously updated computational models representing an individual's mental health status. These avatars would be constructed by AI systems integrating, longitudinal streams of biological data (e.g., genomic profiles, regular blood-based proteomic or metabolomic biomarkers, continuous physiological monitoring from advanced medical-grade wearables, and periodic high-resolution neuroimaging) with psychosocial data (e.g., detailed behavioral logs from smartphone interactions, sentiment and semantic analysis of communication patterns, mapping of real-world social interaction networks, and environmental context sensing through ambient devices).

There are serious challenges in building multimodal AI for mental healthcare. Biological, behavioral, and contextual streams are often sampled at different frequencies and resolutions, making temporal alignment difficult (Kargarandehkordi et al., 2025). Variation in sensor hardware and questionnaire formats and scarce data complicates things (Tanaka, 2025).[40]

Regulation limits sharing raw health data, yet centralizing it is still the default in many deep-learning pipelines. If you consider the necessity for interpretable outputs as well, it is clear why integrated biopsychosocial models remain aspiration than routine practice.

Dubey et al.'s "Federated learning for privacy-enhanced mental-health prediction with multimodal data integration" (2025) offers a way around several of these roadblocks. Working with heart-rate variability and sleep-pattern signals on the biological side, and smartphone/social-media behavior on the psychosocial side, the authors fuse these modalities in a CNN-LSTM model that is *trained entirely on-device via federated learning.* Raw data never leave the user's phone or wearable. This structure satisfies regulatory barriers that can block multimodal mental-health AI.

Although we have discussed various applications of AI in mental healthcare throughout previous sections, predicting developments over the next decade remains largely speculative. Nevertheless, we anticipate that several key themes will prove significant for AI implementation across the following areas of the patient care continuum.

In the domain of treatment, multimodal AI could turn care into a *closed-loop* multimodal continuous care controller. The AI might continuously sense biological (heart-rate variability, sleep quality) and psychosocial (speech tone, location patterns) cues, and decide what matters. This differs from today's open-loo*p* routine, where clinicians prescribe, wait weeks, and revisit. Modality-agnostic transformers will help blend every data stream, and federated learning can keep raw data on the device. You can also picture the system as a personal mental-health copilot or a dynamic therapy coach that never sleeps. The concept of continuity that we mentioned before is highly relevant.

On the frontier for diagnosis, AI will help create a "weather radar" of the mind, combining conversation transcripts, wearable signals, and brain imaging to generate probabilistic, continuously updated computational *phenotypes* that flag relapse risk days early. Contrastive cross-modal pretraining aligns these diverse signals in one latent map, while explainability tools let clinicians zoom in on features.

There seems to be a growing consensus that psychosocial and biological data in one AI model is better. Model architectures vary from multi-stream transformers with fusion of sensor and behavioral features,[41] to graph-enhanced ViT hybrids,[42] to contrastive dual encoders aligning brain signals with text.[43] It will soon be clear that convergent multimodal frameworks outperform single-modality analyses in mental health applications.[44] By combining objective biological markers (brain activity, heart rhythms, etc.) with subjective or behavioral indicators (speech, facial affect, digital behavior), these models can capture the complex biopsychosocial signatures of disorders.

Just as vertebrate brain evolution progressed from simple neural circuits to specialized processing regions like the visual cortex, auditory cortex, and motor areas. And then to the integrative neocortex that unifies them all. AI development has followed a similar path. We began with neural networks and developed specialized systems for processing various data. Now convergent multimodal models represent the emergence of AI's "neocortex" – an integrative architecture that synthesizes all functions into unified understanding.

NOTES

1 Telles-Correia, Diogo, and João Gama Marques. "Melancholia before the Twentieth Century: Fear and Sorrow or Partial Insanity?" *Frontiers in Psychology*, vol. 6, 2015, article 81. https://www.ncbi.nlm.nih.gov/pmc/articles/PMC4314947/.

2 Thara, R. "Schizophrenia – Enhancing Hope with Better Care & Research." *The Indian Journal of Medical Research*, vol. 140, no. 4, 2014, pp. 469–471. https://www.ncbi.nlm.nih.gov/pmc/articles/PMC4277128/.

3 American Psychiatric Association. "DSM History." *American Psychiatric Association*, https://www.psychiatry.org/psychiatrists/practice/dsm/about-dsm/dsm-history. Accessed 3 June 2025.

4 Heckers, Stephan, and Kenneth S. Kendler. "The Evolution of Kraepelin's Nosological Principles." *World Psychiatry*, vol. 19, no. 3, 2020, pp. 381–388. https://www.ncbi.nlm.nih.gov/pmc/articles/PMC7491624/.

5 Engel, George L. "The Need for a New Medical Model: A Challenge for Biomedicine." *Science*, vol. 196, no. 4286, 1977, pp. 129–136. https://doi.org/10.1126/science.847460.

6 Kuang, Junwei et al. "What Symptoms and How Long? An Interpretable AI Approach for Depression Detection in Social Media." *Proceedings of the 57th Hawaii International Conference on System Sciences*, 2024, pp. 2455–2464. https://hdl.handle.net/10125/106681.

7 Chen, Yirong et al. "SoulChat: Improving LLMs' Empathy, Listening, and Comfort Abilities through Fine-tuning with Multi-turn Empathy Conversations." *Findings of the Association for Computational Linguistics: EMNLP 2023*, 2023, pp. 1170–1183. https://aclanthology.org/2023.findings-emnlp.83/.aclanthology.org+5aclanthology.org+5aclanthology.org+5

8 Qiu, Huachuan, Lizhi Ma, and Zhenzhong Lan. "PsyGUARD: An Automated System for Suicide Detection and Risk Assessment in Psychological Counseling." *Proceedings of the 2024 Conference on Empirical Methods in Natural Language Processing*, edited by Yaser Al-Onaizan, Mohit Bansal, and Yun-Nung Chen, Association for Computational Linguistics, 2024, pp. 4581–4607. https://aclanthology.org/2024.emnlp-main.264/.aclanthology.org+7aclanthology.org+7aclanthology.org+7

9 Wang, Liying et al. "Evaluating Generative AI in Mental Health: Systematic Review of Capabilities and Limitations." *JMIR Mental Health*, vol. 12, 2025, e70014. https://mental.jmir.org/2025/1/e70014. Accessed 2 June 2025.

10 Chen, Zhiyu, Yujie Lu, and William Yang Wang. "Empowering Psychotherapy with Large Language Models: Cognitive Distortion Detection through Diagnosis of Thought Prompting." *arXiv*, 11 Oct. 2023. arxiv.org/pdf/2310.07146. Accessed 2 June 2025.

11 Galatzer-Levy, Isaac R. et al. "The Capability of Large Language Models to Measure Psychiatric Functioning." *arXiv*, 3 Aug. 2023. arxiv.org/abs/2308.01834. Accessed 2 June 2025.

12 Singhal, Karan et al. "Large Language Models Encode Clinical Knowledge." *Nature*, vol. 620, no. 7972, 2023, pp. 172–180. https://doi.org/10.1038/s41586-023-06291-2. Accessed 2 June 2025.

13 Yin, Faming et al. "Depression Detection in Speech Using Transformer and Parallel Convolutional Neural Networks." *Electronics*, vol. 12, no. 2, 2023, p. 328. https://doi.org/10.3390/electronics12020328. Accessed 2 June 2025.

14 Jelassi, Mariem et al. "Enhancing Personalized Mental Health Support Through Artificial Intelligence: Advances in Speech and Text Analysis Within Online Therapy Platforms." *Information*, vol. 15, no. 12, 2024, p. 813. https://doi.org/10.3390/info15120813. Accessed 2 June 2025.

15 Suárez, Miguel, Ana M. Torres, Pilar Blasco-Segura, and Jorge Mateo. "Application of the Random Forest Algorithm for Accurate Bipolar Disorder Classification." *Life*, vol. 15, no. 3, 2025, article 394. https://doi.org/10.3390/life15030394. Accessed 3 June 2025.
16 Tu, Sichang et al. "Automating PTSD Diagnostics in Clinical Interviews: Leveraging Large Language Models for Trauma Assessments." *Proceedings of the 25th Annual Meeting of the Special Interest Group on Discourse and Dialogue*, 18–20 Sept. 2024, pp. 644–663. Association for Computational Linguistics, 2024. https://aclanthology.org/2024.sigdial-1.55/
17 Boggavarapu, Lokesh et al. "Evaluating Enhanced LLMs for Precise Mental Health Diagnosis from Clinical Notes." *medRxiv*, 16 Dec. 2024. https://doi.org/10.1101/2024.12.16.24317648.
18 Boggavarapu, Lokesh et al. "Evaluating Enhanced LLMs for Precise Mental Health Diagnosis from Clinical Notes." *medRxiv*, 16 Dec. 2024. https://doi.org/10.1101/2024.12.16.24317648.
19 Rządeczka, Marcin et al. "The Efficacy of Conversational AI in Rectifying the Theory-of-Mind and Autonomy Biases: Comparative Analysis." *JMIR Mental Health*, vol. 12, 2025, e64396. https://mental.jmir.org/2025/1/e64396.
20 Heinz, Michael V., Daniel M. Mackin, Brianna M. Trudeau, Sukanya Bhattacharya, Yinzhou Wang, Haley A. Banta, Abi D. Jewett, Abigail J. Salzhauer, Tess Z. Griffin, and Nicholas C. Jacobson. "Randomized Trial of a Generative AI Chatbot for Mental Health Treatment." *NEJM AI*, vol. 2, no. 4, 27 Mar. 2025. https://doi.org/10.1056/AIoa2400802. Accessed 3 June 2025.
21 Chen, Yujia et al. "MIND: Towards Immersive Psychological Healing with Multi-agent Inner Dialogue." *arXiv*, 27 Feb. 2025, arxiv.org/abs/2502.19860.
22 Wu, Yuqi et al. "WiseMind: Recontextualizing AI with a Knowledge-Guided, Theory-Informed Multi-Agent Framework for Instrumental and Humanistic Benefits." *arXiv*, 28 Feb. 2025, arxiv.org/abs/2502.20689.
23 Chen, Yujia et al. "MIND: Towards Immersive Psychological Healing with Multi-agent Inner Dialogue." *arXiv*, 27 Feb. 2025, arxiv.org/abs/2502.19860.
24 Yin, Hongfan et al. "Mobile-Based Ecological Momentary Assessment and Intervention: Bibliometric Analysis." *Frontiers in Psychiatry*, vol. 15, 2024, article 1300739. https://doi.org/10.3389/fpsyt.2024.1300739.
25 Hiller, Selina et al. "Health-Promoting Effects and Everyday Experiences With a Mental Health App Using Ecological Momentary Assessments and AI-Based Ecological Momentary Interventions Among Young People: Qualitative Interview and Focus Group Study." *JMIR mHealth and uHealth*, vol. 13, 2025, e65106. https://doi.org/10.2196/65106.
26 Dobrushina, Olga et al. "Training Interoceptive Awareness with Real-Time Haptic vs. Visual Heartbeat Feedback." *Psychophysiology*, vol. 61, no. 11, 2024, e14648. https://doi.org/10.1111/psyp.14648.
27 Sezgin, Emre, and Ian McKay. "Behavioral Health and Generative AI: A Perspective on Future of Therapies and Patient Care." *npj Mental Health Research*, vol. 3, article 25, 7 June 2024, pp. 1–6. https://doi.org/10.1038/s44184-024-00067-w.
28 Wen, Junhao, Mathilde Antoniades, Zhijian Yang, Gyujoon Hwang, Ioanna Skampardoni, Rongguang Wang, and Christos Davatzikos. "Dimensional Neuroimaging Endophenotypes: Neurobiological Representations of Disease Heterogeneity Through Machine Learning." *Biological Psychiatry*, vol. 96, no. 7, 1 Oct. 2024, pp. 564–584. https://doi.org/10.1016/j.biopsych.2024.04.017. Accessed 3 June 2025.
29 Jiao, Yong et al. "Deep Graph Learning of Multimodal Brain Networks Defines Treatment-Predictive Signatures in Major Depression." *Molecular Psychiatry*, 31 Mar. 2025. https://pubmed.ncbi.nlm.nih.gov/38886626/

30 Leonardo Tozzi et al. "Personalized Brain Circuit Scores Identify Clinically Distinct Biotypes in Depression and Anxiety." *Nature Medicine*, vol. 30, no. 7, 2024, pp. 2076–2087. https://doi.org/10.1038/s41591-024-03057-9.

31 Haokai Zhao, Haowei Lou, Lina Yao, Wei Peng, Ehsan Adeli, Kilian M. Pohl, and Yu Zhang. "Diffusion Models for Computational Neuroimaging: A Survey." arXiv, 10 Feb. 2025. https://doi.org/10.48550/arXiv.2502.06552. Accessed 3 June 2025.

32 Suárez, Miguel, Ana M. Torres, Pilar Blasco-Segura, and Jorge Mateo. "Application of the Random Forest Algorithm for Accurate Bipolar Disorder Classification." *Life*, vol. 15, no. 3, 2025, article 394. https://doi.org/10.3390/life15030394. Accessed 3 June 2025.

33 Pan, Yi, Pushi Wang, Bowen Xue, Yanbin Liu, Xinhua Shen, Shiliang Wang, and Xing Wang. "Machine Learning for the Diagnosis Accuracy of Bipolar Disorder: A Systematic Review and Meta-Analysis." *Frontiers in Psychiatry*, vol. 15, 2025, article 1515549. https://doi.org/10.3389/fpsyt.2024.1515549. Accessed 3 June 2025.

34 Zhao, Haokai, Haowei Lou, Lina Yao, Wei Peng, Ehsan Adeli, Kilian M. Pohl, and Yu Zhang. "Diffusion Models for Computational Neuroimaging: A Survey." arXiv, 10 Feb. 2025. https://doi.org/10.48550/arXiv.2502.06552. Accessed 3 June 2025.

35 Sterns, Anthony A. et al. "Detecting Tardive Dyskinesia Using Video-Based Artificial Intelligence." *The Journal of Clinical Psychiatry*, vol. 86, no. 3, Sept. 2025, article no. 25m15792. https://www.psychiatrist.com/pdf/detecting-tardive-dyskinesia-using-video-based-artificial-intelligence-pdf/

36 Zhao, Haokai, Haowei Lou, Lina Yao, Wei Peng, Ehsan Adeli, Kilian M. Pohl, and Yu Zhang. "Diffusion Models for Computational Neuroimaging: A Survey." arXiv, 10 Feb. 2025. https://doi.org/10.48550/arXiv.2502.06552. Accessed 3 June 2025.

37 Li, Runda. "Integrative Diagnosis of Psychiatric Conditions Using ChatGPT and fMRI Data." *BMC Psychiatry*, vol. 25, 2025, article no. 145. https://bmcpsychiatry.biomedcentral.com/articles/10.1186/s12888-025-06586-w#:~:text=We%20propose%20a%20novel%20approach,methods%2C%20providing%20detailed%20statistical%20validation

38 Jiao, Yong et al. "Deep Graph Learning of Multimodal Brain Networks Defines Treatment-Predictive Signatures in Major Depression." *Molecular Psychiatry*, 31 Mar. 2025, https://www.nature.com/articles/s41380-025-02974-6?error=cookies_not_supported&code=59f81d80-0c24-4f8f-a03a-0ae957e4d3ee#:~:text=variations%20in%20the%20frontoparietal%20control%2C,Establishing%20Moderators%20and%20Biosignatures%20of

39 Levins, Hoag. "Penn Researcher Awarded $8 Million to Advance Mental Health Diagnostics Using AI." Penn LDI, Leonard Davis Institute of Health Economics, University of Pennsylvania, 28 Apr. 2025. https://ldi.upenn.edu/our-work/research-updates/penn-researcher-awarded-8-million-to-advance-mental-health-diagnostics-using-ai/. Accessed 5 June 2025.

40 Tanaka, Masaru. "From Serendipity to Precision: Integrating AI, Multi-Omics, and Human-Specific Models for Personalized Neuropsychiatric Care." *Biomedicines*, vol. 13, no. 1, Jan. 2025, article 167. https://doi.org/10.3390/biomedicines13010167. Accessed 5 June 2025.

41 Umair, Muhammad et al. "Decentralized EEG-Based Detection of Major Depressive Disorder via Transformer Architectures and Split Learning." *Frontiers in Computational Neuroscience*, vol. 19, Apr. 2025, article 1569828. https://doi.org/10.3389/fncom.2025.1569828. Accessed 5 June 2025.

42 Jia, Xiaowen et al. "Multimodal Depression Detection Based on an Attention Graph Convolution and Transformer." *Mathematical Biosciences and Engineering*, vol. 22, no. 3, Feb. 2025, pp. 652–676. https://doi.org/10.3934/mbe.2025024. Accessed 5 June 2025.

43 Zhang, Xiao et al. "Multimodal Approach to Public Health Interventions Using EGG and Mobile Health Technologies." *Frontiers in Public Health*, vol. 12, Jan. 2025, article 1520343. https://doi.org/10.3389/fpubh.2024.1520343. Accessed 5 June 2025.
44 Hu, Yongquan et al. "Exploring Large-Scale Language Models to Evaluate EEG-Based Multimodal Data for Mental Health." arXiv, 14 Aug. 2024, arXiv:2408.07313 [cs.HC]. https://doi.org/10.48550/arXiv.2408.07313. Accessed 5 June 2025.

Index

A

B

R

S

T

U

V

W

Y

For Product Safety Concerns and Information please contact our EU representative GPSR@taylorandfrancis.com Taylor & Francis Verlag GmbH, Kaufingerstraße 24, 80331 München, Germany